# My First Encounter with an Angel

## Revelations of Ancient Wisdom

by
Sidney Schwartz

**My First Encounter with an Angel**
*Revelations of Ancient Wisdom*
by Sidney Schwartz

Copyright © 1999 Keys of Knowingness L.L.C.
First Edition: *Ancient Wisdom Series*
Published in 1999

Cover Graphics by Linda Deming

Medicine Bear Publishing
P.O. Box 1075
Blue Hill, ME 04614

ISBN# 1-891850-21-0
Library of Congress CCN# 99-074700
Printed in the U.S.A.

# Dedication

This book honors the lives of countless heroic people who have acted as intermediaries between the spiritual and physical worlds. The lives of people endowed with the Gifts of the Spirit, whether they are called prophets, oracles, seers, or mediums are truly difficult. While the Bible immortalized a handful of these gifted people, most of them became targets of hatred and were spurned by society. For reasons which will be chronicled throughout this book, the clergy greatly benefited from isolating the mediums from the people. Churches branded them as evil—torturing and slaughtering untold thousands, silencing the knowledge that came through their gifts.

May this series of books advance the truths these brave and noble people were striving to convey.

Dear Rachel

I pray that the 2 appointed Angels will guide you and yours into forever.

Rev. Carl Hiatt

Dear

I pray that the appointed Angel

will guide you and yours into heaven.

# Table of Contents

# Preface
# A Leap of Faith

**Hear now this, O foolish people, and without
understanding; which have eyes, and see not;
which have ears, and hear not.**
**Jeremiah 5:21 [KJV]**

These ancient words of Jeremiah, which have echoed though time, are reaching us as we enter a new millennium. In a spiritual sense, most inhabitants of the twentieth century still have blind eyes and deaf ears. Few have acquired the understanding Jeremiah discussed.

*My First Encounter with an Angel* strives to illuminate truths about spirituality, mediumship, and prophecy that have been hidden for centuries. This information comes from many books found in our country's research libraries and from mystical sources. Some may not take the latter seriously. Consider taking a leap of faith, as I did many years ago, when an angel came to talk to me through a very well known trance medium. A trance medium is a human bridge from our world to higher realms. Entities residing in these higher realms have access to the present, the future and the past. Therefore, mediumship acts like time machine enabling one to glean information not recorded by historians.

This book asks you to believe in an entity you cannot see or know in a temporal way. AWAN, the Angel Without A Name, contacted me through Rev. Carl Hewitt, a medium I had the great fortune of knowing. Some may think Awan is a figment of my imagination. Others may suggest that Awan is Carl's alter ego. Ultimately, who or what Awan is doesn't matter. What *is* important are the lessons this entity is attempting to teach. Much of this information was available to humanity in the ancient Library of Alexandria, Egypt. Unfortunately, irreplaceable scrolls full of profound wisdom were deliberately destroyed, preventing humanity from reaching the advanced spiritual state of being, we were meant to *collectively* experience.

It is not my goal to convert you to a new belief system, nor is it to prove that Awan's teachings are the "Truth." My goal is to present the truth about what happened to me, my encounters with Awan, and the results of thousands of hours of research verifying Awan's teachings. Please read *My First Encounter with an Angel* with an open mind. Awan challenged me to explore ancient wisdom and truth. I challenge you to do the same.

# Acknowledgments

I have been very fortunate to be surrounded by people who supported and fostered my work as an author. I wish to acknowledge and thank them for being able to see in me what I often could not see in myself.

I first want to thank my wonderful friend and mentor, Rev. Carl Hewitt, who has been the wind at my back, and channeled all of the AWAN information/teachings contained in this book. Carl is a true spiritual brother, selflessly giving of himself to help and serve others. Frequently, the gift of mediumship is difficult to handle. Due to the intense transformation in human consciousness today, heavy demands are placed on a reputable medium's time and energy as people continuously seek solutions to their problems. Some mediums thrive on being the center of attention. When these mediums lose perspective, their egos explode beyond normal boundaries often causing a deterioration of their mediumship. Carl has not fallen into this trap because he does not play into people fantasies that would place him on a pedestal. By respecting this high office, Carl has remained unaffected. He lives a "down to earth life," with his "out of this world gift." He is a most extraordinary individual, and I will always be extremely grateful to him for all that he has done for me.

Next I extend my deep gratitude to Awan—the Angel Without A Name. Although I have never seen him, I felt his intense energy during our first conversation. His unlimited patience became evident as he repeated his explanation of the same concept many times until I could comprehend it. I feel honored to be a direct recipient of Awan's teachings, and to convey some of the wisdom he wishes to bring to our world.

I am very thankful to my mother, Rita Schwartz, and my grandmother, Sylvia Teper for instructing me in the rich traditions of Judaism. I also thank my father, Harry Schwartz, who was a free-thinker. While he was proud of his Jewish heritage, he was not entangled in religious rituals and dogmas. As it turns out, my parents and grandmother served as perfect role models for me to be open to Awan's teachings.

I will always be grateful to Jim Mahone, who taught me how to find and appreciate my positive qualities, and to believe in myself. Without his help, I doubt this book would exist.

When my frustration level was high and the thought of abandoning this project seemed very tempting, Harvey Cohen invariably encouraged me to continue. I will always remember his positive reinforcement, and I am very grateful for his unebbing support.

A very special thanks goes to Suzanne Klein, who volunteered to help edit and refine my manuscript in the early stages. I greatly appreciate her enthusiasm for this extensive task, and thoroughly admire her artistry with words.

I would be totally remiss if I did not acknowledge a very special friend, Bonnie C. Hollis. Bonnie introduced me to Carl, and made my first appointment with him for a psychic reading. I am very grateful for her encouragement, friendship, and support during this project.

Finally, I wish to thank Eleanor Klein. She has been extremely supportive during my frustrations with the writing process, and lengthy search for a publisher. Her nurturing enthusiasm for my transformation to an author has positively affected my work.

For the past twenty years, I have collected specific verses from one hundred sixty different versions of the Bible. Several of these versions are extremely rare, and are only found in major research libraries. I need to express my appreciation two the very helpful librarians who granted me repeated access to these extremely valuable Bibles. I would like to thank Dr. Liana Lupas and the library staff at the American Bible Society of New York City. My gratitude also extends to Dr. Bill Stoneman, in charge of the Shide Library (the rare book library) at Princeton University. Through their cooperation, I examined *original* editions of the earliest English Bibles, which were invaluable to my research and the formation of my opinions.

# A Note to the Readers

On the following pages, I have created a chart of abreviations corresponding to the one hundred and sixty different versions of the Bible I researched. Throughout this book, I use these abreviations to save listing each Bible source in detail. I have also created many smaller charts of verses taken from many of these one hundred and sixty Bibles to help illustrate just how much the original Greek and Hebrew words were changed or distorted by various translators. I found many cases where translators disagreed on the meaning of a particular word and other cases where one translation had a completely opposite meaning of another.

Some of the chapters in this book contain conversations I had with an angel through a trance medium. This angel would not indentify himself by name so I have come to know him as AWAN (Angel Without A Name). To facilitate the reading of these conversations, I have used special icons to label the speakers.

## Symbols For Speakers

 **AWAN** Angel Without A Name

 Sidney Schwartz

The following is a chart of the bibliographic citations for each of the one hundred sixty different Bibles. When I quote from the Bible, I footnote each quotation with chapter and verse. I also indicate which version I am using with an abbreviation inside the brackets. Please refer to this chart to identify which version I am quoting.

| 0 | ABREV. | Translator. Title. Publication Data. |
|---|--------|--------------------------------------|
| 1 | EWYC | Forshall, Josia, Rev., F. R. S. Etc and Madden, Sir Frederic K.H.Y. F.R.S. *The Holy Bible.* Oxford: University Press, 1850. [Reprint of originals 1384]. |
| 2 | LWYC | Same as above |
| 3 | TYND | Tyndale, William. *Tyndale's Old Testament: Being the Pentateuch of 1530, Joshua to 2 Chronicles of 1537 and Jonah.* New Haven and London: Yale University Press, 1992.<br>Tyndale, William. *Tyndale's New Testament: Translated from the Greek in 1534.* New Haven & London: Yale University Press, 1989. |
| 4 | COV | Coverdale, Miles. *The Bible: That is the Holy Scriptures of the Old and New Testament.* Cologne: E. Cervicornus & J. Stoter, 1535. |
| 5 | HOLLY | Hollybushe, Johan. *The New Testament both in Latin and English.* Southwarke: James Nicolson, 1538. |
| 6 | TAV | Taverner, Richard. *The Most Sacred Bible.* London: John Byddell, 1539. |
| 7 | GRT | *The Bible.* Whitchurch, Edward & Grafton, Richard. 1540. |
| 8 | MATT | *The Bible.* London: John Daye, 1549. |
| 9 | JUGG | *The Newe Testament of Our Saviour Jesu Christe. Faithfully Translated Out of the Greek.* London: Richard Jugge, 1552. |
| 10 | GEN | *The Geneva Bible: A Facsimile of the 1560 Edition.* Madison, WI: University of Wisconsin Press, 1969. |
| 11 | BISH | Parker, Matthew. *The Holy Bible.* London: R. Jugge, 1568. |
| 12 | RHEIMS | *The New Testament of Jesus Christ Translated Faithfully into English Out of the Authentical Latin.* Rheims: Fogny, John, 1582. |
| 13 | DOU | *The Holy Bible Faithfully Translated Out of the Authentical Latin.* Douay: Kellam, Lawrence, 1609. |
| 14 | KJV | [Authorized King James Version]. *The Holy Bible Containing the Old and New Testaments.* London: Robert Barker, 1611. |
| 15 | HAAK | Haak, Theodore. *Dutch Annotations Upon the Whole Bible.* London: Henry Hills, for John Rothwell, Joshua Kirton, and Richard Tomlins, 1657. |
| 16 | MACE† | *The New Testament In Greek and English.* London. 1729. |
| 17 | SIMON | Simon, Richard. *The New Testament of Our Savior Jesus Christ According to Ancient Latin Edition.* London: John Pemberton & Charles Rivington, 1730. |

| 18 | WHIS | Mr. Whiston's Primitive New Testament. Part 1 Containing the Four Gospels, with the Acts of the Apostles. Part 2 Containing 14 Epistles of Paul. Part 3 Containing 7 Catholic Epistles. Part 4 Containing the Revelation of John. Stamford & London: printed for the author, 1745. |
|---|---|---|
| 19 | CHAL | [Challoner Revision]. Challoner, Richard. The Holy Bible: Translated from the Latin Vulgate. Dublin, 1750. |
| 20 | WESL† | Explanatory Notes Upon the New Testament. London: William Bowyer, 1755. |
| 21 | PUR | Purver, Anthony. A New and Literal Translation of All the Books of the Old and New Testaments. London: W. Richardson & S. Clark, 1764. |
| 22 | WYNNE | Wynne, Richard A.M. The New Testament. London: R. and J. Dodley in Pall-Mall, 1764. |
| 23 | HAR | Harwood, Edwin D. D. A Liberal Translation of the New Testament. London: T. Becket and P. A. De Hondt in the Strand, 1768. |
| 24 | WORS | Worsley, John. The New Testament of New Covenant of Our Lord and Savior Jesus Christ. London: R. Hett, 1770. |
| 25 | CLEM | [Clementine Edition]. The Holy Bible Translated from the Latin Vulgate Diligently Compared with the Hebrew Greek and other Editions in Divers Languages. Philadelphia: Carey, Stewart and Co., 1790. |
| 26 | GEDD | Geddes, Rev. Alexander, L. L. D. The Holy Bible or the Books Accounted Sacred by Jews and Christians. London: J. Davis, 1792. |
| 27 | RAY | Ray, John Mead. A Revised Translation and Interpretation of the Sacred Scriptures. London: G. Robinson and Co., 1799. |
| 28 | THOM | Thompson, Charles. The Old Covenant, Commonly Called Old Testament: Translated from the Septuagint. Vol. 1 (Gen. -1 Sam.). Philadelphia: Jane Aitken, 1808.<br>Thompson, Charles. The Holy Bible Containing the Old and New Covenant, Commonly Called the Old and New Testament: Translated from the Greek Vol. 2 (2 Sam.-Psalms). Philadelphia: Jane Aitken, 1808.<br>Thompson, Charles. The Old Covenant, Commonly called Old Testament: Translated from the Septuagint. Vol. 3 (Proverbs to Mal.). Philadelphia: Jane Aitken, 1808.<br>Thompson, Charles. The New Covenant; Commonly called the New Testament: Translated from the Greek Vol. 4. Philadelphia: Jane Aitken, 1808. |
| 29 | BELS | Belsham. The New Testament. Boston: Thomas B. Wait and Company, 1809. |
| 30 | FRY | The Holy Bible Containing the Old and New Testaments. London: T. Rutt, Shacklewell, 1812. |
| 31 | BELL | Bellamy, John. The Holy Bible, Newly Translated from the Original Hebrew, with Notes Critical and Explanatory. London: Longman, Hurst, Rees, Orme, and Brown, 1818. |
| 32 | WAKE | Wakefield, Gilbert B. A. Translation of the New Testament. Cambridge: University Press—Hilliard and Metcalf, 1820. |
| 33 | BOTR | Boothboyd, Benjamin, Rev. New Family Bible. London: Hudderesiled: William Moore, 1824. |
| 34 | WEBR | Webster, Noah. The Holy Bible, Containing the Old and New Testaments, in the Common Version. New Haven, CT: N. Webster, 1841. |
| 35 | BREN | Brenton, Lancelot Charles Lee, Sir. The Septuagint Version of the Old Testament According to the Vatican Text. London: Samuel Bagster and Sons, 1844. |

| 36 | CONE | Cone, Spencer H. and William H. Wyckoff. *The Commonly Received Version of the New Testament of Our Lord and Savior Jesus Christ.* New York: Lewis Colby, 1850. |
|----|------|---|
| 37 | MURD | Murdock, James D. D. *The New Testament or The Book of the Holy Gospel of Our Lord and our God, Jesus the Messiah.* New York: Stanford and Swords, 1851. |
| 38 | LEES | Leeser, Isaac. *The Twenty-Four Books of the Holy Bible: Hebrew and English.* London: Trübner & Co., 1856. |
| 39 | SAWY† | *The New Testament, Translated from the Original Greek, with Chronological Arrangement of the Sacred Books, and Improved Divisions of Chapters and Verses.* Boston: John P. Jewett and Company, 1858. |
| 40 | WELL | Wellbeloved, Charles, Rev. *The Holy Scriptures of the Old Covenant in Revised Translation. 3 Vols.* London: Longman, Green, Longman, and Roberts, 1859. |
| 41 | KEN | Kenrick, Francis Patrick. *The Pentateuch.* Baltimore, MD: Kelly, Hedian & Piet, 1860. Kenrick, Francis Patrick. *Historical Books of the Old Testament.* Baltimore, MD: Kelly, Hedian & Piet, 1860. Kenrick, Francis Patrick. *The Book of Job, and the Prophets.* Baltimore, MD: Kelly, Hedian & Piet, 1859. Kenrick, Francis Patrick. *The New Testamentt, translated from the Latin Vulgate.* Baltimore, MD: Kelly, Hedian & Piet, 1862. |
| 42 | YNG | Young, Robert. *The Holy Bible.* Edinburgh, Dublin, and London: A Fullarton & Company, 1863. |
| 43 | BEN | Benisch, Abraham, Dr. *Jewish School and Family Bible Vol. 1: Containing the Pentateuch.* Longman, Brown, Green, and Longmans. Paternoster Row: London, 1864. Benisch, Abraham, Dr. *Jewish School and Family Bible Vol. 2: Containing the Historical Parts.* Longman, Brown, Green, and Longmans. Paternoster Row: London, 1864. Benisch, A. Dr. *Jewish School and Family Bible Volume 3: Containing the Books of Isaiah, Jeremiah, Ezekiel, and the Twelve Minor Prophets.* Longman and Company. Paternoster Row: London, 1856. Benisch, A. Dr. *Jewish School and Family Bible Volume 4: Containing the Hagiography.* Longman and Company. Paternoster Row: London, 1861. |
| 44 | ABU | *The New Testament of Our Lord and Savior Jesus Christ. The Common English Version: Corrected by the Final Committee of the American Bible Union.* NY: American Bible Union; London, Trübner & Co., 1866. |
| 45 | SMITH | Smith, Joseph. *The Holy Scriptures Translated and Corrected by the Spirit of Revelation by Joseph Smith Jr., The Seer.* Philadelphia, PA: Westcott & Thompson, 1867. |
| 46 | HARM | Clark, George W. Rev. *A New Harmony of the Four Gospels in English: According to the Common Version.* Philadelphia, PA: American Baptist Publication Society, 1870. |
| 47 | ALF | Alford, Henry. *The New Testament for English Readers.* Chicago, IL: Moody Press, 1875. |
| 48 | JUSMI | Smith, Julia E. *The Holy Bible Containing the Old and New Testaments Translated Literally from the Original Tongues.* Hartford, CT: American Publishing Co., 1876. |
| 49 | ERV | [Revised Version]. *The Holy Bible Containing the Old and New Testaments Translated Out of the Original Tongues: Being the Version Set Forth A.D. 1611 Compared with the Most Ancient Authorities and Revised.* New York: Thomas Y. Crowell & Co., 1885. |
| 50 | SPUR | Spurrell, Helen. *A Translation of the Old Testament Scriptures from the Original Hebrew.* London: James Nisbet & Co., 1885. |

| 51 | WORD | Wordsworth, Christopher, D. D. *The Holy Bible with Notes and Introduction Vol. 1. Five Books of Moses.* London: 1885.<br>Wordsworth, Christopher, D. D. *The Holy Bible with Notes and Introduction Vol. 2 Josh.-Samuel.* London: 1885. |
|---|---|---|
| 52 | GRANT | Grant, Frederick, W., editor. *The Numerical Bible. The Pentateuch.* NY: Loizeaux Brothers, Bible Truth Depot. 1890.<br>Grant, Frederick, W., editor. *The Numerical Bible. Joshua to Samuel.* NY: Loizeaux Brothers, Bible Truth Depot. 1932.<br>Grant, Frederick, W., editor. *The Numerical Bible. Matthew to John.* NY: Loizeaux Brothers, Bible Truth Depot. 1897. |
| 53 | SHAR | Sharpe, Samuel. *The Holy Bible.* London: Williams and Norgage 14 Henrietta Street, Covent Garden, 1892. |
| 54 | ROTH | Rotherham, Joseph Bryant. *The Emphasized Bible: A New Translation.* Cincinnati, Ohio: The Standard Publishing Co., 1897. |
| 55 | YLT | Young, Robert. *Young's Literal Translation.* Grand Rapids, Michigan: Baker Book House, 1898. |
| 56 | GDBEY | Godbey, W. B. *Godbey's Translation of the New Testament: From the Original Greek.* Cincinnati, OH: God's Bible School. 190? |
| 57 | ASV | [American Standard Version]. *The Holy Bible Containing the Old and New Testaments.* New York: Thomas Nelson & Sons, 1901. |
| 58 | WEY | Weymouth, Richard Francis M. A., D. Litt. *The New Testament in Modern Speech: An Idiomatic Translation into Every-day English from the Text of "The Resultant Greek Testament".* New York: The Baker and Taylor Co., 1903. |
| 59 | CENT | W. H. Bennett, D. D., ed. The New Century Bible*: Genesis Introduction; Revised Version with Notes, Giving an Analysis Showing from which the Original Documents Each Portion of the Text is Taken; index and map.* NY: Oxford University Press, American Branch, 1904.<br>W. H. Bennett, D. D., ed. *The New Century Bible: Exodus Introduction; Revised version with Notes Giving an Analysis Showing from which the Original Documents Each Portion of the Text is Taken; index and map.* NY: Oxford University Press, American Branch, 1908.<br>Rev. A. R. S. Kennedy M. A., D. D., ed. *Leviticus and Numbers.* NY: Oxford University Press, American Branch, 1904.<br>Robinson, H. Wheeler. *Deuteronomy and Joshua.* NY: Oxford University Press, American Branch, n. d.<br>Rev. A. R. S. Kennedy M. A., D. D., ed. *New Century Bible: Samuel 1 & 2: Introduction Revised Version with notes, index and maps.* NY: Oxford University Press, American Branch, 1905.<br>Skinner, Prof. *1 & 2 Kings.* NY: Oxford University Press, American Branch, n. d.<br>Slater, W. F. *St. Matthew, Introduction Revised Version with notes, index and map.* NY: Oxford University Press, American Branch, 1901.<br>Bartlet, J. Vernon M.A., D.D. *St. Mark, Introduction Revised version with notes, index and map.* NY: Oxford University Press, American Branch, 1925.<br>Adeney, Walter F. M. A., D. D. *St. Luke, Introduction Revised Version with notes, index and map.* NY: Oxford University Press, American Branch, 1924.<br>McClymont, J. A., Rev. *St. John, Introduction Revised Version with notes, index and map.* NY: Oxford University Press, American Branch, 1901. |
| 60 | TCNT | *The Twentieth Century New Testament: A Translation into Modern English.* Chicago, IL: Moody Press, 1904. |

| 61 | HORN | Horner. *Coptic Version of the New Testament Vol. 1. The Gospels of St. Matthew and St. Mark.* Oxford: Clarendon Press, 1911.Horner. Coptic *Version of the New Testament Vol. 2. St. Luke.* Oxford: Clarendon Press, 1911. <br> Horner. *Coptic Version of the New Testament Vol. 3. Gospel of St. John.* Oxford: Clarendon Press, 1911. |
|----|------|----|
| 62 | CAMB | Ryle, Herbert E. D. D. *The Cambridge Bible for School and Colleges: The Book of Genesis in the Revised Version with Introduction and Notes.* Cambridge: University Press, 1921. <br> Driver, Rev. S. R. D. D. *The Cambridge Bible for School and Colleges: The Book of Exodus in the Revised Version with Introduction and Notes.* Cambridge: University Press, 1918. <br> Chapman, A. T. M. A. & A. W. Streane, D. D. *The Cambridge Bible for School and Colleges: The Book of Leviticus in the Revised Version with Introduction & Notes.* Cambridge: University Press, 1914. <br> Kirkpatrick, Rev. A. F. B. D. *The Cambridge Bible for School and Colleges: The First book of Samuel with Map, Notes and Introduction.* Cambridge: University Press, 1889. <br> Lumby, Rev. J. Rawson D. D. *The Cambridge Bible for School and Colleges: The First book of Kings with Map, Introduction and Notes.* Cambridge: University Press, 1890. <br> Carr, Rev. A. M.A. *The Cambridge Bible for School and Colleges: The Gospel according to St. Matthew, with Maps, Notes and Introduction.* Cambridge: University Press, 1879. <br> Farrar, F. W. Rev., D. D. *The Cambridge Bible for School and Colleges: The Gospel according to St. Luke with Maps, Notes and Introduction.* Cambridge: University Press, 1889. |
| 63 | PAN | Panin, Ivan. *The New Testament from the Greek Text as Established by Bible Numerics.* New Haven, CT: Bible Numerics Co., 1914. |
| 64 | DARB | Darby, John Nelson. *The Holy Scriptures Containing the Old and New Testaments.* London: G. Morrish, 1920. |
| 65 | FENT | Fenton, Ferrar. *The Holy Bible in Modern English.* NY: Oxford University Press (American Branch), 1922. |
| 66 | MOFF | Moffatt, James. *The Bible: A New Translation.* NY: Harper & Brothers Publishers, 1922. |
| 67 | RIVER | Ballantine, William G. *Riverside New Testament: A Translation from the Original Greek into the English of Today.* NY: Houghton Mifflin, 1923. |
| 68 | OVER | Overbury, Arthur E. *The People's New Covenant (New Testament) Scriptural Writings: Translated from the Meta-Physical Standpoint.* NY: Didion & Company, 1925. |
| 69 | MORD | Richard G. Moulton, M. A. *The Modern Reader's Bible: The Books of the Bible with Three Books of the Apocrypha Presented in Modern Literary Form.* New York: Macmillan Co., 1930. |
| 70 | LAMSA | Lamsa, George M. *The Holy Bible: From Ancient Eastern Manuscripts.* Philadelphia, PA: A. J. Holman Company, 1933. |
| 71 | WADE | Wade, George Wöosung. *The Documents of the New Testament: Translated and Historically arranged with Critical Introductions.* London: Thomas Murby & Co., 1934. |
| 72 | HARK | Harkavy, Alexander. *The Holy Scriptures.* NY: Hebrew Publishing Company, 1936. |
| 73 | GREB | Greber, Johannes. *The New Testament: A New Translation and Explanation Based on the Oldest Manuscripts.* NY: J. Felsberg, Inc., 1937. |

| 74 | SPEN | Spencer, Francis Aloysius. *The New Testament of Our Lord and Saviour Jesus Christ; Translated into English from the Original Greek.* NY: The Macmillan Company, 1937. |
|----|------|---|
| 75 | SMGO | Smith, J. M. Powis, and Goodspeed, Edgar J. *The Complete Bible: An American Translation.* Chicago, Illinois: University of Chicago Press, 1939. |
| 76 | DIAG | Griesbach, J. J., Dr. *The Emphatic Diaglott.* Brooklyn, NY: The Watch Tower Bible and Tract Society, 1942. |
| 77 | KNOX | Knox, Ronald. *The Holy Bible.* New York: Sheed & Ward, Inc., 1944. |
| 78 | MODL | *The Modern Language Bible.* Grand Rapids, Michigan: Zondervan Publishing House, 1945. |
| 79 | SWANN | Swann, George Betts. *New Testament of Our Lord and Savior Jesus Christ: Translated from the Greek Text of Westcott and Hort.* Louisville, KY: New Testament Publishers, 1947. |
| 80 | LETCH | Ford, T. F. and Ford R. E. *The New Testament of Our Lord and Saviour Jesus Christ: The Letchworth Version in Modern English.* Letchworth, Hertfordshire, England: Letchworth Printers Ltd., 1948. |
| 81 | DART | Chamberlin, Roy B. & Feldman, Herman. *The Dartmouth Bible.* Boston, MA.: Houghton Mifflin Company, 1950. |
| 82 | OGN | Ogden, C. K. The Basic Bible: *Containing the Old and New Testaments in Basic English.* NY: E. P. Dutton & Co., Inc., 1950. |
| 83 | WILL | Williams, Charles B. *The New Testament: A Translation in the Language of the People.* Chicago: Moody Press, 1950. |
| 84 | RSV | [Revised Standard Version]. *The Holy Bible: Revised Standard Version Containing the Old and New Testaments.* New York: Thomas Nelson & Sons, 1952. |
| 85 | KLLI | Kleist, James A. and Lilly, Joseph L. *The New Testament, Rendered from the Original Greek with Explanatory Notes.* Milwaukee, WI: Bruce Pub. Co., 1954. |
| 86 | SEPT | Charles Thomson Secretary of the Continental Congress of the United States of America, 1774-1789. *The Septuagint Bible.* Indian Hills, Colorado: The Falcon's Wing Press, 1954. |
| 87 | WEST | [Westminster]. *The Holy Bible.* New York: Hawthorn Books, 1958. |
| 88 | JSOC | *The Holy Scriptures: According to the Masoretic Text.* Philadelphia, PA: The Jewish Publication Society of America, 1960. |
| 89 | NASB | Lockman Foundation. *New American Standard Bible.* Nashville, TN: Thomas Nelson, Publishers, 1960. |
| 90 | SON | Rev. Dr. A. Cohen, M. A., Ph. D., D. H. L. *The Soncino Chumash: The Five Books of Moses with Haphtaroth.* London: Soncino Press, 1960. Rev. Dr. S. Goldman, M. A. Samuel: *Hebrew Text and English Translation with an Introduction and Commentary.* London: Soncino Press, 1966. Rev. Dr. I. W. Slotki, M. A., Litt. D. *Kings: Hebrew Text and English Translation with an Introduction and Commentary.* London: Soncino Press, 1964. |
| 91 | EXPN | Wuest, Kenneth S. *The New Testament: An Expanded Translation.* Grand Rapids, MI: Wm. B. Eedmans Publishing Co., 1961. |
| 92 | NOLI | Noli, Metropolitan Fan Stylian. *The New Testament of Our Lord and Savior Jesus Christ. Translated into English from the Approved Greek Text of the Church of Constantinople and the Church of Greece.* Boston, MA: Albanian Orthodox Church in America, 1961. |

| 93 | NWT | New World Bible Translation Committee. *New World Translation of the Holy Scriptures.* Brooklyn, NY: Watch Tower Bible & Tract Society, 1961. |
|---|---|---|
| 94 | PENTO | Rosenbaum, M., Silbermann, A. M., Blashki, A. and Joseph, L. *Pentateuch with Targum Onkelos, Haphtaroth and Rashi's Commentary: Translated into English and Annotated. Vol. 1. Genesis. Vol. 2. Exodus. Vol. 3. Leviticus. Vol. 4. Numbers. Vol. 5. Deuteronomy.* NY: Hebrew Publishing Co., 1961. |
| 95 | MKJV | *Modern King James Version of the Holy Bible.* New York: McGraw-Hill, 1962. |
| 96 | NORL | Norlie, Olaf M. *The Children's Simplified New Testament: In Plain English—for Today's Reader.* Grand Rapids, MI: Zondervan, 1962. |
| 97 | ANCR | Speister, A. E. *Genesis.* Garden City, NY: Doubleday & Co., Inc., 1964. Milgrom, Jacob. *Leviticus 1-16: A New Translation with Introduction and Commentary.* NY: Doubleday & Co., Inc., 1991. McCarter, P. Kyle, Jr. *1 Samuel: A New Translation with Introduction, Notes & Commentary.* Garden City, NY: Doubleday & Co., Inc., 1980. Albright, W. F. *Matthew:* Introduction, Translation, and Notes. Garden City, NY: Doubleday & Company, Inc., 1971. Fitzmyer, Joseph A., S. J. *Luke 1-9: Introduction, Translation, and Notes.* Garden City, NY: Doubleday & Co., Inc., 1981. Fitzmyer, Joseph A., S. J. *Luke 10-24: Introduction, Translation, and Notes.* Garden City, NY: Doubleday & Co., Inc., 1985. Brown, Raymond E., S. S. *John 1-12: Introduction, Translation, and Notes.* Garden City, NY: Doubleday & Co., Inc., 1966. Brown, Raymond E., S. S. *John 13-21: Introduction, Translation, and Notes.* Garden City, NY: Doubleday & Co., Inc., 1970. |
| 98 | AMP | Lockman Foundation. *The Amplified Bible.* Grand Rapids, Michigan: Zondervan Publishing House, 1965. |
| 99 | CONF | O'Connel, John P., Monsignor. *The Holy Bible: With the Confraternity Text.* Chicago: Illinois: The Catholic Press, Inc., 1965. |
| 100 | JER | Jones, Alexander. *The Jerusalem Bible: Reader's Edition.* Garden City, NY: Doubleday & Company, Inc., 1966. |
| 101 | BARC | Barclay, William. *The New Testament: A New Translation: The Gospels and the Acts of the Apostles. Vol. 1.* London: Collins, 1968. Barclay, William. *The New Testament: A New Translation: The Letters and the Revelation Apostles. Vol. 2.* London: Collins, 1968. |
| 102 | NAB | Catholic Biblical Association of America. *The New American Bible.* NY: P. J. Kennedy & Sons, 1970. |
| 103 | SEPZ | *The Septuagint Version of the Old Testament.* Grand Rapids, Michigan: Zondervan Publishing House, 1970. |
| 104 | ABBR | McCarry, James Leslie and McElhaney, Mark. *The Abbreviated Bible.* NY: Van Nostrand Reinhold, 1971. |
| 105 | LIV | *The Living Bible: Paraphrased.* Wheaton, Illinois: Tyndale House Publishers, 1971. |
| 106 | BYIN | Byington, Steven Tracy. *The Bible in Living English.* Brooklyn, NY: Watchtower Bible and Tract Society of New York, 1972. |
| 107 | PHIL | Phillips, J. B. *The New Testament in Modern English.* NY: Collier Books, 1972. |
| 108 | WMF | Edington, Andrew. *The Word Made Fresh.* Atlanta, GA: John Knox Press, 1975. |

| 109 | BECK | Beck, William F. *The Holy Bible in the Language of Today.* Philadelphia, PA: A. J. Holtman Company, 1976. |
|---|---|---|
| 110 | NEB | Sandmel, Samuel, Ed. *The New English Bible with the Apocrypha: Oxford Study Edition.* NY: Oxford University Press, 1976. |
| 111 | TEV | [Today's English Version]. *Good News Bible: The Bible in Today's English.* New York: American Bible Society, 1976. |
| 112 | NIV | [New International Version]. *The Holy Bible: New International Version.* Grand Rapids, MI: Zondervan Publishing House, 1978. |
| 113 | JBPR | A. J. Rosenberg, ed. *Samuel 1: Judaica Books of the Prophets: A New English Translation of the Text and Rashi, with a Commentary Digest.* NY: Judaica Press, 1980. Rosenberg, A. J., ed. *1 Kings: Judaica Books of the Prophets: A New English Translation: Translation of Text, Rashi,, and commentary.* NY: Judaica Press, 1980. Rosenberg, A. J., ed. *2 Kings: Judaica Books of the Prophets: A New English Translation: Translation of Text, Rashi, and Commentary.* NY: Judaica Press, 1980. |
| 114 | WORR | Worrell, Adolphus Spalding. *The Worrell New Testament: A. S. Worrell's translation with study notes.* Springfield, MO: Gospel Pub. House, 1980. |
| 115 | LIVT | Kaplan, Aryeh. *The Living Torah: The Five Books of Moses.* NY: Maznaim, 1981. Schapiro, Moshe. *The Living Nach: Early Prophets. A New Translation Based on Traditional Jewish Sources. Vol. 1.* NY: Moznaim Pub. Corp., 1994. Schapiro, Moshe. *The Living Nach: Latter Prophets. A New Translation Based on Traditional Jewish Sources. Vol. 2.* NY: Moznaim Pub. Corp., 1996. |
| 116 | ARAON | Aberbach, Moses, & Grossfeld, Bernard. *Targum Onkelos to Genesis: A Critical Analysis Together with an English Translation of the Text: (Based on A. Sperber's Edition).* NY: Ktav Pub. House, 1982. Drazin. Israel. Targum *Onkelos to Exodus: An English Translation of the Text with Analysis and Commentary (based on A. Sperber's Edition).* NY: Ktav Pub. House, 1990. Drazin. Israel. Targum *Onkelos to Leviticus: An English Translation of the Text with Analysis and Commentary (based on A. Sperber's Edition).* NY: Ktav Pub. House, 1994. Drazin. Israel. Targum *Onkelos to Numbers: An English Translation of the Text with Analysis and Commentary (based on A. Sperber's Edition).* NY: Ktav Pub. House, 1998. Drazin. Israel. Targum *Onkelos to Deuteronomy: An English Translation of the Text with Analysis and Commentary (based on A. Sperber's Edition).* NY: Ktav Pub. House, 1982. |
| 117 | NKJV | The Holy Bible: *The New King James Version. Containing the Old and New Testaments.* Nashville, TN: Thomas Nelson Publishers, 1982. |
| 118 | RDB | Metzger, Bruce M., General Editor. *The Reader's Digest Bible: Condensed from the Revised Standard Version, Old and New Testaments.* Pleasantville, NY: Reader's Digest Association, 1982. |
| 119 | CLNT | Knoch, A. E. *Concordant Literal New Testament.* Saugus, CA: Concordant Publishing Concern, 1983. |
| 120 | NLFB | Ledyard, Gleason H. *The New Life Bible, New Testament.* Canby, OR: Christian Literature, 1983. |
| 121 | NJER | Darton, Longman & Todd Ltd. *The New Jerusalem Bible: Reader's Edition.* NY: Doubleday, 1985. |
| 122 | ORIG | Hugh J. Schonfield. *The Original New Testament.* San Francisco, CA: Harper & Row, 1985. |

| 123 | TANK | *Tanakh: A New Translation of the Holy Scriptures.* Philadelphia, PA: Jewish Publication Society of America, 1985. |
|---|---|---|
| 124 | TFFR | Gaer, Joseph, *The Torah For Family Reading: The Five Books of Moses, The Prophets, The Writings.* Northvale, NJ: Jason Aronson Inc., 1986. |
| 125 | ARAM | Chilton, Bruce D. *The Aramaic Bible: The Isaiah Targum: Introduction, Translation, Apparatus, and Notes. Vol. 11.* Wilmington, Del.: Michael Glazier, 1987.<br>Hayward, Robert. *The Aramaic Bible: The Targum of Jeremiah: Translated with a Critical Introduction, Apparatus, and Notes. Vol. 12.* Wilmington, Del.: Michael Glazier, 1987.<br>Levey, Samson H. *The Aramaic Bible: The Targum of Ezekiel: Translated, with a Critical Introduction, Apparatus, and Notes. Vol. 13.* Wilmington, Del.: Michael Glazier, 1987.<br>Cathcart, Kevin and Gordon, Robert P. *The Aramaic Bible: The Targum of the Minor Prophets: Translated, with a Critical Introduction, Apparatus, and Notes. Vol. 14.* Wilmington, Del.: M. Glazier, 1989.<br>Beattie, D. R. G. and McIvor, J. Stanley. *The Aramaic Bible: The Targum of Ruth: Translated, with Introduction, Apparatus, and Notes. The Targum of Chronicles: Translated, with Introduction, Apparatus, and Notes. Vol. 19.* Collegeville, MN: Liturgical Press, 1994. |
| 126 | EB | *The Everyday Bible: New Century Version: Clearly Translated for Life.* Fort Worth, TX: Worthy Publishing, 1987. |
| 127 | ETR | [Easy-to-Read Version]. *Holy Bible: Easy-to-Read Version.* Grand Rapids, Michigan: Baker Book House, 1987. |
| 128 | WBC | Wenham, Gordon J. *Word Biblical Commentary Genesis 1-15.* Waco, Texas: Word Books Publisher, 1987.<br>Durham, John I. *Word Biblical Commentary Exodus.* Waco, Texas: Word Books Publisher, 1987.<br>Hartley, John E. *Word Biblical Commentary Leviticus.* Dallas, Texas: Word Books Publisher, 1992.<br>Klein, Ralph W. *Word Biblical Commentary 1 Samuel.* Waco, Texas: Word Books Publisher, 1983.<br>DeVries, Simon J. *Word Biblical Commentary 1 Kings.* Waco, Texas: Word Books Publisher, 1985.<br>Hagner, Donald A. *Word Biblical Commentary Matthew 1-13.* Dallas, Texas: Word Books Publisher, 1993.<br>Nolland, John. *Word Biblical Commentary Luke 9:21-18:34.* Dallas, Texas: Word Books Publisher, 1993.<br>Beasley-Murray, George R. *Word Biblical Commentary John.* Waco, Texas: Word Books Publisher, 1987. |
| 129 | ARATO | Grossfeld, Bernard. *The Aramaic Bible. Targum Onqelos to Genesis: Translated, with a Critical Introduction, Apparatus, and Notes. Vol. 6.* Wilmington, Del.: Michael Glazier, 1988.<br>Grossfeld, Bernard. *The Aramaic Bible: Targum Onqelos to Exodus: Translated, with Apparatus and Notes. Vol. 7.* Wilmington, Del.: Michael Glazier, 1988.<br>Grossfeld, Bernard. *The Aramaic Bible: The Targum Onqelos to Leviticus ; and, The Targum Onqelos to Numbers: Translated, with Apparatus, and Notes. Vol. 8.* Wilmington, Del.: M. Glazier, 1988.<br>Grossfeld, Bernard. *The Aramaic Bible: The Targum Onqelos to Deuteronomy: Translated, with Apparatus, and Notes. Vol. 9.* Wilmington, Del.: M. Glazier, 1988. |
| 130 | MCORD | McCord, Hugo. *New Testament: McCord's New Testament Translation of the Everlasting Gospel.* Henderson, TN: Freed-Hardeman College, 1988. |

| 131 | MONT | Montgomery, Hellen Barrrett. *The New Testament In Modern English.* Nashville, TN: Holman Bible Publishers, 1988. |
|---|---|---|
| 132 | GNC | Cassirer, Heinz W. *God's New Covenant: A New Testament Translation.* Grand Rapids, Mich., W. B. Eerdmans, 1989. |
| 133 | HIRS | Hirsch, Samson Raphael. *The Pentateuch: Translated and Explained by Samson Raphael Hirsch; Rendered into English by Isaac Levy. Vol. 1 Genesis, Vol. 2 Exodus, Vol. 3. Leviticus part 1, Vol. 3. Leviticus part 2, Vol. 4. Numbers, Vol. 5. Deuteronomy.* 2nd ed. Gateshead: Judaica Press, 1989.<br>Hirsch, Samson Raphael. *The Haftoroth: Translated and Explained by Dr. Mendel Hirsch; Rendered into English by Isaac Levy.* 2nd ed. Gateshead: Judaica Press, 1989. |
| 134 | REB | *The Revised English Bible.* USA: Oxford University Press, 1989. |
| 135 | NRSV | [New Revised Standard Version]. *The Holy Bible: Containing the Old and New Testaments.* New York: American Bible Society, 1990. |
| 136 | NCV | [New Century Version]. *The Holy Bible: New Century Version Containing the Old and New Testaments.* Dallas, TX: Word Bibles, 1991. |
| 137 | REC | Lee, Witness. *The New Testament: Recovery Version.* Anaheim, CA: Living Stream Ministry, 1991. |
| 138 | UNVAR | Gaus, Andy. *The Unvarnished New Testament.* Grand Rapids, MI: Phanes Press, 1991. |
| 139 | ARATJ | Maher, Michael. *The Aramaic Bible: Targum Pseudo-Jonathan, Genesis: Translated, with Introduction and Notes. Vol. 1B.* Collegeville, MN: Liturgical Press, 1992.<br>McNamara, Martin, Hayward, Robert, and Maher, Michael. *The Aramaic Bible: Targum Neofiti 1, Exodus: Translated with Introduction, Apparatus and Notes. Targum Pseudo-Jonathan, Exodus: Translated with Notes. Vol. 2.* Collegeville, MN: Liturgical Press, 1994.<br>McNamara, Martin, Hayward, Robert, and Maher, Michael. *The Aramaic Bible: Targum Neofiti 1, Leviticus: Translated with Apparatus, with Introduction and Notes. Targum Pseudo-Jonathan, Leviticus: Translated with Notes. Vol. 3.* Collegeville, MN: Liturgical Press, 1994.<br>McNamara, Martin, Clarke, Ernest G., Magder, Shirley. *The Aramaic Bible: Targum Neofiti 1, Numbers: Translated, with Apparatus and Notes. Targum Pseudo-Jonathan, Numbers: Translated, with Notes. Vol. 4.* Collegeville, MN: Liturgical Press, 1995.<br>Clarke, Ernest G. *The Aramaic Bible: Targum Pseudo-Jonathan: Deuteronomy: Translated, with Notes. Vol. 5B.* Collegeville, MN: Liturgical Press, 1998.<br>Daniel J. Harrington and Anthony J. Saldarini. *The Aramaic Bible: Targum Jonathan of the Former Prophets: Introduction, Translation, and Notes. Vol. 10.* Wilmington, Del.: Michael Glazier, 1987. |

| 140 | ARATN | McNamara, Martin. *The Aramaic Bible: Targum Neofiti 1, Genesis: Translated, with Apparatus and Notes.* Vol. 1A. Collegeville, MN: Liturgical Press, 1992. McNamara, Martin, Hayward, Robert, and Maher, Michael. *The Aramaic Bible: Targum Neofiti 1, Exodus: Translated with Introduction, Apparatus and Notes. Targum Pseudo-Jonathan, Exodus: Translated with Notes.* Vol. 2. Collegeville, MN: Liturgical Press, 1994. McNamara, Martin, Hayward, Robert, and Maher, Michael. *The Aramaic Bible: Targum Neofiti 1, Leviticus: Translated with Apparatus, with Introduction and Notes. Targum Pseudo-Jonathan, Leviticus: Translated with Notes.* Vol. 3. Collegeville, MN: Liturgical Press, 1994. McNamara, Martin, Clarke, Ernest G., Magder, Shirley. *The Aramaic Bible: Targum Neofiti 1, Numbers: Translated, with Apparatus and Notes. Targum Pseudo-Jonathan, Numbers: Translated, with Notes.* Vol. 4. Collegeville, MN: Liturgical Press, 1995. McNamara, Martin. *The Aramaic Bible: Targum Neofiti 1: Deuteronomy: Translated, with Apparatus and Notes.* Vol. 5A. Collegeville, MN: Liturgical Press, 1997. |
| --- | --- | --- |
| 141 | BBC | McCary, P. K. *Black Bible Chronicles.* NY: African American Family Press, Inc., 1993. |
| 142 | FUNK | Funk, Robert and Hoover, Roy W. *The Five Gospels: The Search for the Authentic Words of Jesus.* San Francisco, CA: HarperCollins, 1993. |
| 143 | GLT | Green, Jay P. Sr. *The Literal Translation of the Holy Bible.* Lafayette, IN: Sovereign Grace Publishers, 1993. |
| 144 | MESS | Peterson, Eugene H. *The Message: The New Testament in Contemporary English.* Colorado Springs, CO: NavPress, 1993. |
| 145 | COMP | Miller, Robert J. , ed. *The Complete Gospels: Annotated Scholars Version.* San Francisco: HarperSanFrancisco, 1994. |
| 146 | KJ21 | *The Holy Bible: The 21st Century King James Version Containing the Old Testament and the New Testament.* Gary, S. D.: 21st Century King James Bible Publishers, 1994. |
| 147 | CCB | Grogan, Patricia. *Christian Community Bible: Catholic Pastoral Edition.* Liguori, MO: Liguori Publications, 1995. |
| 148 | CEV | [Contemporary English Version]. *Holy Bible.* New York: American Bible Society, 1995. |
| 149 | FOX | Fox, Everett. *The Five Books of Moses: Genesis, Exodus, Leviticus, Numbers, Deuteronomy: A New Translation with Introductions, Commentary, and Notes.* NY: Schocken Books, 1995. |
| 150 | GODWD | *God's Word: Today's Bible Translation that Says What it Means.* Grand Rapids, MI: World Publishing, 1995. |
| 151 | INCL | *The New Testament and Psalms: An Inclusive Version.* NY: Oxford University Press, 1995. |
| 152 | NIrV | *New International Reader's Version.* Grand Rapids, Mich.: Zondervan Publishing House, 1996. |
| 153 | ALTER | Alter, Robert. *Genesis.* New York: W. W. Norton, 1996. |
| 154 | LATT | Lattimore, Richard. *The New Testament.* NY: Farrar, Straus, Giroux, 1996. |
| 155 | MITCH | Mitchell, Stephen. *Genesis: A New Translation of the Classic Biblical Stories.* NY: HarperCollins Publishers, Inc., 1996. |

| 156 | NLT | *Holy Bible: New Living Translation.* Wheaton, IL: Tyndale House Publishers, 1996. |
| 157 | STONE | Scherman, Nosson. *Tanach: The Torah/Prophets/Writings: The Twenty-Four Books of the Bible Newly Translated and Annotated.* Stone Edition Tanach. Brooklyn, NY: Mesorah Publications, 1996. |
| 158 | FISCH | Fisch, Harold. *The Jerusalem Bible: The Holy Scriptures.* Jerusalem, Israel: Koren Publishers Jerusalem Ltd., 1997. |
| 159 | WEB | *World English Bible.* [Internet: http://www.bprc.org/], 1997. |
| 160 | CJB | Stern, David H. *Complete Jewish Bible: An English Version of the Tanakh (Old Testament) and B'rit Hadashah (New Testament).* Clarksville, MD: Jewish New Testament Publications, Inc. 1998. |

†*Literature Online: Bible In English.* Version 97:1, Chadwyck-Healey Ltd., 1997.

# ONE

## Psychic Seedlings along a Predestined Path

I could hear the clock slowly ticking. Each second seemed to drag on, an eternity between each tick. Tick... tick... tick... The pitch-black room made it impossible for me to see an inch beyond my nose. As I sat waiting in anticipation, my mind raced at lightning speed. My curiosity was actively feeding a long list of questions to my mind. What was I doing here, sitting silently in the dark with a medium? Why had I been summoned? Tick... tick... tick... Why would an angel want to speak to me? Was I worthy of such an honor? I certainly didn't lead a pious life, as had my great-grandfather, Samuel Frost, a Hasidic Jew.

As the clock rhythmically marked the minutes, I thought about my life and the lives of my ancestors. My paternal grandfather, Max Schwartz, grew up in Russia. Times were difficult, especially for Jews. His family was very poor and to supplement their income, they arranged for Max to apprentice at a tailor's shop. My grandfather worked hard and eventually became an expert tailor. Because of the constant religious persecution in Russia, Max immigrated to the United States. He worked at odd jobs until he had saved enough money to buy cloth to craft a pair of pants. Then he walked into a tailor shop and showed the tailor his craftsmanship. The tailor was impressed and hired him immediately. Max worked long hours and saved his money until he could open his own tailor shop. Soon afterwards, Max married Kate, my grandmother. Their first child was my father Harry. Although Kate was delighted to have a son, she secretly desired a daughter. She went so far as to dress my father as a girl until he was five years old and began school. My grandparents had four more children, but Kate's desire for a daughter was never satisfied. The Schwartz family consisted of five boisterous brothers who grew up in Brooklyn, New York in the early 1900's.

My father had a keen mind, which was a disadvantage in his early life, as he was always six steps ahead of his teachers. Since he was bored, he quit school, and learned to be an expert tailor from my grandfather. At the age of 17, he enlisted in the Coast Guard and went to the academy in New London, Connecticut. He ran a garage and was in the diamond business with his four brothers during World War II. My father was an usual person, some may even consider him a Renaissance man. After watching an expert diamond cutter perform an extremely difficult cut, he could sit down and replicate the same cut. Whether plumbing, fixing a car, or building a house, he could watch someone perform a task and be able to repeat it flawlessly.

My father became disenchanted with city life. The hustle and bustle was irritating to him. He longed for a simple life—to have a farm in the country. He traveled into the country on weekends, finding new places to go fishing. In 1948, he found what he was looking for—a farm with eight acres of land, on US Route 6, in upstate New York. This rural setting was dotted with dairy farms and small houses. A few months after Dad purchased the farm, he married my mother. She had been living in the Bronx and had worked for him when he was in the diamond business. There was a twenty-five year age difference between them.

My mother's family history was very different from my father's. My maternal grandparents lived in Vienna, Austria in the 1930's. They experienced first-hand the cruelty of anti-Semitism. My mother was eleven years old when Hitler annexed Austria in March 1938. My family smuggled across the border to Belgium, where they lived as refugees for over two years, waiting for immigration papers. When the papers finally arrived, the Nazis were already marching to conquer Belgium and my family narrowly escaped. On May 27, 1940, my mother, her parents, and her brother arrived in New York City. That summer my mother attended night school to learn English. In September, she enrolled herself in the seventh grade. When she finished high school, she began working, and eventually worked in my father's diamond business. My parents married in 1949.

I was born in July 1950. I was a difficult infant. I was born with eczema and was allergic to all food, including milk. Each food added to my diet was an experiment. Because of the eczema, my mother had to not only wash, but boil all my clothes and diapers. My childhood must have been taxing for my parents. I am told I had bronchitis and asthma. When I was five years old, I had my tonsils and adenoids removed. It was then that my health improved.

Because my health was so precarious, my parents were afraid to have more children. I grew up as an only child. I would follow my father around, trying to help him with the farm. He had built a number of chicken coops and began operating a chicken farm. I would help collect the eggs, and wash and grade them.

It was lonely growing up in a rural area where large distances separated neighboring farms. If we needed a carton of milk, or ran out of sugar, it meant a seven-mile trip into town. My parents had to drive me everywhere, which made it difficult to have friends. Instead of playing with other children, I learned to entertain myself. I longed for a brother or sister. Often I retreated into a world of make-believe, where I enjoyed creating stories, casting my toys as the characters of intricate plots.

Sometimes I would sit and stare out my second-floor bedroom window. Two tall pine trees stood proudly next to the entrance of our driveway. In the summertime, when the screens were in the windows, I listened to the constant clucking of the chickens. They were a choir, continually singing praises from dawn to dusk. From my window, I had a good view of the highway. I would watch the cars go by, wondering where they were going and who was in them.

Three times a year, my mother and I visited my maternal grandparents, who lived in the Bronx. I thought the trip from our farm to the big city was endless. I felt the drastic contrast between the relaxed, rural setting of our farm and the bustling urban environment. My mother encouraged me to join the children who were playing in the courtyard of my grandparent's apartment building, but I didn't have much experience interacting with other children and was very shy. My grandparents owned a clothing store in Greenwich Village. My mother and I often traveled there on the subway. I remember how small the store was. There was merchandise crammed everywhere—all sorts of clothing for men, women, and children. There were cartons of denim jeans along the walls, and boxes of men's shirts filled shelves from the floor to the pressed tin ceilings. These environments comprised my world.

Religion was always important to my family. Two of our three annual visits to my grandparents were for Jewish holidays, Rosh Hashanah (the Jewish New Year) and Passover. Both holiday celebrations were rich in tradition. I have fond memories of those Passover holidays, even though they were tinged with unspoken sadness. Memories of dear family members murdered at the hands of the Nazis haunted my mother and grandparents.

On Rosh Hashanah, my mother and I would go to my grandparents' temple, which still brings vivid images to my mind. Since it was an orthodox temple, the men and women worshipped separately. A curtain divided the men's section from the women's. Because I was young, I could visit both my grandmother and grandfather during the services. When I was older, and had learned to read Hebrew, my grandfather wanted me to say the prayers aloud with the older men. I didn't understand why I had to say prayers aloud; I felt that saying them in my mind was acceptable. Though I felt God could hear my thoughts, I was much too young to have a theological debate with my grandfather, so I never discussed it with him.

Despite my silent nonconformity, the synagogue services had a mystical aura. The people surrounding me spoke in a language I had never heard spoken on the farm. The ancient Hebrew melodies and chants had traveled through centuries, from generation to generation in an unbroken chain. This link connected me to the Jews of Biblical times.

I began attending Sunday school at the age of four. Learning about the people in the Bible and their relationships to God captivated me. When I was a few years older, we used to play a card game. The teacher had a special deck of cards with questions about Biblical characters. Each card had five or six questions about one Biblical person. I knew every answer to every card in the deck. The Bible fascinated me and made me feel connected to my Jewish heritage.

As a child, my Jewish heritage made me feel uneasy with others. The discrimination and horror my mother's family had experienced during World War II had left an indelible mark on them. My mother often spoke of her terrifying childhood experiences living in Nazi-occupied Austria. Her fear was instilled in me. The community in which we lived was totally Christian. I was the only Jew in my class at public school, and there was only one other Jewish family in our school district. The sense that I was different from everyone else plagued me.

My feelings of isolation intensified at Christmas time. A wave of Christmas spirit engulfed me. Trees and houses full of colored lights twinkled at me seductively, tempting me to be a part of Christmas. These lights were a joy to see, though sadness would envelop me when my conscience reminded me that Christmas was not my holiday. Everywhere, people were singing Christmas carols with their beautifully rich melodies and harmonies. No one, outside of Sunday school, was singing Chanukah songs. Christmas saturated the television and radio, yet I saw no one else celebrating Chanukah.

Perhaps it was my sense of isolation that inspired me to speak out for what I believed in. My art teacher had us make Christmas cards for our parents. I went to her and explained that I celebrated Chanukah. I drew a menorah (the nine branched candlestick) on my card instead of a Christmas tree. In the fifth grade, I made a bulletin board showing a Chanukah menorah and taught the class about my traditions. Although I was outspoken about my heritage, I hid my fear. I was afraid I would experience the same prejudice and hatred my mother had experienced when she was young.

It's interesting that my mother, who grew up orthodox, chose to marry my father. He was Jewish, but had grown up here in America. He had never experienced the prejudice that my mother had. When he was a child, his father sent him to Hebrew school every afternoon for religious instruction. My father detested it. After a few classes, he refused to go and would have nothing more to do with religion. My father considered religion divisive. Each religious group thought the others wrong or evil. This was the origin of many religious wars throughout history. My father felt culturally tied to Judaism, but he practiced none of its rituals.

When I was ten years old, I began attending Sabbath services. Every Saturday morning I went to the synagogue alone. Once I had become familiar with the worship service, I enjoyed it. The repetition created order in my world. Each week was identical to the previous one. We would recite the same prayers, sing the same songs, and practice the same rituals. Only the Torah reading would change from week to week. The *Torah* is the first five books of the Bible's Old Testament. I especially enjoyed this Bible study. The rabbi always explained and interpreted the Torah portion we were to read. Then, as someone chanted the Hebrew words, I would read the English translation. Jewish people love studying the Torah and being philosophical. One little Bible verse would be open to multiple interpretations. People would study and debate each interpretation to determine its truth. This is a strong contrast to Fundamentalist Christians who have only one interpretation of the King James Bible.

I vividly recall an incident that occurred at Sunday school when I was about eleven years old. Though I don't remember what we were studying, I do remember raising my hand to ask this question. "If God spoke to Abraham, and to Moses, and Samuel, and all the prophets, why doesn't God speak to us?"

The answer I received stunned me. "God doesn't talk to us any more because we aren't worthy." I instantly knew that wasn't the truth. The answer just didn't make sense to me, and I could not—*would not* accept it!

At twelve, I began bar mitzvah lessons. A *bar mitzvah* is a ceremony in which a Jewish boy recites blessings and reads a portion of the Torah. It signifies a coming of age, when the boy becomes a man in the eyes of the Jewish community and God. After his bar mitzvah, he is responsible for his actions. From this point on, if he commits sins, he must atone for them on Yom Kippur, Judaism's most sacred holiday. After reading the Torah portion, the bar mitzvah boy chants the *haftorah*.

This is a segment from the remaining books of the Bible (Joshua—Malachi). The haftorah discusses a topic, which corresponds to the topic discussed in that week's Torah portion. Because I had attended Saturday morning Sabbath services regularly, I earned a special honor. At my bar mitzvah, not only would I recite the haftorah, I would lead the congregation through the entire service.

My bar mitzvah was a special event, though I was nervous. My voice still hadn't changed, and my soprano chants of the ancient Hebrew prayers resonated through the congregation. When it was time to recite the haftorah, I became very nervous. My mind suddenly froze. I couldn't remember how to pronounce a certain Hebrew word. It scared me because I had to say it two more times. Somehow I calmed down and continued. When I reached it again, I was able to say it, and complete the rest of my haftorah flawlessly. Many years later, after I had gained an understanding of psychic phenomena, I understood what had happened. Later, I will explain this incident.

Religion was not the only subject that attracted my attention. Parapsychology also fascinated me. During my freshman year in high school, I felt I was becoming psychic. I would have very strong urges to do certain things. I discovered that when I listened to my intuition, events turned out favorably. When I ignored these instincts, the results were not what I wanted, and I wished I had followed my intuition. These experiences inspired me to pick ESP as the topic for my biology research paper. As my research began, I quickly became overwhelmed. Most of the books I read dealt with the scientific laboratory testing of psychics. This was far too technical for me to understand. As a result, I changed the topic of my report.

As each year passed, I felt more and more isolated. My opportunities for socializing were minimal. My mother insisted that I date only Jewish girls. The problem was there were no Jewish girls in my class! My mother allowed me to attend our class dance once a year and a couple of parties. To make matters worse, I couldn't go anywhere alone because I found learning to drive difficult. Our automobile had a standard transmission. I had trouble coordinating the clutch and the gas pedal. After failing my driving test twice, I finally passed it a few days before I left for college.

In 1968, a few months before I began college, my grandmother moved from the Bronx to Brooklyn. My grandfather had died in 1960. In the time since his death the neighborhood in the Bronx had changed. My grandmother no longer felt safe living alone in her apartment building. I have extremely fond memories of my grandparents in their Bronx apartment. To this day, if I dream of my grandmother, she is living in her Bronx apartment, not in Brooklyn.

Once in Brooklyn, my grandmother chose to join an extremely orthodox synagogue a few blocks from her new home. The awe-inspiring services I had experienced in the Bronx did not exist in Brooklyn. In her new synagogue the services were uninspiring. This congregation never spoke English—all the prayers were in Hebrew. The sermons were in Yiddish, a language that is a mixture of Hebrew, German, Russian, and Polish. Although I had often asked to learn Yiddish, my parents had refused to teach me, preferring to speak in Yiddish when they wanted to keep secrets from me. I couldn't understand the rabbi's sermons.

Many of this synagogue's practices disturbed me. A special prayer is said before reading from the Torah. A Jewish person considers the opportunity to say this blessing the highest honor one can have. The name of this blessing is *Aleah*, from the Hebrew word meaning, "to come up," since you are called up by name to say this blessing. Before reading the Torah during the High Holiday services, the president of the synagogue would auction the Aleahs. The winner would be the highest bidder. I felt it was very improper to buy an Aleah on a Holy Day. Jewish law forbids the use of money on these holidays.

Another practice that bothered me was a fund raising activity on Rosh Hashanah. It is the custom to give a donation to the synagogue during the ten day period between Rosh Hashanah and Yom Kippur (the Day of Atonement). This synagogue would announce to the whole congregation the amount each person donated. During my college years, I had the opportunity to attend another Orthodox synagogue. They conducted matters in a more tasteful way. They auctioned their privileges to the Torah *before* the holiday services. During the service, one could make an anonymous donation by folding a card stating the amount one wished to give. These methods were not as commercially blatant and were in keeping with the holiday spirit.

When it came time to choose a college, my main criteria was a large Jewish population. I decided to attend the University of Bridgeport, in Bridgeport, Connecticut. It was a small school, only two hours from home. During the last few months of high school, I had felt trapped and imprisoned. I couldn't wait to leave home, to have some mobility and a social life.

I was very active in Hillel, a Jewish group on campus, and even became president of the organization during my junior year. It was during my presidency that I had the opportunity to help conduct Yom Kippur services. Since my religious feelings were so strong then, it was a high-point of my life. The late sixties and early seventies were turbulent times for college students. I took part in anti-war marches and a student strike at school. Throughout college, though, I felt I didn't really fit in. I knew plenty of people who were smoking marijuana and hash, but I never got involved. The sexual revolution was in high gear, but again, I didn't feel compelled to participate. I remember analyzing the people around me and thinking that I was a throwback to another time because these "in-things" didn't interest me.

For the duration of college, I settled into an uneasy balance of getting by. I did well in courses that interested me but barely passed the required courses. My goal was to become a high school history teacher. I majored in history and minored in education. I found it difficult to deal with the "prima donna" syndrome that most of my history professors displayed. They acted as though they were God's gift to the world, which annoyed me, and often prevented me from doing well in their classes.

The 1972 Summer Olympic games held in Munich, Germany, became the first in a series of events that would shake my religious faith. On September 5, 1972, terrorists kidnapped and murdered eleven Israeli athletes. This happened two days before Rosh Hashanah, the Jewish New Year, and cast a depressing shadow over the holiday. The second event was an argument that occurred between my grandmother and my aunt regarding keeping the rituals of Passover. My aunt was preparing food for the *seder* (dinner). My grandmother didn't like the way she was doing it and a bitter argument ensued. My grandmother refused to eat at the seder. It was the last time my family was together for Rosh Hashanah. The last event that made me question my faith occurred during the High Holiday period. I was praying at my grandmother's orthodox synagogue on Yom Kippur when the Israeli Yom Kippur War began.

These events were difficult for me to accept. The world didn't make sense to me. My mind was filled with questions. I became disillusioned with my religion when it couldn't provide answers. How could a loving God allow so much evil, strife, terrorism, starvation, and unhappiness in our world? Why did bad things happen to good people, while bad people lived their lives free from punishment? How could God have allowed the holocaust to happen? Was there justice in the world?

I continued attending my grandmother's synagogue on the Jewish High Holidays although I didn't enjoy the services anymore. I went for the sake of my mother's and grandmother's feelings. When I was younger, I had experienced dynamic, uplifting, spiritual feelings at synagogue. These feelings had changed to anger, coldness, emptiness, and bitterness. Therefore, I concluded that God did not exist.

As I approached the end of my college years, I was slowly adjusting to the "real" world. I found student teaching extremely nerve-racking. Since I was not secure within myself, standing in front of twenty-five 14 and 16 year olds put me on edge. I was in a constant state of stress, trying to keep one step ahead of the students I was teaching. Yet, on another level, I was having a great time. By trying to teach history on a personal level, I felt I had an opportunity to show young people what life was like in other times.

One night during the ten weeks of my student teaching, the university presented a special program in the student union. Unfortunately I don't remember the name of the speaker, but he was a well-known psychic. My curiosity drove me to attend. I sat close to the stage. The psychic, a middle aged man, had a woman for an assistant. For his first psychic demonstration he took large pieces of cotton off a roll, and put them over his eyes. Then his assistant placed a blindfold over the cotton and taped it to the psychic's face. There was no way he could see. The assistant then went into the audience, asking for personal items. I gave my high school ring to her.

After collecting items from several different people, the assistant returned to the stage. She took one item at a time and held it near the psychic. He lifted his hand and brought it close to the assistant's hand. He didn't touch the item. The assistant held my ring. Within thirty seconds he identified the object as a high school graduation ring!

This demonstration impressed me. It had been many years since I had given psychic phenomena any thought. I had bought a paperback book about improving your ESP at the college bookstore, but I had never had the time to read it. This psychic baffled me. How was he able to identify my ring?

If I had felt baffled before, I was bewildered by the next demonstration he performed. He began talking about reincarnation. He said he could hypnotize a person, and regress him or her to a past life. I had never seriously considered the possibility of reincarnation, although I had studied Hinduism and knew that the Hindus believed one could live many lifetimes.

The psychic chose a woman from the audience and hypnotized her. He took her back to her childhood, and she carried on a conversation as a child would. He then took her further back in time, before her birth, while she was in the womb. Then he took her back even further and asked her where she was. To my astonishment, she was on a Polynesian island. She described her life, and when asked, spoke in her native language. For several weeks my mind returned to this event, pondering the possibility that we might live more than once.

The stress of student teaching forced me to focus on practical things, such as preparing lessons. I remember felt a great sense of relief when student teaching was finally over. Unfortunately, the stress continued after I graduated college.

Finding a job was difficult. I had several interviews, but teaching jobs were hard to come by. The country was in the throes of the Vietnam War, and many people had taken teaching jobs to escape the draft. Few jobs were available.

I had deluded myself. If I couldn't find a job, I would go to graduate school. A friend of mine was studying to become an educational media specialist. I knew that many school districts had openings for that position. I researched college catalogs and discovered that Boston University offered a program in educational media. They would allow me to take eight credits before I applied to the university. I was not enthusiastic about going to graduate school. Although I had worked and contributed to my college education, I didn't want to rely on my parents for more money. I wanted to be independent.

Toward the end of August, with no job in sight, I decided my only alternative was to go to graduate school. I packed a bag and left for Boston University. I registered for course work, secured a part time job, and found an inexpensive apartment.

When I look back now, it amazes me how foolish I was. I thought educational media dealt with making educational videos, filmstrips, and slide presentations. I thought it would be fun. The first class I walked into was a library science class, required for graduation. I was becoming a librarian! I was shocked. I couldn't picture myself as a librarian. To make matters worse, the class involved cataloging books. It was very precise, boring work— a total waste of time. I rebelled.

My rebellion almost caused me to flunk out, but I pulled myself together, and did well. I enjoyed the audio-visual course work. Eventually I came to terms with becoming a librarian, and enjoyed my library science classes.

One spring morning, while I was in the Boston University library looking through *The New York Times* for a teaching position, I discovered an interesting advertisement. A district in New Jersey wanted a teacher who could teach social studies half time and be a media specialist half time. I fit the bill perfectly! I looked up the town in an atlas. To my delight, this town was in the metropolitan New York City area. Immediately I wrote for an application. The school district phoned and asked me to come for an interview, *instead of* completing an application!

I took the train to New York City, and stayed with my grandmother. My aunt drove me to the interview. I was quite nervous, especially after my negative job search experience the year before. As we drove north along the Henry Hudson Parkway to the George Washington Bridge, I said to myself, "Send me a sign if this interview will be successful." I don't know to whom I was addressing this request, nor what I expected to happen. The radio was on and a song just finishing. The next song was Chicago's, *Only the Beginning*. The song lasted into New Jersey. I had my sign. And I did get the job!

My friend Bonnie, a very special person I had met in college, had had a similar experience. She had worked hard getting her Bachelor's degree. She poured her heart and soul into student teaching. After graduation, she couldn't find a teaching job. It devastated her. She felt the injustice of working so hard then not finding a job. The school year had already started when she accepted a position in Waterford, Connecticut as a Title I teacher. This was a federally funded program, which concentrated on giving specialized help to students with learning disabilities.

A year later, I received a phone call from Bonnie. She began very hesitantly, which was unusual for her. She explained that some "strange things" had happened to her. One of her colleagues had described events in Bonnie's life that he had had no way of knowing. He had also described events in some of her friends' lives. It amazed Bonnie that someone who didn't know her well could tell her such precise information. This colleague explained that he could prophesy, as described in the Bible. He had a friend who was a Reverend, who could do the same. He recommended that Bonnie visit his friend. After considering it for a few days, Bonnie made an appointment.

Bonnie is a cautious, level-headed person. She was very skeptical and felt that anyone who could see into a person's future must have a team of researchers gathering information on perspective clients. To avoid investigation, Bonnie had disguised her identity. When she scheduled her appointment, she called from a friend's house. She also gave the fictitious name Susan, and left her friend's phone number instead of her own. Bonnie felt she had covered her tracks—her identity would remain unknown.

A few days later, Bonnie's friend received a phone call asking for Susan. The reverend "had picked up" that Bonnie had given him a fake name and phone number. The annoyed reverend wanted to cancel Bonnie's appointment. After some fast-talking, she managed to persuade him to keep the appointment. It was an astonishing experience for Bonnie. The reverend told Bonnie things that no one else could possibly know about her.

As Bonnie was telling me this story, I interrupted her and asked, "Is this person real? Is he really psychic? Can he see into your future?" Bonnie replied that he was. "Then make an appointment for me, as soon as possible," I replied. This is how I came to meet Carl Hewitt, and have my first psychic reading.

\* \* \* \* \*

*How many minutes had I been sitting in the dark waiting for this angel to speak? I could hear Carl's slow breaths, but the angel still hadn't uttered a word. It was easier to think about what had brought me to this point in my life, than to wonder what this angel would say to me. I began thinking about my first encounter with Carl Hewitt.*

# TWO

## My First Psychic Reading

Columbus Day 1975 was a bright, crisp autumn day. Crimson and gold leaves glimmered in the sunlight, and there was an invigorating chill in the air. It was the day I had been waiting for—my appointment with the Reverend Carl Hewitt. As I left my New Jersey apartment, I was filled with conflicting thoughts: Could the reverend really see into my future? What would he see? I hoped he wouldn't see things that I didn't want him to see! Would I be changing jobs? Would I find the love of my life soon? What's a nice Jewish boy doing visiting a reverend? I hoped he wouldn't try to convert me to Christianity.

As this litany of thoughts rolled through my mind, I completely lost track of the present. When I finally awoke from my mind's wanderings, I found myself about twenty minutes from Bonnie's apartment. I had been so engrossed in thought, I had no recollection of where I had been during the last 2 hours of driving. Thank God I hadn't had an accident.

Shortly after I arrived at Bonnie's place, it was time to leave for my appointment. As we drove to the reverend's office, I told Bonnie about the questions that were rambling through my mind. I had no idea that the experience I was about to have would alter my life. A new door was about to open, one that would lead me on a path that I'd never dreamed of travelling.

We arrived at the Reverend Carl Hewitt's office. After Bonnie introduced us, he showed her where to wait. Then he and I went into his private office. He pointed to a chair, then he sat opposite me on the other side of his desk. After a few seconds he said, "I think you need a glass of water." He stood up and left his office.

Curious, I examined his office from my seat. A portrait of the reverend hung on a wall. A large bookcase filled with books lined another. A familiar title caught my eye. It was Yigael Yadin's book "Masada." Masada was a fortress in ancient Israel where a group of zealous Jews had committed suicide rather than surrender to the Roman army. It surprised me to see this book in the reverend's library. Was he interested in Jewish history? There were books on many different topics, including ancient Egypt. My curiosity peaked when I saw all the Bibles in his bookcase. I wondered why the reverend had so many different Bibles. I dismissed the thought, surmising he must lead a Bible study group.

The reverend returned with a glass of water. He was a pleasant man. I studied his face. His complexion was fair and he had golden blond hair. His eyes were magnetic. Not only were they an unusual ice-blue, they seemed to express wisdom. I was intrigued.

"Do you have any knowledge of the work I do?" the reverend asked me.

"Well, I was told that you can see into people's futures," I responded.

"That is a part of what I do, but perhaps in your case, it might be easier for you to understand if I have you do some reading."

He stood up and walked over to his bookcase. His hand seemed to select a book automatically. He thumbed through it, paused, then handed it to me. It was the King James Bible. "Read the part that is highlighted." he said.

I began reading silently, 1 Kings 14:1-10.

> At that time Abijah the son of Jeroboam fell sick And Jeroboam said to his wife, Arise, I pray thee, and disguise thyself, that thou be not known to be the wife of Jeroboam; and get thee to Shiloh: behold, there is Ahijah the prophet, which told me that I should be king over this people. And take with thee ten loaves, and cracknels, and a cruse of honey, and go to him: he shall tell thee what shall become of the child. And Jeroboam's wife did so, and arose and went to Shiloh, and came to the house of Ahijah. But Ahijah could not see; for his eyes were set by reason of his age. And the LORD said unto Ahijah, Behold, the wife of Jeroboam cometh to ask a thing of thee for her son; for he is sick: thus and thus shalt thou say unto her: for it shall be, when she cometh in, that she shall feign herself to be another woman. And it was so, when Ahijah heard the sound of her feet, as she came in at the door, that he said, Come in, thou wife of Jeroboam; why feignest thou thyself to be another? for I am sent to thee with heavy tidings. Go, tell Jeroboam, Thus saith the LORD God of Israel, Forasmuch as I exalted thee from among the people, and made thee prince over my people Israel, And rent the kingdom away from the house of David, and gave it thee; and yet thou hast not been as my servant David, who kept my commandments, and who followed me with all his heart, to do that only which was right in mine eyes; But hast done evil above all that were before thee: for thy hast gone and made thee other gods, and molten images, to provoke me to anger, and hast cast me behind thy back: Therefore, behold, I will bring evil upon the house of Jeroboam and will cut off from Jeroboam him that pisseth against the wall, and him that is shut up and left in Israel, and will take away the remnant of the house of Jeroboam, as a man taketh away dung, till it be all gone.

Verses 12 and 17 were also highlighted.

> Arise thou therefore, get thee to thine own house: and when thy feet enter into the city, the child shall die. And Jeroboam's wife arose, and departed, and came to Tirzah: and when she came to

**the threshold of the door, the child died.**

When I finished reading, I looked up from the Bible. The reverend explained, "In this passage we find that King Jeroboam and his wife were desperate to find out the fate of their son. In Biblical times, Hebrews frequently consulted prophets concerning events in their futures. However, prophets were afraid to tell the king the truth. Often, if the king didn't like the prophet's message, the prophet would be killed or imprisoned."

Then he handed me a copy of the New American Standard Bible, and told me to turn to 2 Chronicles 16:10 and read aloud.

> **Then Asa [king of Judah] was angry with the seer and put him in prison, for he was enraged at him for this.**

The reverend said, "Let me continue to explain the other verse. Jeroboam didn't want to get a sugar-coated, or fictitious story from the prophet—that is why he asked his wife to disguise herself. He wanted to make sure that Ahijah would not give the queen special treatment, nor tell her only things that she wanted to hear.

"In the meantime, God told the blind prophet, Ahijah, that the queen would be coming for a consultation. Ahijah was instructed as to what to say. When the queen arrived, Ahijah foretold the destruction that would befall King Jeroboam's family, including the exact timing of his son's death."

"So what does this have to do with you, reverend?" I asked. "Are you a prophet?"

"I choose to call myself a *seer*," the reverend explained, "although the words *prophet* and *seer* can be used interchangeably." As he moved to get another Bible, he said, "Please don't stand on ceremony with me, young man, call me Carl." Then he handed me the Today's English Version Bible and said, "Read 1 Samuel 9:9."

> **At that time a *prophet* was called a *seer*, and so whenever someone wanted to ask God a question, he would say, "Let's go to the seer."**

"But wait a minute, Carl," I said. "If you are a seer, according to this Bible passage, that would mean you can talk with God."

"That depends on your definition of God," he replied. He retrieved another Bible from his bookcase. "Read the same verse in The Confraternity Bible," he suggested.

> **Now in time past, in Israel when a man went to consult God he spoke thus: Come, let us go to the seer. For he that is now called a prophet, in time past was called a seer.**

I looked up from the Bible and Carl continued, "Throughout history, there have been people who could talk to the inhabitants of other realms. Centuries ago, people were very class conscious. If a peasant spoke to a nobleman, he would call him *your lordship* or *my lord*. This was done to show respect to a person of a higher class. Turn to Genesis, chapter 31 in that King James Bible and read aloud how Rachel addressed her father in verse 35."

> **And she said to her father, Let it not displease *my lord* that I cannot rise up before thee; for the custom of women is upon me. And he searched, but found not the images.**

"Do you think Rachel thought her father was God Almighty? No, *my lord* was a term of respect. Now read Genesis 44:5 to me for another example."

> **Is not this it, in which *my lord* drinketh? and whereby indeed he divineth? Ye have done evil in so doing.**

"In this verse, Joseph's servant is talking about his master. Obviously there was a difference in social class, and that's why the servant referred to Joseph as *my lord*. People who spoke to entities that they could hear, but not see, or even those they could see, would address them using the word *lord*. The title *Lord* expressed the respect Biblical characters had for these entities as superior beings. Turn to Genesis, chapter 16 in that King James Bible. Read verses 9-13 aloud to me."

> **And the *angel* of the LORD said unto her, Return to thy mistress, and submit thyself under her hands. And the *angel* of the LORD said unto her, I will multiply thy seed exceedingly, that it shall not be numbered for multitude. And the *angel* of the LORD said unto her, Behold thou art with child, and shalt bear a son, and shalt call his name Ishmael; because the LORD hath heard thy affliction. And he will be a wild man; his hand will be against every man, and every man's hand against him; and he shall dwell in the presence of all his brethren. And she called the name of the LORD that spake unto her.**

Carl continued, "Hagar was having a conversation with an angel. The Bible tells us that three times. So why didn't she call out the name of the angel? The Bible says, *'She called the name of the Lord that spake unto her.'* The word *Lord* was used here as a sign of respect. Hagar knew she was speaking to an entity from another realm, and she paid him homage by using the word *Lord*. Now turn to the second book of Kings, chapter 4, in that King James Bible. Read verses 14-17."

I quickly turned to the page and read a conversation between Elisha and Gehazi, his servant.

> **And he [Elisha] said, What then is to be done for her? And Gehazi answered, Verily she hath no child, and her husband is old. And he said, Call her. And when he had called her, she stood in the door. And he said, About this season, according to the time**

**of life, thou shalt embrace a son. And she said, Nay, *my lord*, thou man of God, do not lie unto thine handmaid.**

Carl interrupted, "Do you see, the woman called Elisha *lord*? Notice that the word is not capitalized in this case. Do you think that the woman thought Elisha was God Almighty?"

"No," I replied.

"Then why did she call him *lord*?" Carl asked.

"I guess, as you said, as a sign of respect."

"Exactly. Now read the next verse."

**And the woman conceived, and bare a son at that season, that Elisha had said unto her, according to the time of life.**

"Elisha was also a seer. He could see this woman's future and told her exactly when she would have a child. Obviously, the woman didn't think she was able to have a child. That's why she accused Elisha of placating her by telling her what she wanted to hear. But Elisha insisted that what he saw would come to pass, and it did."

I began feeling as though I were back at school. Examining all these Bibles, was beginning to relax me. As Carl continued, however, I became a bit confused and startled.

"References to the kind of work I do can be found throughout the Bible. I don't know your religious background. It's not important. What we discuss here can be used as an accessory to what you already believe. Many people have told me after their sessions that they have a much deeper understanding of their religious beliefs, and of the Bible.

It's important that you don't get hung up on labels. The Bible has many names for people like me: *soothsayer*, *seer*, *prophet*, *sorcerer*, *wizard*, and *witch*. In primitive societies, I would be called a *shaman*; in ancient Greece, an *oracle*. Today, the three most popular names are *psychic*, *medium* and *instrument*. I don't like to refer to myself as psychic. Everyone is psychic to some degree or another."

"You must realize," Carl continued, "that the word "psychic" comes from the word *psychikos*, which is a Greek word meaning *soul, mind*, and *spirit*. Since everyone has a soul, and everyone has a mind, everyone is psychic. Therefore, anytime we use psychic phenomena we are using the phenomena of the soul. Some people are more psychic than others, just as some people have a talent for painting, but not for playing the piano.

"A *medium* is more unique than a psychic. A medium communicates with entities that are invisible to most people. When the word *medium* describes a psychic person, it indicates that the person acts as an intermediary between people living in the physical world and people living in the Spirit World. Most people call the Spirit World, heaven.

"Spirit people often call their medium an *instrument*. A violin has the potential to create beautiful music, but it takes an outside force, the musician, to produce the music. The musician has the potential to produce beautiful music, but he can not create it without the violin. Music can only be created though the combined effort of the instrument and the musician. Through the use of a medium, Spirit can transmit messages from the Spirit World to a person on the earth plane.

"The medium can't receive the message without the help of Spirit, just as Spirit cannot send the message without the use of a medium. The cooperation of both is needed.

"It really doesn't matter what word you use—*prophet, seer, psychic, medium, instrument, man of God, oracle*—they all mean the same. As Shakespeare said: 'What's in a name? That which we call a rose by any other name would smell as sweet.'

"What is important is not what I call myself, but that I am in contact with the Spirit World; that I give guidance that can help you make decisions in your life."

"How do you communicate with this unseen Spirit World?" I asked.

"There are two main ways that Spirit communicates with a medium. The first is *clairaudience*. This is when Spirit talks to the medium, who hears its voice coming from the Spirit World. The second is *clairvoyance*, when the medium has a vision, projected by Spirit.

"Different people use different names for Spirit. I refer to them as *Spirit, Spirit controls*, or *guides*. The American Indians talked of the *Great White Spirit*. Religious people often speak of *saints, angels, comforters*, and *paracletes*. Many ancient people, like the Greeks and Romans, worshipped *gods* and *goddesses*. In Biblical days, a person who could hear the voice of Spirit always addressed that Spirit as *the Lord*. There are other terms for Spirit like *ghosts* and *poltergeists*. Regardless of the name used, all guides from the Spirit World are actually the souls of people who once lived here on earth.

The Spirit World is timeless—time, as we know it, does not exist. This enables Spirit to see our future, our past, and our present simultaneously. During a psychic reading, issues of time can be confusing. Unless Spirit is very specific, the medium doesn't know when something will happen. For example, if a medium were to see you selling your house, he or she might say, I see the sale of your house when the apples are red. That doesn't tell you if it is this fall, next fall, or two falls from now. Another example might be seeing a new job in a period of three. That could be three days, weeks, months, or years. To the medium it all looks the same. It is unusual for a medium to be more specific than that concerning time."

Carl went on to explain that everyone has guardian angels, or Spirits watching over them. My guardian angels would talk to Carl and clairvoyantly show him images. This is how Carl would know about my past, present, and future. Carl explained that his guardian angel was a Tuscarora Native American chief, named Lone Eagle. This chief had lived nearly 400 years ago in the same area of North Carolina that Carl had grown up in. Carl called this Native person his *control*, because he controlled which Spirits could have access to Carl. Just as there are good and bad people on earth, there are good and bad Spirits in the Spirit World. It is the chief's job to shield Carl from negative Spirits.

Now that I had some understanding about the process of mediumship, it was time for my reading. Carl asked me to give him either the watch or the ring I was wearing. I gave him the ring that I had received on the day of my bar mitzvah. It had belonged to my grandfather, and I had worn it for twelve years. Carl explained that he needed to hold the ring to keep attuned to my vibration, and not wander off to another. People are like radio stations. Just as everyone has a unique fingerprint, everyone's vibrational rate, or frequency, is unique. Being a medium, Carl can adjust himself to tune into another's vibration. Just as you can lose a station on a radio, a medium can drift from the frequency of the person he or she is reading. Holding a piece of jewelry, which has already recorded its owner's vibration, anchors the medium so he or she won't drift off to another frequency.

My counseling session began. What follows are excerpts from the tape of my reading.

> Carl:   I don't know what you do. But I see Philadelphia and Washington D. C. over your head in the future. You have several opportunities. This is confusing; I see electronics around you, yet I don't see them around you. This is not what you do in your field. Are you in teaching or instructing?
>
> Sid:   Yes.

Carl knew only my first name. Without any prior knowledge of me, he was able to determine my profession.

> Carl:   Something's coming up in Philadelphia and Washington D. C. I see a drawing board—do you know if some company like RCA, in conjunction with 3 or 4 other companies, is working on some kind of learning process for advanced students? Great deal of electronics involved here. I see kids with earphones on, and monitors in front of them. You're going to have a chance to be in on the ground floor with this. It pertains to higher education. There will be a pilot school, or class, in motion in Washington D. C. RCA is in Philadelphia and Camden, New Jersey. It looks very modernistic, tomorrow's classrooms.

It seems this still lies in my future, despite the fact that this reading happened over twenty years ago. What is described sounds very close to what is happening in the '90's. With the thrust for technology in the classroom, there are now many classrooms where computers with CD Roms and headsets are being used.

> Carl:   I see a tremendous amount of changes around you. I connect you with Connecticut, New York and New Jersey? All three of them at one time? Do you have any relatives here in Connecticut?

**Sid:** No, I went to college in Bridgeport, and have friends who live in Connecticut. My relatives are in New York, and I live in New Jersey.

**Carl:** Tell me, have you been having dreams that are quite startling?

**Sid:** Not that I can remember.

**Carl:** You know, you are quite psychic yourself, but it was only recently that you could begin to take this kind of work seriously. Am I right? There was quite a long time, during which you never paid attention. While talking to someone, doors suddenly opened to you. Things have happened in your life that have left you wondering whether Spirit caused the events, or it was your imagination. You're going to have some startling experiences, nothing you should fear—you draw Spirit very strongly.

I see a man that looks like a rabbi next to you. Do you know a rabbi, or was there a rabbi in the family someplace? In the distant past? A relative way back?

**Sid:** Yes, my great grandfather, and generations before him, were all Hassidic people. (They would look like rabbis, with a long beards, and a black hats and coats).

**Carl:** I want to go to that era. There is a rabbi that comes from the Spirit World, who seems to stand by you, the way Lone Eagle stands by me. He is waiting for you to develop. A medium develops his psychic over time. As a rose bud opens—petal by petal in its own sweet time, so does the medium blossom when he's ready. No one can hurry the process.

I do not know why I want to count 1, 2, 3, 4, 5, 6. I wanted to count them up this way for some reason. What does six weeks, months, or years have to do with you? Six years from now, will you be thirty or thirty-one?

**Sid:** Thirty-one

Carl correctly stated my age.

**Carl:** That's right, by the time you get to your thirty-first birthday, you will have achieved a great deal in this work. And, believe it or not, I see you in front of a lot of people lecturing, about psychic phenomena. You might push this aside now, you might not want to accept it, but this man that comes from the Spirit World will be using you, and you will have no control, just as I have

Sid:    no control over it.
Sid:    I had an interesting experience when I was in Israel, and I'd like to know if my grandfather had anything to do with it?
Carl:   Is your grandfather in Spirit?
Sid:    Yes.
Carl:   I'm seeing the Star of David with him, was he Jewish?
Sid     Yes.
Carl:   I don't know what happened, but your grandfather had something to do with this. The incident happened to you when you were in Jerusalem, was it Jerusalem?
Sid:    Yes.

Jerusalem! I had deliberately asked my question without divulging the specific location. I had wanted to see if Carl would know the location of this event. I had only talked about this experience to one other person, the mother of a college friend. Carl was telling me information that no one else knew! He was correct again.

Carl:   Was it very dry and hot when you were there? Is this why I feel like I'm in sweltering heat?
Sid:    Yes.
Carl:   They're not showing me what happened, but they are showing me the weather conditions. This event has caused you to think a great deal about psychic matters, right?
Sid:    Yes.

In the summer of 1972, I had taken a trip to Israel. At that point in my life, my feelings toward Judaism varied. Occasionally I thought God did not exist, yet at other times, I felt quite religious. My visit to the Western Wall, Judaism's holiest site in Jerusalem, was a mystical experience. My emotions were running high. The tradition, when one visits the wall, is to write a request of God on a small piece of paper, and cram it in a crack between the blocks of stone. Supposedly, God will receive these requests and answer them. I couldn't accept that as possible. Yet, as I stood before the wall, hundreds of pieces of paper crammed into the cracks. I felt a very strong need to pray, however I didn't have a prayer book. I also wanted to put on phylacteries. After my bar mitzvah, at 13, I had recited morning prayers wearing phylacteries—two boxes with a prayer inside. One box sits on the forehead with a leather strap around the head, going over the shoulders. The other box is placed around the left arm, near the heart, and the leather strap is wound around the arm in a particular pattern. Jewish men put on phylacteries each morning before saying prayers, except Saturday mornings.

I had stopped this practice when I went to college. Now I felt a need to perform this ritual. Suddenly, from out of no where, I heard a voice. "Would you like to put on phylacteries?" I turned and there was one of the Hassidic Jews, with a long beard

and a dark black coat. A bit shaken, I said, "Yes." It seemed he had read my mind.
He escorted me, helped me put the phylacteries on, and handed me a prayer book. I
said my prayers, still wondering how this had happened.

Carl:  There is someone else who comes to you, a male from
the Spirit World who gives you thoughts. It is part of
the training you have to go through. I feel very good
about this, very good. This ring belongs to you, or does
it belong to someone else? I'm getting vibrations from
another person.

Sid:   It was my grandfather's ring.

Not even Bonnie knew that my ring had belonged to my grandfather. Carl had to
be a genuine medium to be giving me this much correct information.

Carl:  Is this the one who is in Spirit?

Sid:   Yes.

Carl:  This person feels good. He was a smart man, but he
had a few mishaps. He thought a lot of you. Did he
pass about 4-5 years ago?

Sid:   No, he passed 15 years ago.

Carl:  What happened four years ago with your grandfather?
Did you have an experience? Did you have a dream
about him?

Sid:   Every once in a while I dream about him.

Carl:  Were you having a struggle, at that particular time in
college, and you had a dream one night?

Sid:   Not that I remember.

Carl:  This is what I see. Were you in college four years ago?

Sid:   Yes.

Carl:  Were you struggling? Was there something you were
having a problem with? This man came to you in a
dream, whether you remember the dream or not. Many
people do not remember their dreams. He came to you
in a dream to give you courage to go on. Because you
rode that storm out, you came out on top.

Sid:   I wonder if that had anything to do with student
teaching?

Carl:  It was teaching. Remember I asked you if you were in
college at the time? I saw you not as a student, sitting
with the rest of the students, but up in the front of a
room. It was college, but you were teaching. It was
definitely during that time. There was a time when you
thought of going in another direction, because you
were discouraged. You finally decided to hold on to

what was good. That was a good choice. You are going
to be stepping in on the ground floor of something new.
This person will help you a great deal. This man was
not only good, but also shrewd. It's as if he could see
around the bend before he got there. That's what he's
showing me about this new venture, you'll be involved
with.

After this experience, I was hungry for more knowledge. I began to read all the
books I could get on the subject. Many dealt with reincarnation. It made sense to me.
The soul would reincarnate many times to gain knowledge and to pay karmic debts.
For example: Sebastian was a priest in the 1500's who burned witches at the stake.
He might reincarnate in the 1970's as a fire fighter and die in a burning building.
There seemed to be a sense of balance with this theory. If you were bad in this life,
you would pay for it in another. If you were poor in one life, you might be rich the
next. I was fascinated with this concept. Three months later, I was having some
difficulty with work. I decided to ask Carl for advice. Most of this reading concerned
my job and questions I had about my past lives.

Three months after that, I had another reading. This time I found out more about
the Spirits who were around me. It was at the end of this reading that this
conversation occurred:

Carl:   Too bad you live so far away, because I would like to
        invite you to be part of my psychic development class.
Sid:    Well don't let that stop you. I would drive up for your
        classes.

A look of disbelief crossed Carl's face. I lived two and a half-hours away. I
wasn't aware of any real mediums in the metropolitan New York City area. I knew
Carl was genuine. It was worth the long drive to learn more about the Gifts of the
Spirit, and perhaps to become psychic myself.

# THREE

## Evaluating Readings: How Accurate Are They?

It has been over twenty years since my first reading with Carl. Since then I have had about thirty readings with him, as well as with other mediums. To present a balanced picture, I need to discuss the accuracy of psychic readings. This is more involved than, "Yes, that prediction did happen," or "No, it didn't happen."

A psychic reading is similar to traveling down a country road—one comes to a crossroad and makes a choice: left, right, straight ahead. Each road leads to a different destination. For example, I have been told many times in my readings that I would change jobs. This still hasn't happened. A skeptical person would say the medium was incorrect. The medium said I would change jobs several times but I'm still at the same job. Why? I *chose* to remain there. Whether it is insecurity, or a resistance to change, I can look back and say I never pursued leads to new jobs, I never put energy into changing my job, except on one occasion, and then I changed my mind. This is one of the areas where I can control my decision. Since I chose to go left when the medium said I would go right, it's not the medium's mistake.

On other subjects Carl was 100 per cent right. When he described how my father and grandmother would pass on, he was very accurate. The death of a relative is an event that no one can change. Here, predestination comes into play, and Carl's insights greatly helped me to cope with that traumatic period of my life.

How accurate does a medium have to be, to be considered correct? That depends on one's degree of skepticism. Let me give you an example. One evening Bonnie and I walked into our psychic development class. Carl greeted us, looked at Bonnie, and said, "Congratulations, I see you're carrying a child." Bonnie's mouth dropped open. "Oh my God," she said, "I just went to the doctor for a pregnancy test, but haven't gotten the results back yet." Sure enough, a day or two later, the doctor confirmed that Bonnie was pregnant.

A few weeks later Bonnie confronted Carl. "OK, if you know I'm pregnant before my doctor does, tell me when this baby will be born, and if it will be a boy or a girl." Carl paused then replied, "I see you being handed a piece of paper with the date August 26th on it. You will have a baby girl."

In one sense, Carl was wrong, yet he was right. Bonnie's little girl, Jennifer, was born on August 23rd, much to Bonnie's disbelief as she went into labor. Through the pain, Bonnie thought, "This can't be happening today. Carl said I would give birth on the 26th." Bonnie had to stay in the hospital a few days. When the nurse handed

Bonnie a hospital release form, Bonnie understood what had happened. The date on the release form was August 26th. Carl didn't see the birth certificate, as we had thought, but Bonnie's hospital release form. Would you say that Carl had accurately predicted the birth? That would be your decision.

Five years passed, and Bonnie and her husband moved to New Jersey. Bonnie was pregnant again. Carl and I went to visit her. "OK," Bonnie said, "you did so well with Jennifer, let's try it again. When will this baby be born? Will it be a boy or a girl?" This time Carl said, "Let me see a calendar." Bonnie gave him a calendar. Carl thumbed through it, and pointed to the 17th of April. "I feel very good with this date, and you will have a baby boy."

"Are you seeing the release date or the birth date?" Bonnie asked.

"I just feel good about April 17th." On April 17th, Michael was born.

Sometimes in phone conversations, Carl gives me information that he picks up psychically. On one occasion, I was expecting the delivery of a piano. As I was talking to Carl that morning, he said he saw the deliverymen arriving at my apartment at 11:30. Well, 11:30 came and went, and the whole day seemed to drag. Finally, at 5:00, the men arrived to deliver my piano. The next day, I spoke to Carl again. "Well you didn't get this one right," I said. "They didn't come until 5:00."

Carl responded, "Yes, but think about this. Flip 11:30 around, and it will become 5:00. Sometimes images that mediums see are in reverse, or negative form, especially with issues of time. Remember, the Spirit World is a timeless dimension. Any predictions concerning time can be considerably inaccurate."

The choice of a medium is important. Carl can't read for himself. Mediums are too emotionally involved in their problems to be able to read for themselves. Carl had been having another medium, Catherine, read for him. He thought she was fantastic. Everything she told him happened. Carl highly recommended her as a medium. Bonnie had a couple of readings with her, and was impressed with her work. Eventually, I went to her too. I didn't find her that accurate. Since every one has a different vibration, I think a medium is able to connect more effectively with one individual than another. While I would never question Catherine's abilities as a medium, my connection with Carl was stronger. Yet, Bonnie connected with both.

I have had varied experiences with readings from mediums other than Carl. I am often skeptical in my approach to a new medium. As I did with Carl, I'll ask questions and leave out details to see if the missing information comes through. If it does, then my confidence in the new channel grows. If it doesn't, then I don't take the reading too seriously.

I had a fascinating experience with an astrologer who lived in Providence, Rhode Island. I had heard about her from one of Carl's clients. I was curious, so I made an appointment. She asked me my first name, place of birth, date of birth, and time of birth. She then gave me directions to her house. My appointment came two weeks later.

Minutes after the start of my reading I was astonished. She had drawn up my astrological chart. She looked at it and began talking. It seemed as if she had picked up a book entitled, "This is your life Sidney Schwartz," and began reading from it. Everything she said was accurate. She described details from my childhood, giving my age for different events. Every detail was 100 per cent correct. This reading amazed me.

A few days after I began to write this book, Carl received a letter. Two women had come to his office for an appointment. While the first lady was having her reading, the second wrote this letter documenting the accuracy of Carl's readings. This is one of the hundreds of testimonials that Carl has on file in his office. I think it sums up the topic of the accuracy of psychic readings.

July 6, 1994

Dear Carl,

From a very young age, I was open to the extraordinary, or should I say, paranormal. At the ripe old age of 10, I saw patterns in my life—things falling into place, lessons being learned at the precise moment I needed one to be taught in order to progress to the next level. It wasn't until years later I heard about the concepts of "synchronicity" and "everything happening for a reason."

Through much thought, a lot of reading, and, dare I say, spiritual guidance, I have discovered many truths that many others whom I come in contact with are totally unaware of. I have learned, sometimes the hard way, not to ignore my intuition, and to tune into my "God-within" to ask for guidance in how to live my life.

This spiritual search is intense—since I am intensely curious. I am pleased to say that you have been a catalyst for much of the positive growth and development I've experienced in my life.

I first came to see you in 1982 while I was in the midst of a very difficult relationship. Although it wasn't clear at that time, your reading did point to many of the positive changes I would experience in the future. In 1983, you told me, I would leave my relationship and that a much better relationship was ahead. You said this man would have lighter hair than mine, he would be about 2-3 years older, his work involved engineering or architecture, and he had a mustache. You were wrong on only one account—*he had just shaved off his mustache!* In 1985, I met this man who has been the light of my life, a solid rock upon which to lean, and a port in the storm. We are very different, and, in many ways, so compatible. He is blond, two and one-half years older than me, a mechanical engineer who had been a builder for ten years, and a delightful person. This relationship is truly different from any I have experienced in the past. You also said we would have known each other in a previous life. Upon initially meeting me, Michael told me that he had an impulse to hug me—almost as if he had known me before. You also said the name Bill comes around this person. Bill was his roommate, continues to be his best friend, and was the best man at our wedding.

You are truly miraculous. Your readings have served to affirm my own beliefs on the meaning of life, and my faith in the afterlife.

I would say 90 per cent of the details that were relayed to me in my readings have been on target and amazingly accurate. The only things that have not been too accurate have been the timeframes. It's usually a longer period of time than what you predict.

I saw you in March of this year. I was very apprehensive about having a child. You told me that I would conceive and you saw me with a healthy child—in fact, you saw me with two healthy children down the road. I'm not sure about two, but I am pregnant right now. Everything seems to be fine. I am saying the prayer you gave me and visualizing the best. I will let you know, sometime in December, what the outcome is.

I wish you the very best, and I hope that you continue to be a light for others as you have been for me.

Love,
Deborah Korval

# FOUR

## Psychic Development Classes

The 3:30 p.m. bell rang. School was finally over for the day. A sense of excitement permeated through me. I got into my car to drive from New Jersey to Connecticut. I weaved in and out of traffic, crossed the George Washington Bridge and headed for the New England Thruway. I coundn't believe the night was finally here! I was off to my first psychic development class! As the car made its way up the highway, my mind wandered. What was this class going to be like? Would I really be able to become a psychic?

As I navigated the highway, I thought about how Carl's church had begun. In 1976, Carl had decided to follow the command of Spirit. Many years before, he had had a vision of establishing a church based on the twelfth chapter of 1 Corinthians. He was to name his church The Gifts of the Spirit Church. Psychic phenomena would be practiced as part of the service. Carl had been reluctant to carry out Spirit's command, for he had seen the difficulties other mediums had encountered with their churches. After much urging by Spirit, he began the process. Carl's church was different from other churches in that he sent a copy of the bylaws to the United States Government and to the State of Connecticut. Both levels of government submitted the bylaws to committees made up of priests, ministers, and rabbis. The committees approved The Gifts of the Spirit Church as a new religion not to be considered a sect, or a cult. The United States government and the State of Connecticut followed suit and recognized Gifts of the Spirit Church as an official religion. In 1977, after this founding process was complete, Carl held his first church service.

Before I knew it, I had arrive in New London, and was making the intricate series of turns to Bonnie's apartment. As she opened her door, a look of excitement was on her face, for this was her first psychic development class.

We sat down to dinner exchanging our ideas of what class would be like. Bonnie said, "If our parents knew about this they would kill us." After dinner, we began our trip. We watched the clock. Carl locked the doors at 7:30 and we didn't want to miss our first class!

We arrived at the chapel in plenty of time. Other people were already there. There were more women than men in the class. We introduced ourselves. Most of these people had attended Carl's previous classes, so were not new students. Carl had arranged the class in a circle. As 7:30 approached, he directed us to our seats, and began the first part of the class with discussion about psychic phenomena. Over the course of the next three years, I attended these weekly classes.

Often Carl spoke about the Bible. He claimed the major characters of the Bible demonstrated psychic gifts. This theory fascinated me, although I was skeptical at first. After a while it started to make sense. I learned that Carl was *clairaudient*, meaning he could hear Spirit voices. The Bible said God talked to Abraham and Moses. Exactly how did this conversation take place? I had never thought about it. Obviously not everyone could hear or see God. It seemed logical that Abraham and Moses heard the voice of God because they were also clairaudient.

Often during his lectures, Carl would start talking to someone else. He would turn his head and say, "I heard you," to some entity invisible to the rest of us.

A period of meditation followed Carl's talk. He had us close our eyes in the darkened room, and listen to relaxing music. This process of relaxing, centering, and "going within" had a very calming affect on me. Meditation is the most crucial step in psychic development.

After meditation we had a psychic demonstration. Carl would have the students practice their psychic gifts, or he would demonstrate his own. This was my favorite part of the class. Frequently, Carl would demonstrate *deep trance*. This Gift of the Spirit is extremely fascinating and occurred frequently in Biblical times. Carl always stressed that the Bible was a book of psychic history. As we learned, each Gift of the Spirit, he showed us examples of that gift in the Bible. For trance, Carl read from the book of Samuel:

**And the Spirit of the LORD will come upon thee, and thou shalt prophesy with them, and shalt be turned into another man.**[1]

To demonstrate deep trance, Carl would lie on the floor in the middle of our circle. He appeared to go to sleep. Carl's soul would leave his body. Another soul, or Spirit, from the Spirit World would enter his body. This Spirit would speak to us through Carl. Many different Spirits spoke to us during the series of classes I attended. My favorite Spirit was Nathaniel, who had once lived in Kent, England. He would come through with a British accent and say, "A jolly good evening." It was such a marked change from Carl's normal speaking voice. When Carl went into deep trance, it was evident that he was *turned into another man*.

The Spirit that took over Carl's body would lecture us, explaining some aspect of psychic phenomena or philosophy. Sometimes the Spirit would *prophesy* future events.

After the lecture, the Spirit would allow each of us to ask a question. Many people chose to ask personal questions that pertained to their lives. Others chose to ask philosophical, historical questions, to clarify events that had happened during another time.

It was extremely important for us to remember that when Carl was in a deep trance state, no one could say his name as that would summon his Spirit to re-enter his body. This sudden jarring of the Spirit could be dangerous, even fatal, as it could send him into a state of shock.

---

[1] 1 Samuel 10:6 [KJV].

I once attended a class during the early summer. Carl had locked the screen, but left the door ajar. He was in a deep trance state. One of the class members arrived late, knocked, and called Carl's name. Instantly Carl's Spirit flew back into his body, and he began shaking like a leaf. His heart was racing, but luckily, after about 15 minutes, he was back to his normal self. Carl expelled that student from his class.

Carl also showed us how to use the gift of *healing*. Carl would go into a meditative state, then he'd have someone sit in a chair before him. He would ask to become an instrument of healing. Spirit people assembled and channeled healing energy from the Spirit World into Carl's body. Carl would place his hands on the person sitting in the chair to transfer the healing energy to him.

One night after a year or so of attending classes, Carl said he needed a healing for himself. He called on me to be the healer. I was dumbstruck. He told me to clear my mind, then gave me basic instructions, including the correct placement of my hands. Once my hands made contact with him, it was important not to break the contact until the healing was over. If I felt inspired to move my hands to another location, I was to move them one at a time. I followed all of Carl's instructions carefully. I tried to focus and clear my mind. The healing lasted about five minutes. As I cleared my mind, my hands became very warm. I was thrilled that I had been chosen to be the instrument that night. It was an event I will never forget.

Carl taught us *psychometry*, which is the ability to receive an impression of a person by holding one of his or her personal belongings, usually a piece of jewelry or a watch. Carl had us close our eyes and meditate. Then he placed objects in our hands. When he placed an object in my hands, I began to see pictures that described the object, or its owner. My experiences with psychometry varied. On one occasion a lady gave me her watch to hold. I immediately saw beautiful paintings, a mountain landscape dissolved into a seascape. Next, I saw a painting of colorful flowers. I asked if she painted. When she responded that she hadn't, I suggested she consider painting as a hobby. About three years later, this same lady came to church with three of the pictures she had just finished. She had taken Spirit's advice and was now painting beautiful landscapes.

Over the three years that I attended these classes, I met many interesting people. After a class met for a while, a bond formed, as if we were all interconnected. Carl said our vibrations had blended. Each of us would become a cell in one big battery.

This bond was not always permanent. I saw many students come and go. Some showed promise, but became impatient with their slow process of developing their gifts. A few even tried to fake a trance state. Since Carl was clairvoyant, he was able to see a Spirit leave or enter the body. There was no point in trying to fake a trance, since he could tell if it were genuine or not. Some became egotistical. They felt they were so advanced they no longer needed Carl's classes. I was to learn that this was the norm in psychic development classes throughout history.

# FIVE

## The Trip to Lily Dale

The sun shone brightly as Bonnie and I drove to Carl's church. This time we weren't going to a psychic development class. At Carl's we would board a bus for an eleven-hour ride to Lily Dale, a small village in upstate New York where many psychics had summer homes. Carl had arranged this trip for our class as well as several other people. We were enthusiastic about what we were learning in Carl's classes. The more knowledge we acquired about psychic phenomena, the more we realized there was so much more to learn. This is a vast subject, with hundreds of facets. With our insatiable appetite for more knowledge, and more psychic experiences, we eagerly boarded the bus.

We had a fantastic time on the bus ride. We joked and sang songs. The hours seemed to fly by. At last we arrived at Lily Dale. As our bus approached the arched gate, we read the boldly lettered sign: **LILY DALE, THE LARGEST SPIRITUALISTS CAMP IN THE WORLD.** Spiritualism is a religion with two main tenets: the soul survives after death, and communication is possible with departed souls through mediumship.

Lily Dale was 88 years old. Most of the buildings wore their age without pride. There was a whisper of days of grandeur—days long gone. We were staying at the Maplewood Hotel, located in the northwest corner of the grounds. I felt I was travelling back to the turn of the century. The bright summer sun had made the rooms quite stuffy, and there were no fans to help escape the heat. Once we had settled in, we met Carl in the lobby for a tour of the grounds.

Although most of us were just beginning to develop our psychic abilities, it was apparent to all of us that Lily Dale had a unique vibration. It was puzzling. I scanned the grounds. It looked like an ordinary small village, with little streets branching out in all directions. It resembled thousands of other small towns that dot the countryside. What made Lily Dale feel so different?

The medium's cottages gave Lily Dale its special flavor. Like a multi-colored patch-work quilt, some were painted in bright, cheerful colors, while others were faded. What caught our attention were the signs on the doorways of each medium's house. Each sign listed the medium's name and special psychic gift such as trance or healing.

As we continued our tour of Lily Dale, we began to notice the many specialized buildings on the grounds. They varied in size, shape, and purpose. The largest building was the auditorium, which held about 700 people. The stateliest building in

Lily Dale was the library, with its majestic columns adorning the entry doors. When I had a chance to explore it, I discovered most of the books were about psychic phenomena and the history of Spiritualism. The archives had books dating back to the 1850's.

During the summer, an intensive schedule of lectures, psychic demonstrations, and classes kept visitors to Lily Dale very busy. When a medium was not busy with a scheduled assignment, he or she conducted private readings.

On our first night, our whole group attended a service. This service followed the same format as Carl's church services. It began with a lecture. As the lecturer began speaking, Carl nudged me and whispered, "You know he's in trance?"

"He is?" I said, "But he's standing up and his eyes are open. How can he be in trance?"

"A medium can be standing and still be in a trance state. The average person couldn't tell."

Later Carl explained to me that many Biblical prophets were in a trance when they prophesied. The Bible describes the trance-state as follows:

> **And the Spirit of the LORD will come upon thee, and thou shalt prophesy with them, and shalt be turned into another man.**[2]

This clearly shows that the prophet's Spirit had left his body, so the Spirit of the Lord could speak through it. This is why the Bible used the phrase, *and shalt be turned into another man*. Often the Spirit would have another accent, use different grammatical syntax, or different enunciation than the prophet used in his natural state of consciousness. As these *men of God* prophesied in public, many people might have thought the words the prophet spoke were coming from his own consciousness instead of from the Spirit that had taken over his body.

The second part of the service at Lily Dale was a message service in which the medium would act as bridge between a Spirit and a person in the congregation. It is essential for the person receiving the Spirit message to respond to the medium. The person should say, "Good morning," or "You are welcome," even if the person does not recognize the Spirit. If the person remains silent, the Spirit will not communicate. Spirit Messages are similar to telephone calls. If a person answers the phone and remains silent, the caller will hang-up, terminating the communication.

Message work can be very emotional, especially the first time a person contacts a deceased loved one. This is a sample of the type of communication that may occur during a message service:

| | |
|---|---|
| Medium: | I would like to come to the lady wearing the pink blouse. I need to hear your voice. |
| Woman: | Good evening. |
| Medium: | Yes, thank you. As I am picking up on your vibration, I see the word "Roy" around you. Did you know a man |

---

[2] 1 Samuel 10:6 [KJV].

|          | named Roy, who would be on the Spirit side of life? |
|----------|---|
| Woman:   | Yes, he was my husband. |
| Medium:  | He is handing you a vase with four beautiful red roses in it. |
| Woman:   | Tell him he can keep his damn roses. He was an alcoholic, and he drank Four Roses whiskey. He drank himself to death. If he wasn't a drunk, he'd still be alive, here with me. |

The first lesson a medium receives from Spirit is about symbolism. It is an ancient language that Spirit uses, since, like sign language, it transcends all languages and cultures. Sometimes a Spirit can only speak a language that is foreign to the medium. By using symbolic pictures, the Spirit can communicate to the medium, who can then pass on the information to the person. In this message, the medium saw the symbol of four roses, which symbolized the husband's favorite brand of whiskey. It was a perfect symbol for his identification.

Messages may come through involving people's health, lost objects, and from loved ones who have passed on. Sometimes they're serious and sometimes very funny.

|          |   |
|----------|---|
| Medium:  | The light is moving to a young gentleman in the back of the room. You are wearing a green and white striped shirt. |
| Man:     | Yes, you are welcome. |
| Medium:  | As I move into your vibration, I am aware of a gentleman coming to you. He was heavyset, and quite tall. He has jet black hair and is wearing an army uniform. |
| Man:     | Yes, my father was in the army. He died in the Korean War. |
| Medium:  | As he comes around you, sir, he places his arms around you. He is now showing me the image of a toy train. |
| Man:     | Just before he left for the war, he bought me a train set. I still have it. |
| Medium:  | Yes, he is smiling because you still remember that. He is concerned about a health condition. He is telling me that you need to be careful. Have you had a physical lately? |
| Man:     | No, I haven't. |
| Medium:  | Your father is saying that unless you see a doctor within the next 10 days, and start taking blood pressure medicine, you will be joining him in the Spirit World. He is quite concerned, since it is not your time to cross over. |
| Man:     | Well, I will have it checked out. |

| | |
|---|---|
| Medium: | Thank you. I am now leaving your vibration, and I would like to come to the gray haired woman sitting in the second row. |
| Woman: | Good evening. |
| Medium: | There is a man here who is laughing. All he's showing me is a jar of peanut butter, and a jar of cold cream. Does that mean anything to you? |
| Woman: | Yes, as a matter of fact, it does. |
| Medium: | Now I see the man emptying the jar of cold cream and filling it with peanut butter. |
| Woman: | That's exactly what he did. We were on vacation and he put peanut butter in my cold cream jar. When I went to put the cream on my face in the dark, I put the peanut butter on instead. It was really funny, and we had a good laugh. I was so embarrassed that I never told a living soul about it. |

At Lily Dale, it seemed the medium came to people who were new to the meeting. Most of the people in our group received messages. Finally, Spirit came to me. The message I received spoke of a time when I would become an instrument of Spirit. This excited me greatly, as I had developed a great deal of respect for mediumship.

One of Spiritualism's main doctrines was becoming clear to me. After death, our Spirit continues to live. Death is not the end. It is actually a birth into a new world. Heaven, or the Spirit World, is not detached from us, above or below us. The Spirit World (heaven) is not above us. It exists on a higher frequency than our sences can detect.

It was comforting to know that loved ones who had passed on could communicate with us. This new philosophy removed the mystery and fear surrounding death. Death was merely a transition, the severing of the silver cord that connects the physical body and soul. The Bible also explains that we have two bodies—one for each world. Although I was unaware of it at the time, it was in The New Testament:

> It is sown a physical body; it is raised a spiritual body. If there is a physical body, there is also a spiritual body.[3]

> I tell you this; my brothers: an earthly body made of flesh and blood cannot get into God's kingdom. These bodies are not the right kind to live forever.[4]

---

[3] 1 Corinthians 15:44 [RSV].

[4] 1 Corinthians 15:50 [LIV].

When the soul leaves the body, it enters the Spirit World. Then it has access to *all* its memories, not only of the last life, but all of previous lives.

Being around so many mediums and hearing these messages was inspiring and educational. It was evident, being submersed in a community where the Gifts of the Spirit were practiced on a daily basis, that we were witnessing a principle Carl had taught us. Often during our psychic development classes, he stressed that the laws of psychic science have not changed, what is true today was true in Biblical times. At Lily Dale we could see this for ourselves.

Although the terminology has changed over the centuries, the process of receiving spiritual guidance from a *prophet*, or *medium*, existed in Biblical times. One of the most famous "readings" that occurs in the Bible is when Jesus read for a Samaritan woman at Jacob's well.[5] Jesus had come to Jacob's well, and was tired and thirsty. At the same time a Samaritan woman approached the well. Jesus ask her for a drink. We discover in verse 11:

> **"Sir," the woman said, "you have no bucket and this well is deep."[6]**

Jesus did not have a bucket. The woman drew Jesus water from the well with her water jar and handed it to him. As he held the jar, he saw images of her life. This is exactly what happened when Carl had us practice *psychometry*. All objects record the vibration of their owner. Because Jesus was a medium, he was sensitive to the vibrations of the water jar. Jesus began telling the woman about her life and gave her spiritual advice. This is exactly what a psychic reading is. It is receiving spiritual advice from a medium.

Just like the mediums of Lily Dale, Jesus told the woman information that he had no way of knowing except through his psychic ability.

> **Jesus replied, "Go home, call your husband and come back." She answered, "I have no husband." "You are right, said Jesus, 'in saying that you have no husband, for, although you have had five husbands, the man with whom you are now living is not your husband; you told me the truth there."[7]**

We know this information was accurate by the woman's response.

> **"Sir," replied the woman, "I can see you are a prophet."[8]**

This is clearly a psychic reading. Again, we find evidence towards the end of this episode.

---

[5] John 4:6-30.

[6] John 4:11 [NEB].

[7] John 4:16-18 [NEB].

[8] John 4:19 [NEB].

> **The woman put down her water-jar and went away to the town, where she said to the people, "Come and see a man who has told me everything I ever did. Could this be the Messiah?"**[9]

The King James Bible does not use the word *Messiah* in this verse. It says:

> **Is not this the Christ?**[10]

The fact that the woman left her water jar further implies that she had given it to Jesus to drink from. She was obviously excited by her "reading," since the information that came through Jesus was accurate. Besides, it was not every day that a woman from her social class had a reading with a prophet. Usually only royalty or the wealthier classes could afford such a luxury.

There are two more salient points that occur in this particular Bible story. The first is that Jesus reveals a great truth in this conversation. He simply states:

> **God is spirit, and those who worship him must worship in spirit and in truth.**[11]

This statement is a great truth. God is Spirit, because God is the spiritual energy that resides with in us, as the soul. Many people think Jesus is God. They believe that when they die, Jesus will sit in judgment of their lives, and decide if their souls will live in heaven or hell. This is far from the truth, as this Bible story demonstrates.

Because Jesus held the woman's water jar, he sensed that the woman was living with a man without the benefit of being married. To put it in modern day terms, she was living in sin. Jesus did not judge this woman. He didn't say to her, "Listen lady, you are a terrible sinner for living with a man without being married. You must do penitence and say the Act of Contrition." Nor did Jesus say, "You must ask for forgiveness." Jesus made no comment about this woman's behavior. Careful analysis reveals that Jesus didn't judge her at all!

If an obvious sinner (according to the custom of that era) received no condemnation from Jesus, then there is strong evidence that Jesus did not believe in judging people. After all, wasn't it Jesus who said:

> **Pass no judgment, and you will not be judged. For as you judge others, so you will yourselves be judged, and whatever measure you deal out to others will be dealt back to you.**[12]

---

[9] John 4:28-29 [NEB].

[10] John 4:29 [KJV].

[11] John 4:24 [NEB].

[12] Matthew 7:1-2 [NEB].

That was his philosophy. Very simply stated, the priests became ventriloquists, using their God as a wooden puppet, projecting their falsehoods through their God's mouth.

The reading I had while at Lily Dale was as emotionally charged as the one the woman received at the well. I am sure I will never forget it for as long as I live. The medium I went to was flamboyant and charismatic. His house was a deep burgundy red. His readings lasted fifteen minutes. He was a very popular medium, and I was lucky to get an appointment with him. I was his last client for the day. Mediums have different styles, just as teachers do. Some can be quite funny as they deliver their message, while others can be quite blunt. This medium was confrontational. He made me look at issues in my life that I had been afraid to examine. It was a harrowing experience. I felt as though I were on the witness stand, being crossed examined. When I left, I was so shaken that the medium had to remind me to give him his fee. The reading had lasted 45 minutes.

Bonnie had an upsetting reading too. The medium had told her things that distressed her. We decided to talk to Carl about it. He explained that there are different types of mediums. Some are fantastic, others not. He told Bonnie to forget about her reading, since he wouldn't recommend that medium. He told me the medium I had seen was probably correct in what he saw, but that he could have been a bit more tactful in his presentation.

The Lily Dale community is near a wooded area. Several meeting places are in the woods, because trees help to increase psychic energy. The largest natural meeting area was called the *Forest Cathedral*. The day after we arrived at Lily Dale, another group arrived. Surprisingly, the medium for that group was Emily Hewitt, from Paterson, New Jersey. Emily Hewitt and Carl Hewitt weren't related to each other. Emily was a very feisty, elderly lady. When we had the opportunity to hear her give messages, we discovered she didn't pull any punches. She spoke her mind, and the minds of her Spirit guides, with no regard to the receiver's feelings. Carl and Emily decided to hold a joint meeting for both our groups, at midnight in the *Forest Cathedral*.

I'll never forget our march into the woods that dark, starry night. Carl had wrapped himself in an Indian blanket. He resembled what I'd imagined his control, Chief Lone Eagle, looked like. When we arrived, the other group was already there. Emily Hewitt's Spirit control was also Native American. These two Native Spirits decided to have some fun. They treated us to a pow-wow. Each Native American took over his respective medium. Each wanted to out-do the other. We had a spectacular demonstration of deep trance mediumship. The lectures that both these Spirits delivered through their mediums were superb. It was interesting that everyone could hear both voices. There was no amplification system out in the woods, but the voices of both mediums boomed through the air. The next day Carl explained that the Spirits had made an adjustment, so the sound carried.

The trip to Lily Dale lasted three days. It was an inspirational experience for me. I learned so much. I witnessed many Spirit Messages, and discovered the great variations between mediums—some being better than others. I had also encountered a philosophic difference between the mediums. Many mediums at Lily Dale focused on proving the continuation of life. The readings and messages they gave from Spirit were geared toward proving an afterlife. Carl's readings were different, because he didn't share that focus. He brought in many Spirits connected to the sitter during a reading, but he went far beyond that. He focused on spiritual advice and guidance. Being forewarned of an upcoming event sometimes means that one is better prepared for a situation. I can say this was true in my case.

During this trip, I had a religious reawakening. Spiritual feelings overwhelmed me, and I felt a need to pray. I went to the library and asked if they had a Jewish prayer book. Unfortunately they didn't. So I walked toward the *Forest Cathedral*. As I walked, the interplay of light and shadow drew my eyes. I studied the light filtering through the trees. I imagined myself as an early settler walking through the virgin woods of a seemingly uninhabited continent.

Deeper into the woods, I came to the *Forest Cathedral*. There were many long, white, wooden benches. I sat down on one and basked in the peaceful light. The beauty of nature surrounded me. I began to drift off, to go within. It's easy to meditate, to communicate with the God within in such a tranquil setting. As I sat I realized the architect of this great cathedral was not a man, but Mother Nature. As I looked up into the crystal blue sky, there was nothing to hinder my view.

The hustle and bustle of urban life had drained me. I felt depleted because I had lost my connection with God. The warmth of the sun, the clean smell of the air, and the chirping of the birds all held me in their embrace. I felt my soul being recharged.

A man-made cathedral is a holy site for one particular group of people. The *Forest Cathedral* had no sign labeling its denomination. All could worship at this holy site.

I found myself praying. I had found my way back to God. I could now see a pattern in the universe. I found the answers to all those questions that troubled me during my college years. Reincarnation gave new meaning to life. The thought of life after death removed my fear of death. The experience of spiritual mediumship brought me a great sense of purpose and peace.

As I continued sitting in that magnificent cathedral, I realized what made Lily Dale such a special place was its history. The hallowed grounds were full of ghostly imprints left by people who had come to communicate with God, for almost one hundred years. The grounds held the memory of the thousands of people, endowed with the Gifts of the Spirit, who had reached through the veil to retrieve timeless knowledge. The grounds had absorbed the joy of the many people who had had the opportunity to speak to their departed loved ones. Their heart-felt relief in learning that life continued after death permeated the grounds of Lily Dale, charging the atmosphere with holy reverence and joy.

# SIX

## My First Encounter with an Angel

One morning in December, before I left for work, the phone rang. Carl was on the line, his voice full of excitement. He began by saying, "I have something I need to share with you. For the last two weeks, I have been awakened by an angel at 3:00 AM. This angel is lecturing me, on different subjects. It's extremely interesting. This morning this entity asked me if I would call you. It seems he wants to talk to you. He has asked me to ask you to be here Saturday morning. At that time, I will go into a trace state, and he will speak directly to you. Could you be here bright and early on Saturday morning?"

"Sounds interesting," I replied. "You bet I'll be there!"

Bright and early on Saturday morning I arrived at Carl's office. He had made all the preparations. His office was darkened, a large pitcher of water and the tape recorder were ready. Carl sat in his chair, closed his eyes, and began to meditate. After a few moments, he said this prayer, "Lord God of my being, unto the Father within, come forward this moment, this hour, and allow me to become the instrument between the two dimensions of life. I ask only that which is good, true and helpful to pass through these lips. So be it!"

There was silence for a minute. Suddenly Carl's body went into spasms. He flinched three times, then relaxed in the chair. Carl began to speak, but his voice sounded very different. His southern accent was gone, and the tone of the voice was different from his natural speaking voice.

My blessings to you. Are you able to hear my voice clearly?

Yes, I can, very clearly in fact.

I'm glad since this is my first attempt to use this medium. I have called you here, young man, to talk with you. However, before I get to the main part of my discussion, I need to make something perfectly clear to you.

I am an unknown friend. Because of past experiences, I have decided to keep my identity to myself. In the past, after humans have spoken with angels, they have put us on a pedestal, turned us into minor deities, then bombarded us with prayers and wishes to be fulfilled. I do not desire to be worshiped, nor do I wish to be at anyone's beck and call. Neither do I wish to be the inspiration for the start of another religion. There are already more than twelve thousand different religions in existence.

In recent years many of us have appeared to people all over the world. Perhaps you are aware that people are currently seeing angels quite often. Alas, not all of these angels are imparting information that will enlighten people.

 [I was stunned by what I had just heard!] You're an angel?

 That is correct.

 How could that be? I've been in the presence of this medium while he was in deep trance at least a hundred times. Many different entities have spoken through him. Never has anyone claimed to be an angel. Why should I believe you?

 You remind me of your cousin.

 What do you mean by that?

 Are you familiar with the *Book of Books*?

 Which one do you mean?

 When I use the term *Book of Books*, I am referring to what many people call the *Holy Bible*. You are familiar with it?

 I am. I loved to study Bible stories when I was a child, but being Jewish, I only read the Old Testament.

 In the Bible, Moses, your very distant cousin, also had a problem accepting the "messenger." *Messenger* is the literal translation of the Hebrew word, מַלְאָךְ (*mal âk*), which is most often translated as *angel*. After this session, read of Moses' first encounter with an angel at the burning bush. Notice that at first Moses thought he was speaking with an angel, and later he thought it was God. As the conversation continued, Moses realized he was speaking to a highly evolved being.

*When this deep trance session ended, I found the verses the angel had referred to.*

And the *angel* of the LORD appeared unto him in a flame of fire out of the midst of a bush: and he looked, and, behold, the bush burned with fire, and the bush [was] not consumed. And Moses said, I will now turn aside, and see this great sight, why the bush is not burnt. And when the LORD saw that he turned aside to see, God called unto him out of the midst of the bush, and said, Moses, Moses. And he said, Here *am* I. And he said, Draw not nigh hither: put off thy shoes from off thy feet, for the place whereon thou standest *is* holy ground.[13]

 Your world is now in the "end-times," which means the end of the *Age of Ignorance*. It was prophesied thousands of years ago. I have chosen this time to return to teach those who are ready to think for themselves. I have information I wish to share with people. Most of this knowledge is not new. Centuries ago, it was destroyed by a few who found it threatening to the goals they wished to achieve. I feel the time has come for people to have access to this wisdom again, it is essential for the spiritual growth and survival of humanity.

I don't understand. Could you be more specific?

Religious leaders have altered the Bible for their own purposes. They have inserted laws into the book and claimed they were God's laws. Priests wanted these laws in place create fear and to control the masses.

That can't be true. The Bible is the word of God. It has never been changed. I have a friend who is a Christian. She thinks that mediumship is the work of the devil. Are you the devil, trying to disguise yourself as an angel to deceive me?

I will be very candid with you, my brother. I am not the devil. There is no devil. Theologians invented the devil to instill fear in the minds of the people. This fear kept them enslaved, and digging deeper into their pockets to put money in the collection plates. The priests lived in a grand style on the backs of the masses. If you subscribe to this concept of devil, can you prove that the invisible entities that spoke to your ancestors Abraham, Isaac, Jacob, Joseph, Moses, Samuel, Elijah, Elisha, Isaiah, Jeremiah, and all the other prophets were not the devil?

Again, I object. The Bible is the word of God.

---

13 Exodus 3:2-5 [KJV].

Let's change the subject for a minute. Think back to your bar mitzvah ceremony. Did anything unusual happen?

 Yes, as a matter of fact. I was reading my haftorah, and my mind froze. I couldn't pronounce a Hebrew word.

 Yes, I know.

 How would you know?

 I was there. Do you remember what book you were reading from?

 Yes, my haftorah was chapters 2, 3, and 4 of the Book of Zechariah.

 Isn't it interesting that those chapters are the Biblical record of conversations between the prophet Zechariah and an angel? It was not an accident that your Hebrew schoolteacher assigned this particular haftorah to you. I influenced him. I wanted you to read this before your whole synagogue. It would mirror what you would do later in your life—conversing with an angel. I was there on the day of your bar mitzvah. Your mind froze on that word because I prevented you from saying it.

 You did?

 Yes, and when you became so upset, I allowed you to say the word the other two times.

 Why would you do such a thing?

 I knew you were a person who valued the truth. You see, just as happened to Jeremiah, I knew you before you were born.[14] While in Sprit World, we had arranged that you would meet my medium, that we could have these conversions.

 That's difficult to believe.

---

14 Jeremiah 1:5.

Do you remember what word you were not able to say in your haftorah?

 No.

 It was the word שָׂטָן (*Satan*). I wouldn't allow you to speak the name of a non-existent being. There is no all-powerful evil being. I knew that one day you would want proof of my identity. I did this so I could prove to you that I'm not the devil.

*I later reread my haftorah and discovered that the angel was correct. The word I couldn't say was שָׂטָן (*Satan*). That name **did** appear three times.*

 Millions of people believe that Satan exists.

 And how many millions believe in the Easter Bunny and the Tooth Fairy?

 But those are only children.

 In effect, all the people in your world are children because so little of their brains are functioning. Let me ask you another question. Why did you keep coming to my medium for readings and classes?

 Because I found him so interesting and I was learning information I couldn't find elsewhere.

 Do you feel you are being deceived, or does this medium speak the truth when he is the instrument of Spirit?

 I think he speaks the truth.

 Then why do you think I might be the devil? Isn't the devil the great deceiver? Apparently you don't feel you are being deceived.

 When you tell me that the Bible has been changed, I have to question. I don't believe it.

In the New Testament, Paul discuses the Gifts of the Spirit.[15] One of the gifts Paul describes is "the ability to distinguish true Spirits from false."[16] You have this gift. You know if information coming from Spirit is accurate. This is why you feel the truth comes though this medium.

*As the angel continued to speak, there was an unexpected, dramatic change in the room. I felt his intense power. I felt insignificant and intimidated by his masterful voice. I empathized with Moses, how he must have felt as he stood in utter amazement before the burning bush.*

 Let me tell you more about myself. I realize that for me to remain nameless would be difficult for you. Humans are addicted to labeling and categorizing everything. Once it is labeled, it is judged. Very few people consider how limited their point of view may be, and that this process of labeling and judging truly limits the possibilities in their lives. To make it easier for you, you may address me as **AWAN** — Angel Without A Name." Awan will be your name for me, yet I am still nameless to you.

What just happened, Awan? I've never experienced this with any other Spirit who spoke through the medium. Quite frankly, you're making me nervous.

You wanted proof that I'm an angel. I allowed you to feel my vibration. You experienced a little of my energy, my brother, but do not be afraid. I will not harm you. Perhaps now you can accept that I am an angel.

I certainly can. Where do you come from?

That's a simple question, yet it will take a lengthy explanation. I come from a marvelous world only a breath away from you – but I might as well be light years away.

Awan, I'm confused. Don't angels live in Heaven?

What is your concept of Heaven?

---

15 1 Corinthians 12.

16 1 Corinthians 12:10 [NEB].

Heaven is where we go after we die, if we've lived a good and righteous life. It's where God lives. And it's the place where angels live, too.

 Have you ever studied the teachings of Jesus?

 No, Awan, I have never read the New Testament.

 You should read The New Testament, for Jesus revealed a wondrous truth, one that the churches choose to ignore. Jesus taught, **"Behold, the kingdom of God is within you."**

*Awan was quoting Luke 17:21.*

 Awan, you come from the kingdom of God, isn't that correct?

 Yes, I do.

 If the kingdom of God is within me, how can I hear your voice coming from outside of me?

 To visit your plane of existence, I have to travel down many frequencies. I despise visiting your frequency. It is very dense, because so much ignorance abounds. As I lower my frequency, the medium raises his. The medium's spiritual (etheric) body vacates his physical body and hovers nearby. I then step into the medium's body and use his vocal cords to speak to you.

Since my spiritual body vibrates at a higher rate than the spiritual body of the medium, my increased speed of vibration taxes his mind and physical body. That's why he's so tired after he has been in a deep trance. This is a very simplistic explanation. A thorough explanation would be much more complex.

 Awan, please tell me more about the Kingdom of God.

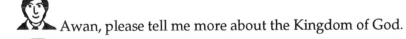 Before you can understand the world I live in, you have to learn new concepts. Be patient. By the end of this conversation you should understand. I have lived many lifetimes and in many places. The place I originally came from, and enjoy revisiting, is located in what became known as the Plains of Sharon. It is on the beach, close to the shores of the Mediterranean Sea. It is my favorite place, and is now known as Joppa. When I lived there, the climate was different than it is today.

It was a tropical paradise then, not a desert. We did not have the communication machines you have today, the ones that speak, and the ones that speak with pictures.

Do you mean radios and televisions?

Yes. Radios and televisions work on similar principles. I will discuss the radio first. How are you able to hear someone through your radio who is not there to talk to you?

I don't know all the details. Someone at the radio studio speaks into a microphone, and those sound waves get amplified, broadcast, and they come through the radio.

In simple terms, that's true. Do you realize those radio sound waves are present in this very room? If you turned on your radio, you would hear them.

I never thought about it.

Radio signals are here in the room right now. They traveled from the radio station, went right through the solid walls of this building, and are surrounding you at this very moment. So, why do you need a radio to listen to them? Why don't you hear them all the time?

I don't know.

Human ears and eyes can only hear and see a limited range of frequencies. Radio and television waves surround the planet entirely. Yet, because your eyes and ears cannot detect them, they remain imperceptible to you. The only way you can intercept these waves and understand them is to use a receiving machine—your radio or television. These devices are attuned to these higher frequencies. They intercept these waves, and modulate, or slow them down, and reissue them on lower frequencies, which human eyes and ears can interpret. You receive the invisible information because these instruments lower the vibrational rate of the signal.

I understand what you're saying. The radio lowers the frequency of the radio signals to a range that I can hear. The same process happens to TV signals.

Precisely. And these signals surround your body this very moment, yet you are unaware of them.

OK, I understand that.

My realm of being exists at a frequency that is higher than television and radio signals—frequencies that you cannot presently perceive. My world surrounds your world. We can occupy the same space because my world vibrates much faster than your world. Our worlds are actually intermeshed. Since I vibrate so fast, I can walk through the slow moving molecules of your solid walls.

 I'm beginning to understand.

Are you familiar with the Christmas song, "Angels We Have Heard On High?"

 I've heard it many times.

This is the true meaning of the song: the angels that were heard, were on a higher frequency than human beings. Unfortunately, theologians taught their congregations to address their prayers and thoughts to a higher world, a place in the sky, where "Heaven" is supposed to be. This is a false teaching. As Jesus said, "the Kingdom of God is within," but it exists at a higher frequency.

 Awan, now I'm confused. If I need a radio to hear radio waves, or a television to hear and see television waves, what kind of instrument is needed to hear or see angels?

Throughout time, there have been people who have been used as instruments to relay messages from my realm. These people have an innate ability to receive the thoughts, or sound waves, that are broadcast from my kingdom. To be more precise, a center in their brains is functioning which is dormant in most people. This brain center acts as a receiver, just as that small radio that you have is the receiver of radio waves. These people can hear the angels, and can then deliver our messages. Your Bible is full of people who heard the inhabitants of our kingdom.

Are you talking about Abraham, Isaac, and Jacob, who talked with God?

Yes, though you have named just a few. Have you forgotten the names of those you call the *prophets*? They communicated with my realm. Your ancestors, people of Jewish lineage, have a rich history of communicating with my world. We have also communicated with many other people from many other cultures. One case that you will easily find in your history books is of a young girl from France. You call her Joan of Arc. She heard our voices, and followed most of our instructions. Are you familiar with her?

 Yes, I am. But I never understood why she had to die for following your instructions.

 That was her choice. Her mission was over once her dauphin Charles VII (the uncrowned King of France) was crowned King of France. That was her mission. She didn't heed our warnings to go home. She wanted to liberate all of France from English control, so, she continued leading the troops into battle. She was captured, and the rest can be found in your history books.

 Why didn't you stop her?

 It is not our way to rule and command you. We are here to guide those who are open to our guidance. We cannot force you to do anything. We can influence you in certain matters, but the ultimate decisions in your life are yours, not ours.

 If she were a saint, bringing God's message to the world, why wasn't she spared such a horrific death?

Have you ever thought about who made her a saint, and when?

Being Jewish, I never gave it much consideration.

It was Pope Benedict XV who canonized Joan of Arc as a saint, 489 years after her death. Now think about this. If she were a saint, why didn't the church recognize that fact while she was alive? Why did the church mandate her death? Why did it take the church over four centuries to discover she was a saint? After all those years, what facts did church officials use to determine Joan's sainthood? On whose authority was she canonized? Sainthood is annoying to me and one of the reasons I choose not to identify myself. Joan of Arc utilized her psychic abilities of clairvoyance and clairaudience. She was open to other realms of being.

Please describe your realm. What is Heaven like?

What makes you think I exist in a place called *Heaven*?

Don't angels live in Heaven?

 We don't use that term. You said before that to get into Heaven you would have to live a good and righteous life. Tell me what you meant by that.

 A person would have to lead a good life, do good deeds, and follow the rules of their religion.

 What do you do that would allow you to enter Heaven after you die?

 I try to be honest with people. I try to help people. However, I don't do many of the rituals that Judaism asks me to do. I don't eat only kosher food, except during Passover.

 What is Passover? What exactly do you eat during Passover?

 Passover is a Jewish holiday that occurs near Easter. It's when the Jewish people celebrate their liberation from slavery in Egypt as recorded in the Book of Exodus. I only eat the foods that are permitted during the holiday. It is forbidden to eat wheat, barley, spelt, rye, and oats, and any product that is leavened (containing yeast), or fermented. For example, I would not be allowed to eat bread, only matzah.

 And how do you know when to stop eating bread and begin eating matzah?

 At 10:00 A.M. on the morning before Passover starts, we must stop eating bread. Its an important tradition. However, you must not eat matzah until that evening at the celebration of the seder. A *seder* is a special service conducted at home, retelling the story of how the Hebrews left their enslavement in Egypt. So from 10:00 A.M. until the evening seder, you must eat only certain foods like vegetables.

 And how long does Passover last?

 Eight days.

 Do you believe that not eating leavened foods during the eight days of Passover will help you gain entry into Heaven?

It's supposed to.

 I have been watching you for quite some time. I know you are an intelligent person. What would happen if you broke this tradition and ate bread during Passover?

 It says in the Bible that I would be committing a sin. By eating leavened food during Passover, I would be cut off from the Jewish people.[17]

 So tell me, how does this work? Does God sit on a magnificent golden throne, next to a giant clock? When the clock strikes 10:00 does he begin to write down the names of the people who are eating bread in a big book? How would God set his clock? Would he use Greenwich mean time, and set it by Big Ben in London? Or would he set it by the clock in the Vatican, or one in Jerusalem? Perhaps he would use Eastern Standard Time or Pacific Standard? Perhaps he decides to split himself into 24 parts, so he can watch for people eating bread in each of the different time zones.

Do you really think that eating matzah instead of bread makes you a more righteous or holy person? Would God love you more because of the food you ate?

If you were a Catholic instead of a Jew, do you think it would make any difference? How would the eating of matzah effect your entrance into Heaven?

 Catholics aren't supposed to eat matzah, just Jews.

 But I understand Catholics weren't supposed to eat meat on Friday, until the church changed its mind, and it was allowed except on Good Friday. So, all the people who disobeyed this rule and ate meat on a Friday before the Vatican said it was allowed, went straight to hell. But today if you eat meat on Friday, you can still get into heaven. The same piece of meat can condemn you to hell, or not be a problem depending on whether you ate it before or after the Vatican granted permission.

When did the Vatican change the rule? Did Jesus return and proclaim a new set of rules? Let us continue discussing the changing of rules. What's the most important food for you to avoid if you want to be kosher all the time?

 Pork.

 Why is that?

---

[17] Exodus 12:19.

Because in the Bible, God forbid us to eat pork.

 That's correct. God forbids the touching or eating of pork in the Old Testament.[18] The both the followers of Islam and the Jews accept the Old Testament as divine revelation. Therefore, they obey the Old Testament and don't eat pork. Christians also accept the Old Testament as part of their Bible. Yet the Christians have changed the rules, and enjoy their ham and eggs on a regular basis. They even enjoy playing football, which were made of pigs' skin. Does that mean that anyone who plays football, or eats bacon and eggs, will be denied entry into Heaven?

 Awan, you are confusing me.

 A little confusion may be good for the soul. You and many others have been regimented by your religious leaders to believe a set of rules. Few of you have questioned these rules to determine if they make sense. Eating a certain food at a certain time does not make you a holy person, or guarantee you entry into a place named *Heaven!*

 Then why does the Bible say that God said if the Jews did not observe the proscriptions of Passover, they would be cut off from their people?

 How do you know God said that?

 What do you mean?

 How do you know an almighty God decided a thing as trivial as a bit of food is so important?

 It's in the Bible.

 I know, but you have to realize that the Bible has been changed over the course of the centuries.

 I still have a difficult time accepting that claim.

---

[18] Deuteronomy 14:8.

Tell me, what are your views of slavery?

 I think it's terribly wrong for one human being to own another.

 Then why would eating pork, or meat on Friday, or bread on Passover, keep you out of heaven, but owning a slave would not? According to the Bible, God says it's permissible to own slaves. Now tell me, which sin is worse—owning another human, or eating bread on Passover?

 Owning a human. So why would God say that owning a slave was permissible?

 He didn't. That's just one example of theologians inserting laws into the Bible to satisfy their own needs. Pope Gregory II owned over a thousand slaves. He was having the Bible rewritten. Since the Bible is many separate books combined into one, Gregory assigned different books to different cardinals to rewrite.

During this time, one of Pope Gregory II's slaves, being bold and outspoken, asked the Pope, "Master, is it really right, in God's eyes, for you to own us body, soul, and mind?" Pope Gregory replied, "Let me ponder this a while. I will answer your question in two days."

At that moment, the book of Leviticus was being edited upstairs. Gregory went to the scribe who was rewriting Leviticus. The scribe inserted words that sanctioned slavery. He wrote the Lord's proclamation into the chapter he was working on.[19] Pope Gregory II went back to speak to the slave and said, "It is God's word, it is in the Bible." He brought the newly written book down to the slave. The slave couldn't read so he had to take the Pope's word for it. It was a cardinal who wrote that one man could enslave another, and called it God's will. If God gave His divine approval to the institution of slavery, no human could argue with it. To this very day, those words are still in the Bible.

 I still don't believe the Bible was changed.

 And what makes you so adamant?

 I can only speak for the Jewish Bible, especially the Torah. When a Torah scroll is copied, the scribes must count each and every letter. They know how many *A's* there are and how many *B's*. They also know how many times the name *Abraham*, or *Moses* appears in the scroll. They count it, and scrutinize it, to make

---

[19] Leviticus 25:44.

sure there are no mistakes. If the Bible were changed, it would have to have been the Christian Bible, not the Jewish one.

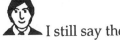 I hate to disillusion you, but you are mistaken. And in time, you will discover just how mistaken you are. A few minutes ago, I told you about one of my lifetimes when I lived in your world. I lived one of my lives in a place called Ebla. Archeologists recently found the ruins of this ancient city. Among the ruins were hundreds of clay tablets. These tablets contain information that powerful religious organizations are trying to keep secret because so much of the information on these tablets contradicts what is written in the Bible. The knowledge contained in the Dead Sea Scrolls is also being kept away from the general public. The knowledge recorded on these tablets and scrolls is the truth, not what is presently written in your Bible.

That can't be. I can't believe theologians have altered the Bible.

You wish a more detailed explanation. I want you to realize that the teachings I wish to share with you are sequential. It's like learning mathematics. You can't learn how to multiply before you know how to add. I can't teach you everything in one session. You need to understand the energy I'm using. Being in deep trance is very taxing on the medium's body and uses energy that is stored in his cells. It is very important that I not keep this body entranced for too long, depleting all the energy available in this human "battery." With all the work to be done, we don't want anything to happen to this instrument. I cannot afford to keep this medium entranced much longer.

I cannot teach you everything in one session. Even if I could, you would not be able to digest it all. Let me say this: A few theologians created Satan to put fear into the minds of humankind. This fear allowed them to control the general population. The only way to escape the control of these theologians is through mediumship. That is why certain verses were inserted into your Bible. Just as they made God seem to sanction slavery, they had God outlaw mediumship. In time you will have a complete understanding of this.

I still say the Bible has not been changed.

I challenge you to prove me wrong. Find evidence that the Bible has not been changed. Look at different Bibles.

The energy that I am using is becoming depleted. We will continue this discussion another time. It has been a pleasure to talk with you today. You have just had your first *close encounter of the Divine kind!* My peace be with you.

*This ended the first conversation with Awan.*

A transition began, as Awan left Carl's body. I saw Carl's body go into spasms. He coughed and was extremely groggy. His throat was parched, as if he had been in a desert for a day without water. I brought him a glass of water.

"Did anything come through?" Carl asked.

While in deep trance, Carl's Spirit relinquishes his body. Since his consciousness is out of his body, he has no knowledge of whose Spirit has entered his body, or what has been said through him.

"Yes, an angel gave me lot of information." I replied. Then I summarized what Awan had said.

Later, I thought about Awan's message to me, especially what he said just before he left: "My peace be with you." What peace? I was in turmoil, not peace. Talking with an angel was not what I had thought it was going to be. Awan was telling me that the very concepts I grew up with, and had held so dear for most of my life, were all lies and deceptions. That couldn't be true!

I suddenly felt very much akin to Jacob, an ancient ancestor of mine. Jacob had had a confrontation with an angel, and the wrestling match that ensued had changed his life.[20] Jacob's angel had also refused to tell his name, just as Awan had.

> **And Jacob asked him [the angel], and said, Tell me, I pray thee, thy name? And he [the angel] said, Wherefore is it that thou dost ask after my name? And he blessed him there.[21]**

Although my conversation with Awan was intellectual, I felt depleted. How could a divine being have such radical and almost anti-religious views, and still be an angel? How could Awan say that the Bible had been changed? I felt frustrated and confused. After talking it over with Carl, I decided to probe further into some of the questions Awan had raised. The primary one was: *Had the Bible, in fact, been changed?*

---

[20] Genesis 32:24.

[21] Genesis 32:29 [KJV].

# SEVEN

## Proof in a Rare Book Library

From my first psychic reading with Carl, I had found many of the concepts he taught me were compatible with Judaism. Others were a radical departure. For months, my conversation with Awan haunted me. Whenever I had free time, my mind inevitably wandered back to the many questions he had raised. Was it possible the Bible had been changed? Had theologians tampered with it, changing and inserting passages to justify slavery and prohibit mediumship? These ideas were so flagrantly opposed to those I had learned in Sunday school, that they were difficult for me to accept.

Whenever I had the opportunity, I discussed this with Carl. Carl agreed with Awan. I would argue the same points, over and over trying to win. It became a major source of irritation for me. I felt troubled, never at peace. It was like walking with a pebble in your shoe— I'd take my shoe off and beat it on the ground to loosen the pebble and get it out of my shoe. I'd put my shoe back on and continue my journey, only to discover the pebble still there.

I finally decided to go to a library to find evidence that Awan was wrong. Choosing to mix research with pleasure, I went to Boston, where I planned to do some sightseeing, see old friends, and visit the Boston Public Library.

Little did I know I would leave the Boston Public Library a changed man. I was about to discover evidence that would remove the cornerstone of my doubt. I would see with my own eyes that the Bible had, in fact, been altered, although I wouldn't comprehend the extent of the innumerable changes, nor what motivated Bible translators to make such modifications.

I don't recollect of how I began my research that August day when I climbed the steps of the regal Boston library. I only remember that one topic lead to another, and I found myself looking for *The Bible of Today* in the rare book collection. The Reverend John Chadwick, minister of the Second Unitarian Church of Brooklyn, New York, wrote the book in 1879. It seemed odd to me that this particular book was part of the rare book collection.

If you've never been to the rare book collection of a large research library, it's quite an experience. You need to register, listing your name and address. Some libraries want to know if you're planning to publish a book. At the end of the registration process you receive a list of rules you must follow. You're not allowed to use a pen to take notes, only a pencil. You must hang your coat in a particular closet. The list of restrictions can be quite long. Once you have gained entry into the rare book department, you need to fill out a call slip, listing the author, title, publisher, date of publication of the book you want, and your name and address. You then give it to the librarian who retrieves the book.

While I was waiting for the librarian to bring *The Bible of Today*, I browsed in the card catalog. This catalog contained only catalog cards for the rare book collection. After scanning several drawers, I pulled out a drawer that contained the cards for the many Bibles of the rare book collection. Much to my surprise, the Boston Public Library had a copy of the Coverdale Bible, published in 1535. I quickly filled out a call slip for this early edition of the English Bible.

When the Coverdale Bible arrived at my desk, I felt a jolt of electricity flow through my body. I realized I was about to touch a book that was over four hundred fifty years old! My mind raced back to the year 1535. Henry VII was king of England. This book existed before Henry VIII broke away from the Catholic Church. It existed before the Pilgrims left for Massachusetts, before the Revolutionary and Civil Wars. The historical significance flooded my mind.

I reached out and touched the Bible's ancient cover, and carefully opened it. "OK," I thought, "now what should I look up?" I slowly scanned different verses. These ancient pages were difficult to read, since the publisher had used Old English lettering. As I randomly thumbed through this centuries-old volume, I turned to 1 Samuel 28—the chapter that would totally change my perception of the Bible. Later, I would learn this is the chapter where Bible translators performed the most "scripture twisting," altering the Bible's text to suit their own beliefs. This may seem a radical statement to some readers. I certainly didn't believe it as I began reading the Coverdale Bible. Today, I can easily agree with Rev. Chadwick's statement, in his book *The Bible of Today*.

> **The text of Samuel is more "corrupt" than that of any other book; that is to say, more mistakes have occurred in the transcription of manuscripts and more liberties have been taken by transcribers.[22]**

One probable reason for all the "scripture-twisting" is that the 28th chapter of the first book of Samuel documents an event most Bible translators wish to hide. This chapter contains a record of the séance where Samuel, who had died, talked to King Saul through the medium of Endor. The word *séance* is a French word meaning *sitting*. A séance is a sitting, or gathering of two or more people, to communicate with the Spirit World. Jesus described a séance when he said:

> **For where two or three are gathered together in my Name, there am I in the midst of them.[23]**

Jesus was in a trance state when he made this statement. It was not Jesus who spoke these words, but Spirit who spoke through him. Therefore the word "I" in this

---

[22] Chadwick, John White, Rev. *The Bible of Today*. New York: G. P. Putnam's Sons 1879. p. 59.

[23] Matthew 18:20 [KJV].

passage is referring to Spirit, not Jesus. Most Bible translators want to hide this fact, for many reasons that I will discuss in a latter chapter. These translators did their best to disguise the psychic manifestations that occurred in Biblical times by twisting the words they used. In fact, this is one of the two chapters with the most changes I have found in the Bible. Two Hebrew words were translated *52 different ways*. A quick example would be the chapter heading used in some Bibles for story. The New International Bible labels this passage, "Saul and the Witch of Endor." Surprisingly, the Anchor Bible correctly labels it as, "The Séance at Endor."

Before we have our translator's vocabulary lesson, let me set the stage, and retell the story of the medium of Endor. The Hebrew people were accustomed to the Gifts of the Spirit. The Old Testament, a history of the Hebrews, is crammed full of individuals such as Abraham, Isaac, Jacob, Moses, Samuel, Elijah, and the other prophets who spoke with God. It was not unusual for these Biblical figures to have two-way conversations with God, the way we talk to people today on the telephone. These Hebrews also sought guidance from non-Hebrew prophets.

Priests didn't approve of mediumship, because they wanted to be the intermediaries between God and the people. They persuaded Saul to institute a religious reform. He gave gifted people the choice to leave Israel or be killed. Before Samuel's death, he and Saul didn't get along, because Saul continued to do things that God didn't sanction. Using Samuel as his instrument, God told Saul that he would no longer help him. To further show his abandonment, God commanded Samuel to anoint David as king.

The Philistines, Saul's enemies, decided to attack Israel. Saul received word that they were on the march to attack. Saul began to panic. His first thought was to consult God for help, as this was the custom of the time. Saul went through the socially approved channels to contact God for advice. The King James Version says:

**And when Saul enquired of the LORD, the LORD answered him not, neither by dreams, nor by Urim, nor by Prophets.**[24]

This is an important point to remember: Saul sought advice *from God* through the approved channels—the *Urim* (special stones) which Priest's used to divine answers from God; the *prophets* who provided no answer; and through *dreams*. God didn't answer Saul's plea for help, since He was angry with him.

The translators of the Bible were so intimidated by mediumship, they accused Saul of all kinds of wickedness. In the King James Bible, 1 Chronicles 10:13-14 seems to directly contradict 1 Samuel 28:6.

---

[24] 1 Samuel 28:6 [KJV].

| 1 Samuel 28:6 [KJV] | 1 Chronicles 10:13-14 [KJV] |
|---|---|
| And when Saul *enquired of the Lord*, the Lord answered him not, neither by dreams, nor by Urim, nor by Prophets. | So Saul died for his transgression which he committed against the Lord, even against the word of the Lord, which he kept not, and also for asking counsel of one that had a familiar spirit, to enquire of it. *And enquired not of the Lord:* therefore he slew him, and turned the kingdom unto David the son of Jesse. |

First the Bible says that Saul tried to consult the Lord, who would not answer him. Then the Bible says that Saul did not consult the Lord. Many Christians insist the Bible is the word of God and is 100 per cent accurate. Therefore, they claim the Bible doesn't contradict itself. In this example, the Bible depicts Saul as evil because he consulted a medium. This is the message traditional Church leaders wish to give, because mediumship threatens their very existence.

Let's continue the story of the medium of Endor. Saul's panic continued to grow, especially since he received no guidance from the Spirit World. He asked two of his servants if they knew a medium, so he could receive guidance from the Spirit World. The servants knew of a medium in Endor. Previously, King Saul had established a law forbidding mediumship, because he didn't want anyone to know more about the future than he did. He knew if he went to Endor in the daylight, people would see him going to the medium's house, breaking the very law he had established. Despite his sense of urgency, Saul waited for the cover of darkness. Then, he and his two body guards disguised themselves as beggars and traveled to Endor to consult the medium.

They arrived at the medium's house, which was near a cave. Saul knocked on the door. The woman answered, "What do you want?"

"I have come for a reading," King Saul replied.

"You are the king! You have set a trap for my life. That is why you are here," the woman angrily replied. King Saul had promised to kill anyone who performed the Gifts of the Spirit.

Saul said, "I promise you, as your Lord, your God, lives, no harm will come to you, if you will let me in and do for me that which I ask." He managed to convince her that he meant her no harm. Cautiously, the women opened the door and let him into her humble home. He asked her to summon the Spirit of Samuel who had died. She sat down and closed her eyes. Slowly she slipped away into a deep trance, allowing the Spirit of Samuel to enter her body and speak to King Saul. Samuel told him that he and his sons would be in the Spirit World with Samuel the very next day. That night, the Philistine army declared war on King Saul and his kingdom. The next day in battle, King Saul and his sons died as Samuel had prophesied the day before.

Let us examine how Bible translators have worded this story. When I opened the Coverdale Bible to the 1 Samuel 28, this is what I found:

| Verse | Coverdale Bible 1535 | King James Version 1611 |
|-------|----------------------|--------------------------|
| 1 Sam 28:7 | Then said Saul unto his servants: Seek me *a woman which has a spirit of soothsaying,* that I may go unto her and ask at her. | Then said Saul unto his servants, seek me *a woman that hath a familiar spirit,* that I may go to her, and enquire of her. |

A cold chill ran down my spine as these words raced through my mind: "Oh my God, Awan was right!" The phrase *a spirit of soothsaying* is certainly clearer, and easier to understand, than *a familiar spirit*.

A *soothsayer* is:

> **a compound of the Old English *soth*, "true," and *sayer*, "to say," literally meaning "one who says the truth." A soothsayer is one who claims or pretends to have the power of foretelling future events.[25]**

It is easy for the Spirit working with a *soothsayer* to provide information about our future, because Spirit lives in a realm where the past, future and present are all one point in time. True mediums do not *pretend* to know the future. Mediums simply relay information about future events that they hear from a Spirit.

A *familiar spirit* has a different meaning.

> **The word *familiar* is from the French *familier*, literally meaning "pertaining to one's family," for the word ultimately derived from the Latin *familia*, "family." If something is familiar then it is intimate, well acquainted, private, in constant or close association, personal or common. Thus a familiar spirit is a spirit that is in intimate communication with someone.[26]**

From these definitions, we can conclude a *familiar spirit* is an ancestral spirit, who comes to communicate with a family member, still living in the physical world.

When the translators of the King James Bible chose to replace Coveredale's "a spirit of soothsaying" with the phrase "a familiar spirit," they altered the meaning of the verse! A *familiar spirit* would have been a deceased family member, while a Spirit of soothsaying would not have to be a blood relative of the medium. I had the evidence before my eyes. Awan's theory that the Bible had been changed was being proved!

Returning to the Coverdale Bible, these are the verses from the story of the Medium of Endor which contain psychic information:

---

[25] Vance, Laurence M. *Archaic Words and the Authorized Version.* Pensacola, FL: Vance Publications, 1997. p. 312.

[26] Vance, Laurence M. *Archaic Words and the Authorized Version.* Pensacola, FL: Vance Publications, 1997. p. 135-136.

| Verse | Coverdale Bible 1535 | King James Version 1611 |
|---|---|---|
| 1 Samuel 28:3 | So Saul had driven the *soothsayers and expounders of tokens* out of the land. | And Saul had put away those that *had familiar spirits, and the wizards* out of the land. |
| 1 Samuel 28:6 | And he asked council at the Lord. But the Lord gave him no answer, *neither by dreams, nor by the lights, nor by prophets.* | And when Saul enquired of the Lord, the Lord answered him not, *neither by dreams, nor by Urim, nor by Prophets.* |
| 1 Samuel 28:7 | Then said Saul unto his servants: Seek me *a woman which has a spirit of soothsaying,* that I may go unto her and ask at her. | Then said Saul unto his servants, seek *me a woman that hath a familiar spirit,* that I may go to her, and enquire of her. |
| 1 Samuel 28:8 | *Prophecy unto me I pray thee through the spirit of soothsaying,* and bring me him up whom I shall name unto thee. | And he said, I pray thee *divine unto me by the familiar spirit,* and bring me him up whom I shall name unto thee. |
| 1 Samuel 28:13 | I see Gods coming up out of the earth. | I saw gods ascending out of the earth. |
| 1 Samuel 28:14 | He said: How is he shaped? She said: There cometh up an old man, and *is clothed with a long garment.* Then perceived Saul that it was Samuel, and bowed himself down with his face to the ground, and worshipped him. | And he said unto her, What form is he of? And she said, An old man cometh up; *and he is covered with a mantle.* And Saul perceived that it was Samuel, and he stooped with his face to the ground, and bowed himself. |

As you can easily see, the translators of the Bible frequently altered the wording. That hot August day in 1981 marked the beginning of a new hobby for me. I began collecting Bible verses. For the next 15 years I visited used bookstores wherever I travelled. If I found a different edition of the Bible, I bought it. I currently own 110 versions. Still there were many versions I had not collected. I found many of the older Bibles in the Scheide Rare Book Library at Princeton University; Wesleyan University Library in Middletown, Connecticut; Boston Public Library; New York Public Library; and The American Bible Society in New York City, which has the largest Bible collection in North America.

To make it easier to collect verses at these research libraries, I bought a portable computer. I compiled a data base of Bible verses that either portray the Gifts of the Spirit, or show how the priests tried to outlaw these gifted people. I have collected

44,389 verses from the Old Testament, and 30,044 from the New Testament—all from 160 Bible translations!

What follows is a complete listing for 1 Samuel 28:7 from 107 different versions of the Bible. The three or four letter abbreviation in the first column is the abbreviation for the particular Bible. For complete listing of the bibliographic information of these abbreviations, see the Note to the Readers in front of this book. Notice the diverse wording for this one verse!

# 1 SAMUEL CHAPTER 28 VERSE 7

| Bible | Date | Text |
|---|---|---|
| EWYC | 1384 | And Saul said to his servants, Seeketh to me a woman *having a charming ghost*; and I shall go to her, and ask by her. |
| LWYC | 1395 | And Saul said to his servants, Seek ye to me a *woman having a fiend speaking in the womb*; and I shall go to her, and I shall ask by her. |
| COV | 1535 | Then said Saul unto his servants: Seek me a woman which *has a spirit of soothsaying*, that I may go unto her and ask at her. |
| TYND | 1537 | Then said Saul unto his servants: seek me a woman that *is a mistress of a spirit of prophecy*, that I may go to her and ask of her. |
| TAV | 1539 | Then said Saul unto his servants: seek me a *woman having a spirit of prophecy*, that I may go to her and ask of her. |
| GRT | 1540 | Then said Saul unto his servants: seek me a woman that *hath a spirit of prophecy* that I may go unto her and ask of her. |
| MATT | 1549 | Then said Saul unto his servants: seek me a woman that is *a mistress of a spirit of prophecy*, that I may go to her and ask of her. |
| GEN | 1560 | Then said Saul unto his servants, seek me a woman that *hath a familiar spirit*, that I may go to her, and ask of her. |
| BISH | 1568 | Then said Saul unto his servants, Seek me a woman that *hath a familiar spirit*, that I may go to her, and ask of her. |
| DOU | 1609 | And Saul said to his servants: Seek me a woman that *hath a pythonical spirit*, and I will go to her, and will ask by her. |
| KJV | 1611 | Then said Saul unto his servants, seek me a woman that *hath a familiar spirit*, that I may go to her, and enquire of her. |
| HAAK | 1657 | Then said Saul unto his servants, Seek me a woman that *hath a soothsaying spirit*, that I may go to her, and enquire by her. |
| CHAL | 1750 | And Saul said to his servants: Seek me a woman that *hath a divining spirit*, and I will go to her, and enquire by her. |
| PUR | 1764 | Then he said to his Servants, Seek out for me a Woman who *has a familiar Spirit*, that I may go to her, and enquire of her. |
| CLEM | 1790 | And Saul said to his servants, "Seek me a woman who *hath a divining spirit*, and I will go to her, and enquire by her." |
| GEDD | 1792 | Saul, therefore, said to his servants: "Seek out, for me, *a woman skillful in necromancy*, that I may go and consult her." |
| RAY | 1799 | Then said Saul to his servants, Seek me a woman *that speaketh from the belly* that I may go to her, and enquire of her. |
| THOM | 1808 | Then Saul said to his servants, seek out for me a woman *who is a belly speaker* and I will go to her and consult her. |
| FRY | 1812 | Then said Saul unto his servants, seek me a woman that *hath a familiar spirit*, that I may go to her and enquire of her. |
| BELL | 1818 | Then Saul said to his servants, Seek ye for me a woman, *to raise a basilisk*; for I will go to her, and I will enquire before her. |

| BOTR | 1824 | Then said Saul to his servants, "Seek out for me, *a woman skillful in necromancy*, that I may go to her, and inquire of her." |
|------|------|-------------------------------------------------------------------------------------------------------------------------------|
| WEBR | 1841 | Then said Saul to his servants, seek me a woman that *hath a familiar spirit*, that I may go to her, and inquire of her. |
| BREN | 1844 | Then Saul said to his servants, Seek for me a woman who *has in her a divining spirit*, and I will go to her, and enquire of her. |
| LEES | 1856 | Then said Saul unto his servants, Seek out for me a woman that *hath a familiar spirit*, that I may go to her and inquire of her. |
| KEN | 1860 | And Saul said to his servants: Seek me a woman who *hath a divining spirit*, and I will go to her, and inquire by her. |
| WELL | 1861 | Then said Saul to his servants, "Seek me *a woman skilled in necromancy*, that I may go to her and enquire of her." |
| YNG | 1863 | And Saul saith to his servants, 'Seek for me *a woman possessing a familiar spirit*, and let me go unto her, and inquire of her.' |
| BEN | 1864 | Then said Saul unto his servants, Seek me *a woman owner of a familiar spirit*, that I may go to her and inquire of her. |
| SMITH | 1867 | Then said Saul unto his servants, seek me a woman that *hath a familiar spirit*, that I may go to her and enquire of her. |
| JUSMI | 1876 | And Saul will say to his servants, Seek out for me a woman, *mistress of necromancy*, and I will go to her and inquire of her. And his servants will say to him, Behold, a woman mistress of necromancy in the Fountain of Dor. |
| ERV | 1885 | Then said Saul unto his servants, Seek me a woman that *hath a familiar spirit*, that I may go to her, and inquire of her. |
| SPUR | 1885 | Then said Saul unto his servants: Seek me a woman who *hath a familiar spirit*, that I may go to her and enquire of her. |
| WORD | 1885 | Then said Saul unto his servants, seek me a woman that *hath a familiar spirit*, that I may go to her and enquire of her. |
| CAMB | 1889 | Then said Saul unto his servants, Seek me a woman that *hath a familiar spirit*, that I may go to her and inquire of her. |
| SHAR | 1892 | Then said Saul to his servants, 'Seek me a woman that is the *owner of a speaking bottle*, that I may go to her, and inquire of her.' |
| ROTH | 1897 | Then said Saul unto his servants—Seek me out a woman that *owneth a familiar spirit,* that I may even go unto her and enquire of her. |
| YLT | 1898 | And Saul saith to his servants, 'Seek for me a woman *possessing a familiar spirit*, and I go unto her, and inquire of her.' |
| GRANT | 1899 | Then said Saul unto his servants, seek me a woman that *hath a familiar spirit*, that I may go to her and enquire of her. |
| ASV | 1901 | Then said Saul unto his servants, Seek me a woman that *hath a familiar spirit*, that I may go to her and inquire of her. |
| CENT | 1905 | Then said Saul unto his servants, Seek me a woman that *hath a familiar spirit*, that I may go to her and inquire of her. |
| DARBY | 1920 | Then said Saul to his servants, Seek me a woman that *has a spirit of Python*, that I may go to her and inquire of her. |
| FENT | 1922 | Consequently Saul said to his officers, "Seek me *a woman who possesses a divining spirit*, and I will go and enquire of her." |
| MOFF | 1922 | Then Saul said to his courtiers, "Find me *a witch* that I may go and consult her." |
| MORD | 1924 | Then said Saul unto his servants, Seek me a woman that *hath a familiar spirit*, that I may go to her and inquire of her. |
| HARK | 1928 | Then said Saul unto his servants, Seek me a woman that *hath a familiar spirit*, that I may go to her and inquire of her. |
| LAMSA | 1933 | Then said Saul unto his servants, seek me a woman who *has a familiar spirit*, that I may go to her and inquire of her. |
| SMGO | 1939 | "Seek for me a woman who *has a divining talisman* that I may go to her and inquire of her." |
| KNOX | 1944 | At last he bade his servants to find him some *woman that was an enchantress*, so that he could go and question her. |

| MODL | 1945 | Then Saul told his attendants, "Find me *a woman who contacts spirits*, so I may go and consult her." |
|------|------|--------|
| DART | 1950 | Then said Saul unto his servants, seek me a woman that *hath a familiar spirit*, that I may go to her and inquire of her. |
| OGD | 1950 | Then Saul said to his servants, Get me *a woman who has control of a spirit* so that I may go to her and get directions. |
| RSV | 1952 | Then Saul said to his servants, "Seek out for me *a woman who is a medium*, that I may go to her and inquire of her." |
| SEPT | 1954 | Then Saul said to his servants, Seek out for me a *woman who is a trance-speaker*, and I will go to her and consult her. |
| WEST | 1958 | And Saul said to his servants: Seek me a woman that *hath a divining spirit*, and I will go to her and inquire by her. |
| JSOC | 1960 | Then said Saul unto his servants: 'Seek me *a woman that divineth by a ghost*, that I may go to her and inquire of her.' |
| NASB | 1960 | Then Saul said to his servants, "Seek for me *a woman who is a medium*, that I may go to her and inquire of her." |
| NWT | 1961 | "Seek for me *a woman who is a mistress of spirit mediumship*, and I will go to her and consult her." |
| MKJV | 1962 | Then said Saul to his servants, seek me a woman who *has a familiar spirit*, so that I may go to her and inquire of her. |
| HIRS | 1963 | Not translated |
| AMP | 1965 | Then Saul said to his servants, Find me *a woman who is a medium [between the living and the dead]*, that I may go to her and inquire of her. |
| CONF | 1965 | And Saul said to his servants: seek me a woman that *hath a divining spirit*, and I will go to her and inquire by her. |
| JER | 1966 | Then said Saul to his servants, "Find *a woman who is a necromancer* for me to go and consult her." |
| NAB | 1970 | Then Saul said to his servants, "Find me *a woman who is a medium*, to whom I can go to seek counsel through her." |
| SEPZ | 1970 | Then Saul said to his servants, Seek out for me *a woman who has in her a divining spirit*, and I will go to her, and enquire of her. |
| ABBR | 1971 | Saul inquired concerning the whereabouts of *a woman who could converse with the spirits of the dead.* |
| LIV | 1971 | Saul then instructed his aides to try to find *a medium* so that he could ask her what to do. |
| BYIN | 1972 | And Saul said to his officers "Look me up *a medium* that I can go to and inquire of her." |
| WMF | 1975 | Then Saul said to one of his servants, "Locate me *a fortune teller or a medium* that I may go and get some inside information." |
| BECK | 1976 | "Find me *a woman medium*," Saul told his servants, "Then I'll go to her and find out something from her." |
| NEB | 1976 | So he said to his servants, 'Find me *a woman who has a familiar spirit*, and I may go and inquire through her.' |
| TEV | 1976 | Then Saul ordered his officials. "Find me *a woman who is a medium*, and I will go and consult her." |
| SON | 1977 | Then said Saul unto his servants: Seek me *a woman that divineth by a ghost*, that I may go to her and inquire of her. |
| NIV | 1978 | Saul then said to his attendants, "Find me *a woman who is a medium* so I may go and inquire of her." |
| ANCR | 1980 | "So Saul said to his servants find me *a ghostwife*, so I may go make my inquiry through her!" |
| NKJV | 1982 | Then Saul said to his servants, Find me *a woman who is a medium*, that I may go to her and inquire of her. |
| RDB | 1982 | "Seek out *a woman who is a medium*," Saul said to his servants, "that I may go and inquire of her." |

| WBC | 1983 | Saul instructed his servants, "Seek out for me *a woman dealing with ancestral spirits* since I want to go to her and inquire of her." |
|---|---|---|
| JBPR | 1984 | And Saul said to his servants, "Seek for me a *necromanceress*; and I shall go to her and inquire of her." |
| NJER | 1985 | Saul then said to his servants, '*Find a necromancer* for me, so that I can go and consult her.' |
| TANK | 1985 | Then Saul said to his courtiers, "Find me *a woman who consults ghosts*, so that I can go to her and inquire through her." |
| TFFR | 1986 | Then said Saul to his servants. "Seek out for me *a woman who divines by a spirit,* that I may go and inquire of her." |
| ARATJ | 1987 | And Saul said to his servants; "Seek for me *the woman who knows how to bring up lying oracles*, and I will go unto her and inquire of her." |
| EB | 1987 | Then Saul said to his servants, "Find me *a woman who is a medium*. I'll go and ask her what will happen." |
| ETR | 1987 | Finally, Saul said to his officers, "Find me *a woman who is a medium*. Then I can go ask her what will happen in this war." |
| REB | 1989 | So he said to his servants, 'Find *a woman who has a familiar spirit*, and I will go and enquire through her.' |
| NRSV | 1990 | Then Saul said to his servants, "Seek out for me *a woman who is a medium*, so that I may go to her and inquire of her." |
| NCV | 1991 | Then Saul said to his servants, "Find me *a woman who is a medium* so I may go and ask her what will happen." |
| BBC | 1993 | Not translated |
| GLT | 1993 | And Saul said to his servants, Seek out for me *a woman possessing a familiar spirit [a medium],* and I will go to her and inquire of her. |
| KJ21 | 1994 | Then said Saul unto his servants, "Seek me *a woman who hath a familiar spirit*, that I may go to her and inquire of her." |
| LIVT | 1994 | Then Saul said to his servants, "Find me *a medium of an ov*, and I will go to her and inquire of her." |
| CCB | 1995 | Then Saul said to his servants, "Find me *a woman who consults the spirits of the dead*, that I may go and consult her." |
| CEV | 1995 | Then Saul told his officers, "Find me *a woman who can talk to the spirits of the dead.* I'll go to her and find out what's going to happen." |
| FOX | 1995 | Not translated |
| GODWD | 1995 | Saul told his officers, "Find me *a woman who conjures up the dead.* Then I'll go to her and ask for her services." |
| NIrV | 1996 | Saul spoke to his attendants. He said, "Find me *a woman who gets messages from those who have died.* Then I can go and ask her some questions." |
| NLT | 1996 | Saul then said to his advisers "Find *a woman who is a medium,* so I can go and ask her what to do." |
| STONE | 1996 | So Saul said to his servants, "Seek out *a woman who practices necromancy*, and I will go to her and inquire through her." |
| FRISH | 1997 | Then said Sha'ul to his servants, Seek me a woman who is *a medium*, that I may go to her, and inquire of her. |
| WEB | 1997 | Then said Saul to his servants, Seek me *a woman who has a familiar spirit,* that I may go to her, and inquire of her. |
| CJB | 1998 | Then Sha'ul said to his servants, "Try to find *a woman who tells the future by communicating with the dead;* I want to go and consult with her." |

The actual Hebrew for the boldface words in the chart above is בַּעֲלַת אוֹב (*ba aals ôwb*).[27] Translators of the Bible seem to have difficulty with

---

[27] Kohlenberger, John R., III. *The NIV Interlinear Hebrew-English Old Testament. Vol. 2.* Grand Rapids, MI: Zondervan,

this phrase. In the one hundred seven versions of the Old Testament, there are *fifty-two* different phrases to translate בַּעֲלַת אוֹב (*ba aals ôwb*). To help synthesize this information, I have reduced the quotes, leaving just the phrase that translates בַּעֲלַת אוֹב (*ba aals ôwb*).

| Phrase # | Version | Date | Phrase בַּעֲלַת אוֹב |
|---|---|---|---|
| 1 | THOM | 1808 | a belly speaker |
| 2 | WMF | 1975 | a fortune teller |
| 3 | ANCR | 1980 | a ghostwife |
| 4 | RSV | 1952 | a medium |
| | NASB | 1960 | a medium |
| | NAB | 1970 | a medium |
| | LIV | 1971 | a medium |
| | TEV | 1976 | a medium |
| | NIV | 1978 | a medium |
| | NKJV | 1982 | a medium |
| | RDB | 1982 | a medium |
| | EB | 1987 | a medium |
| | ETR | 1987 | a medium |
| | BYIN | 1972 | a medium |
| | FRISH | 1977 | a medium |
| | NRSV | 1990 | a medium |
| | NCV | 1991 | a medium |
| | NTL | 1996 | a medium |
| 5 | AMP | 1965 | a medium [between the living and the dead] |
| 6 | LIVT | 1994 | a medium of an ov |
| 7 | TYND | 1537 | a mistress of a spirit of prophecy |
| 8 | NWT | 1961 | a mistress of spirit mediumship |
| 9 | JER | 1966 | a necromancer |
| | NJER | 1985 | a necromancer |
| 10 | JBPR | 1984 | a necromanceress |
| 11 | DARBY | 1920 | a spirit of python |
| 12 | SEPT | 1954 | a trance-speaker |
| 13 | MOFF | 1922 | a witch |
| 14 | BECK | 1976 | a woman medium |
| 15 | KNOX | 1944 | an enchantress |
| 16 | GODWD | 1995 | conjures up the dead |
| 17 | TANK | 1985 | consults ghosts |
| 18 | CCB | 1995 | consults the spirits of the dead |
| 19 | MODL | 1945 | contacts spirits |
| 20 | ABBR | 1971 | converse with the spirits of the dead. |
| 21 | WBC | 1983 | dealing with ancestral spirits |
| 22 | TFFR | 1986 | divines by a spirit |
| 23 | JSOC | 1960 | divineth by a ghost |
| | SON | 1977 | divineth by a ghost |
| 24 | NIrV | 1996 | gets messages from those who have died |

| 25 | SMGO | 1939 | has a divining talisman |
|---|---|---|---|
| 26 | PUR | 1764 | has a familiar spirit |
|  | LAMSA | 1933 | has a familiar spirit |
|  | MKJV | 1962 | has a familiar spirit |
|  | NEB | 1976 | has a familiar spirit |
|  | REB | 1989 | has a familiar spirit |
|  | WEB | 1997 | has a familiar spirit |
| 27 | COV | 1535 | has a spirit of soothsaying |
| 28 | OGD | 1950 | has control of a spirit |
| 29 | BREN | 1844 | has in her a divining spirit |
|  | SEPZ | 1970 | has in her a divining spirit |
| 30 | CHAL | 1750 | hath a divining spirit |
|  | CLEM | 1790 | hath a divining spirit |
|  | KEN | 1860 | hath a divining spirit |
|  | WEST | 1958 | hath a divining spirit |
|  | CONF | 1965 | hath a divining spirit |
| 31 | GEN | 1560 | hath a familiar spirit |
|  | BISH | 1568 | hath a familiar spirit |
|  | KJV | 1611 | hath a familiar spirit |
|  | FRY | 1812 | hath a familiar spirit |
|  | WEBR | 1841 | hath a familiar spirit |
|  | LEES | 1856 | hath a familiar spirit |
|  | SMITH | 1867 | hath a familiar spirit |
|  | ERV | 1885 | hath a familiar spirit |
|  | SPUR | 1885 | hath a familiar spirit |
|  | WORD | 1885 | hath a familiar spirit |
|  | CAMB | 1889 | hath a familiar spirit |
|  | GRANT | 1899 | hath a familiar spirit |
|  | ASV | 1901 | hath a familiar spirit |
|  | CENT | 1905 | hath a familiar spirit |
|  | MORD | 1924 | hath a familiar spirit |
|  | HARK | 1928 | hath a familiar spirit |
|  | DART | 1950 | hath a familiar spirit |
|  | KJ21 | 1994 | hath a familiar spirit |
| 32 | DOU | 1609 | hath a pythonical spirit |
| 33 | HAAK | 1657 | hath a soothsaying spirit |
| 34 | GRT | 1540 | hath a spirit of prophecy |
| 35 | EWYC | 1384 | having a charming ghost |
| 36 | LWYC | 1395 | having a fiend speaking in the womb |
| 37 | TAV | 1539 | having a spirit of prophecy |
| 38 | ARATJ | 1987 | knows how to bring up lying oracles |
| 39 | MATT | 1549 | mistress of a spirit of prophecy |
| 40 | JUSMI | 1876 | mistress of necromancy |
| 41 | BEN | 1864 | owner of a familiar spirit |
| 42 | ROTH | 1897 | owneth a familiar spirit |
| 43 | FENT | 1922 | possesses a divining spirit |
| 44 | YNG | 1863 | possessing a familiar spirit |
|  | GLT | 1993 | possessing a familiar spirit [a medium] |
| 45 | STONE | 1996 | practices necromancy |

| 46 | BELL | 1818 | raise a basilisk |
|----|------|------|------------------|
| 47 | WELL | 1861 | skilled in necromancy |
| 48 | GEDD | 1792 | skillful in necromancy |
|    | BOTR | 1824 | skillful in necromancy |
| 49 | RAY | 1799 | speaketh from the belly |
| 50 | CEV | 1995 | talk to the spirits of the dead |
| 51 | CJB | 1998 | tells the future by communicating with the dead |
| 52 | SHAR | 1892 | the owner of a speaking bottle |
|    | HIRS | 1963 | Not translated |
|    | BBC | 1993 | Not translated |
|    | FOX | 1995 | Not translated |

The actual Hebrew words are embedded with psychic meaning, which is only partially captured in the translated English versions. The *Theological Wordbook of the Old Testament* translates בַּעֲלַת (*ba aals*) as:

> **Female owner.** Used infrequently, *ba ala* signifies owner of something... Or like *ba'al* [which is masculine] it is used to characterize a person (e.g. enchantress, literally "possessor of charms")... In contrast to *ba'al*, *ba ala* is not used in the Old Testament of a goddess...[28]

So we discover that בַּעֲלַת (*ba aals*) is the feminine form of the word בַּעַל (*baal*), which was also the name of a Phoenician god, Baal. The exact translation of אוֹב (*ôwb*) is as interesting. *The New Strong's Complete Dictionary of Bible Words* explains that:

> אוֹב (*ôwb*) from the same as [אָב (*âb*) *father*] (apparently through the idea of *prattling* a father's name); probably a *mumble*, i.e. a water-skin (from the hollow sound); hence a *necromancer* (ventriloquist, as from a jar):—bottle, familiar spirit.[29]

From this source we learn that אוֹב (*ôwb*) is a talking father, whose voice is a bit hollow. From a psychic point of view, the true meaning of אוֹב (*ôwb*) describes mediumship. A medium is one who can bring the words of a dead father, through the veil that separates the two realms. Two types of mediumship could be described by a "hollow sound." Perhaps the father's voice is hollow because it is coming through a deep trance medium. Sometimes if the psychic energy is low, the voice may sound very weak. The voice would not sound identical to the father's voice. The second would be a trumpet medium, where the voice is amplified by a metal cone shaped device (similar to a megaphone). The voice can have a "tinny, hollow" quality. Both types of mediumship will be discussed in length in latter chapters.

---

[28] Harris, R. Laird, ed. *Theological Wordbook of the Old Testament Vol. 1.* Chicago: Moody Press, 1980. p. 120.

[29] Strong, James. *The New Strong's Complete Dictionary of Bible Words.* Nashville, TN: Thomas Nelson Publishers, 1996. p. 300, 295.

Now as we combine the meanings, it is not farfetched to translate בַּעֲלַת אוֹב (ba aals ôwb) as the female owner of a father/god (or ancestral god). We discover that the translators of **WBC** were quite accurate with their phrase *a woman dealing with ancestral spirits*. Using 21st century psychic terminology, בַּעֲלַת אוֹב (ba aals ôwb), would be a *trance/trumpet medium*. This translation is confirmed by **SEPT**'s translators, who use the phrase *a trance-speaker*.

Since Jesus taught that "God is Spirit"[30] and since there is also a connection to the Phoenician god Baal, this demonstrates that mediums are in contact with divine entities living in a higher realm. It was the bias of the Hebrew priests, who wanted to monopolize the Hebrews' contact with the Spirit World, which caused them to infuse the Hebrew language (which seeped into the English), with negative connotations for בַּעֲלַת אוֹב (ba aals ôwb). This abhorrence of mediumship is the reason many Bible translators bring their own "anti-medium bias" into their translations.

**LWYC** was written in 1395, when people were seeing devils, witches and fiends everywhere they looked. This would account for **LWYC**'s phrase *having a fiend speaking in the womb*. **DOU**'s *hath a pythonical spirit* is a reference to the Greek Oracle of Delphi. It was thought that python snakes empowered her ability to predict the future. According to Christian theology, a snake was a euphemism for Satan. This reinforced the church's claim that mediumship was the work of the devil. **THOM**'s *a belly speaker* is implying that a medium is a ventriloquist, who could project his or her voice, or speak from the belly. Its phraseology is an attempt to cast a negative shadow over mediumship. **BELL**'s *raise a basilisk* refers to a mythological animal whose breath or glance would kill a human. Such imagery was employed to frighten people from seeking a medium's guidance.

When **SHAR** translates בַּעֲלַת אוֹב (ba aals ôwb) as *the owner of a speaking bottle* the translator is showing his ignorance of psychic science. *Wineskin* (hence *bottle*) is a correct translation of the Hebrew word אוֹב (ôwb). However, what Mr. Sharpe failed to realize is the word אוֹב (ôwb) in this verse needs to be used figuratively instead of a literally. A medium can be referred to as a vessel for Spirit to fill and use. An אוֹב (ôwb) was a vessel to store new wine. The medium would be the vessel to store, and utilize psychic energy.

When **MOFF** used *witch* in his translation, he is exposing his flagrant contempt of mediumship. The Hebrew word for *witch* is כָּשַׁף (kashshâph). The Hebrew words in this verse are בַּעֲלַת אוֹב (ba aals ôwb) **NOT** כָּשַׁף (kashshâph). **MOFF**'s use of *witch* illustrates and proves Awan's claim that the Bible translators altered the text of the Bible to corroborate their own beliefs.

**ANCR**'s *a ghostwife* is tying to express and imitate the *familiar* connection between the Spirit control and the medium. Yet, *a ghostwife* seems to imply that the two are married, and creates a confusing image.

Many of the newer versions attempt to translate בַּעֲלַת אוֹב (ba aals ôwb) in a more positive light. **MODL**'s *contacts spirits*, **ABBR**'s *converse with the spirits of the dead*, **JSOC**'s *divineth by a ghost*, **TFFR**'s *divines by a spirit*, **NIrV**'s *gets messages from those who have died* are accurate translations of the Hebrew.

---

[30] John 4:24.

We will use the same detailed technique to examine of the third verse of this chapter. This verse informs us Samuel had died, and Saul had all the mediums banished or executed. Notice the words for *mediums* keep changing in this verse.

## 1 SAMUEL CHAPTER 28 VERSE 3

| Bible | Date | Text |
|---|---|---|
| EWYC | 1384 | And Saul took away dyuynours and **keepers of devils** from the land, and slew them that had **charmers of devils in the womb**. He slew them that had charmers of devils in their womb. |
| LWYC | 1395 | And Saul did away from the land, **witches** and **false dyuynours** and he slew them that had **charmers of devils in their womb.** |
| COV | 1535 | So Saul had driven the **soothsayers** and **expounders of tokens** out of the land. |
| TYND | 1537 | And Saul had put the women that had **spirits of prophecy** and **sorcerers** out of the land. |
| TAV | 1539 | And Saul had put the women that had **spirits of prophesy** and the **sorcerers** out of the land. |
| GRT | 1540 | And Saul had put the women that had **spirits of prophecy** and **soothsayers** out of the land. |
| MATT | 1549 | And Saul had put the women that had **spirits of prophesy** and the **sorcerers** out of the land. |
| GEN | 1560 | Saul had put away the **sorcerers** and **soothsayers** out of the land. |
| BISH | 1568 | Saul had put away the **sorcerers** and the **soothsayers** out of the land. |
| DOU | 1609 | And Saul took all the **magicians** and **soothsayers** out of the land. |
| KJV | 1611 | And Saul had put away those that had **familiar spirits**, and the **wizards** out of the land. |
| HAAK | 1657 | And Saul had put away the **sooth-sayers** and the **wizards** out of the land. |
| CHAL | 1750 | And Saul had put away all the **magicians** and **soothsayers** out of the land. |
| PUR | 1764 | Saul also had put away those who had **familiar Spirits**, with the **Sorcerers**, out of the Country. |
| CLEM | 1790 | And Saul had put away all the **magicians** and **soothsayers** out of the land. |
| GEDD | 1792 | And Saul had expelled from the country the **necromancers** and **soothsayers**. |
| RAY | 1799 | And Saul had put away necromancers out of the land, **speakers from the belly**, and **magicians**. |
| THOM | 1808 | And Saul had driven from the land the **belly speakers** and the **diviners**. |
| FRY | 1812 | And Saul had put away those that had **familiar spirits,** and the **wizards** out of the land. |
| BELL | 1818 | And Saul had removed the **basilisks**, and the **prognosticators**, from the land. |
| BOTR | 1824 | And Saul had removed from the land, **necromancers** and **prognosticators**. |
| WEBR | 1841 | And Saul had put away those that had **familiar spirits**, and the **wizards** out of the land. |
| BREN | 1844 | And Saul had removed those who had in them **divining spirits**, and **wizards** out of the land. |
| LEES | 1856 | And Saul had removed those that had **familiar spirits**, and the **wizards** out of the land. |
| KEN | 1860 | And Saul had put away all the **magicians** and **soothsayers** out of the land. |
| WELL | 1861 | And Saul had put away the **necromancers**, and the **wizards**, out of the land. |
| YNG | 1863 | And Saul had turned aside those who have **familiar spirits**, the **wizards** also, out of the land. |

| BEN | 1864 | And Saul had removed those that had *familiar spirits*, and the *wizards* out of the land. |
|---|---|---|
| SMITH | 1867 | And Saul had put away those that had *familiar spirits,* and the *wizards* out of the land. |
| JUSMI | 1876 | And Saul took away the *necromancers* and the *wizards* from the land. |
| ERV | 1885 | And Saul had put away those that had *familiar spirits*, and the *wizards* out of the land. |
| SPUR | 1885 | And Saul had put away those that had *familiar spirits*, and the *wizards* out of the land. |
| WORD | 1885 | And Saul had put away those that had *familiar spirits,* and the *wizards* out of the land. |
| CAMB | 1889 | And Saul had put away those that had *familiar spirits*, and the *wizards* out of the land. |
| SHAR | 1892 | And Saul had put away the *speaking bottles [of ventriloquists]*, and the *wizards* out of the land. |
| ROTH | 1897 | Saul moreover had put away them who had *familiar spirits* and them who were *oracles* out of the land. |
| YLT | 1898 | and Saul hath turned aside those having *familiar spirits*, and the *wizards*, out of the land. |
| GRANT | 1899 | And Saul had put away those that had *familiar spirits* and the *wizards* out of the land. |
| ASV | 1901 | And Saul had put away those that had *familiar spirits,* and the *wizards* out of the land. |
| CENT | 1905 | And Saul had put away those that had *familiar spirits,* and the *wizards* out of the land. |
| DARBY | 1920 | And Saul had put away the *necromancers* and the *soothsayers* out of the land. |
| FENT | 1922 | And Saul drove away the *spirit-raisers,* and the *soothsayers* from the country. |
| MOFF | 1922 | Now Saul had cleared the *mediums* and *wizards* out of the country. |
| MORD | 1924 | And Saul had put away those that had *familiar spirits,* and the *wizards* out of the land. |
| HARK | 1928 | And Saul had put away those that had *familiar spirits,* and the *wizards* out of the land. |
| LAMSA | 1933 | Saul had put away the *diviners* and the *wizards* out of the land. |
| SMGO | 1939 | And Saul had put the *mediums* and the *wizards* out of the land. |
| KNOX | 1944 | When Saul purged the country of *soothsayers* and *diviners.* |
| MODL | 1945 | And Saul had driven the *mediums* and the *fortunetellers* out of the country. |
| DART | 1950 | And Saul had put away those that had *familiar spirits,* and the *wizards* out of the land. |
| OGD | 1950 | And Saul had put away from the land all those who had *control of spirits* and *who made use of secret arts.* |
| RSV | 1952 | And Saul had put the *mediums* and the *wizards* out of the land. |
| SEPT | 1954 | And Saul had driven from the land the *belly speakers* and the *diviners.* |
| WEST | 1958 | And Saul had put away all the *magicians* and *soothsayers* out of the land. |
| JSOC | 1960 | And Saul had put away those that *divined by a ghost* or *a familiar spirit* out of the land. |
| NASB | 1960 | And Saul had removed from the land those were *mediums* and *spiritists.* |
| NWT | 1961 | As for Saul, he had removed the *spirit mediums* and the *professional foretellers of events* from the land. |
| MKJV | 1962 | And Saul had put away those that had *familiar spirits*, and the *wizards* out of the land. |
| AMP | 1965 | And Saul had put the *mediums* and the *wizards* out of the land. |
| CONF | 1965 | And Saul had put away all the *magicians* and *soothsayers* out of the land. |

| JER | 1966 | Saul had expelled the *necromancers* and *wizards* from the country. |
|---|---|---|
| NAB | 1970 | Meanwhile Saul had driven *mediums* and *fortune-tellers* out of the land. |
| SEPZ | 1970 | And Saul had removed those who had in them *divining spirits*, and the *wizards*, out of the land. |
| ABBR | 1971 | Before this, Saul had ordered all such people [who could *converse with the spirits of the dead*] executed. |
| LIV | 1971 | King Saul had banned all *mediums* and *wizards* from the land of Israel. |
| BYIN | 1972 | And Saul had expelled from the country all the *spirit-mediums of different kinds*. |
| WMF | 1975 | Saul had passed a law against *fortune tellers, witches, mediums*, or *people using ESP*. |
| BECK | 1976 | Saul had rid the land of *mediums* and *wizards*. |
| NEB | 1976 | And Saul had banished from the land all who *trafficked with ghosts* and *spirits*. |
| TEV | 1976 | Saul had forced all the *fortunetellers* and *mediums* to leave Israel. |
| SON | 1977 | And Saul had put away those that *divined by a ghost* or *a familiar spirit*, out of the land. |
| NIV | 1978 | And Saul had expelled the *mediums* and the *spiritists* from the land. |
| ANCR | 1980 | And Saul had banished *necromancers* and *mediums* from the land. |
| NKJV | 1982 | And Saul had put the *mediums* and the *spiritists* out of the land. |
| RDB | 1982 | Not translated |
| WBC | 1983 | Meanwhile Saul had removed the *(images of) ancestral spirit* and *ghosts* from the land. |
| JBPR | 1984 | Now, Saul had abolished *necromancers* and those who *divine with the Jidoa bone* from the land. |
| NJER | 1985 | Saul had expelled the *necromancers* and *wizards* from the country. |
| TANK | 1985 | And Saul had forbidden *[recourse to] ghosts* and *familiar spirits* in the land. |
| TFFR | 1986 | And Saul had put away the *wizards*, and those who *divined by spirits*. |
| ARATJ | 1987 | And Saul removed *lying oracles* and *necromantic apparitions* from the land. |
| EB | 1987 | And Saul had forced out the *mediums* and *fortune-tellers* from the land of Israel. |
| ETR | 1987 | Earlier, Saul had forced the *mediums* and *fortune-tellers* to leave Israel. |
| REB | 1989 | And Saul had banished from the land all who *trafficked with ghosts* and *spirits*. |
| NRSV | 1990 | And Saul had expelled the *mediums* and the *wizards* from the land. |
| NCV | 1991 | And Saul had forced out the *mediums* and *fortune-tellers* from the land. |
| BBC | 1993 | Not Translated |
| GLT | 1993 | And Saul had taken away the *mediums* and *spiritists* out of the land. |
| KJ21 | 1994 | And Saul had put away those who had *familiar spirits*, and the *wizards* out of the land. |
| LIVT | 1994 | Saul had removed the *ovoth* and *yidonim* from the land. |
| CCB | 1995 | Meanwhile, Saul had driven those who *consult spirits of the dead* and *fortunetellers* out of the land. |
| CEV | 1995 | Meanwhile, Saul had been trying to get rid of everyone who *spoke with the spirits of the dead*. |
| FOX | 1995 | Not Translated |
| GODWD | 1995 | Saul had rid the land of *mediums* and *psychics*. |
| NIrV | 1996 | Saul had gotten rid of people *who get messages from those who have died*. He had also gotten rid of people who *talk to the spirits of the dead*. He had thrown all of them out of the land. |
| NLT | 1996 | And Saul had banned all *mediums* and *psychics* from the land of Israel. |

| STONE | 1996 | Saul had banished the **necromancers** and the **Yidoni-diviners** from the Land. |
| FRISH | 1997 | And Sha'ul had put away the **mediums** and the **wizards**, out of the land. |
| WEB | 1997 | Saul had put away those who had **familiar spirits,** and the **wizards**, out of the land. |
| CJB | 1998 | Also Sha'ul had expelled from the land those who tell the **future by communicating with the dead** or with a **demonic spirit**. |

When we examine *1Samuel* 28:3 in the *Interlinear Hebrew-English Old Testament*,[31] a Bible that translates the Hebrew word for word, we find the following: There are two Hebrew words used in the passage—הָאֹבוֹת (*haovos*), which is translated as *mediums*, and הַיִּדְעֹים (*hayid'onim*), which is translated *spiritists*. However, Peter Ackroyd translates הָאֹבוֹת as *beings that know the future*, and הַיִּדְעֹים as *Spirit control*.[32]

Further examination of the Hebrew will reveal additional meaning. The ה (*hay*) in הָאֹבוֹת (*haovos*) and הַיִּדְעֹים (*hayid'onim*) adds the word *the* onto both words, which happen to be plural. The singular form would be אֹוב (*ôwb*) and יִדְעֹנִי (*yiddônî*). The *Theological Wordbook of the Old Testament* states:

> **The word [יִדְעֹנִי] yidoni is derived from the root "to know"**
> **(יָדַע *yâda*).**[33]

*The New Strong's Complete Dictionary of Bible Words* explains יָדַע (*yâda, to know*) as:

> **a primitive root: *to know* (properly to ascertain by *seeing*).**[34]

Therefore, הַיִּדְעֹים (*hayid'onim*) were people who knew things by seeing them, or *the knowing ones by seeing*. Today, we would simply say that הַיִּדְעֹים (*hayid'onim*), means *clairvoyants*. By carefully studying Hebrew reference books, the translation of the Hebrew word הַיִּדְעֹים (*hayid'onim*) becomes clear. Yet, none of the professional Bible translators chose to use the word *clairvoyants*. It becomes sadly evident that they have no knowledge of psychic science, yet they have been allowed to relate the history of very psychically gifted people. Is it any wonder that translators constantly rephrase so many passages that describe psychic events? Since they do not understand the psychic events they are reading, how is it possible for them to accurately translate them?

*The New Strong's Complete Dictionary of Bible Words* states that יִדְעֹנִי (*yiddônî*) means:

---

[31] Kohlenberger, John R., III. *The NIV Interlinear Hebrew-English Old Testament. Vol. 2.* Grand Rapids, MI: Zondervan, 1980. p. 241.

[32] Ackroyd, Peter R. *The Cambridge Bible Commentary on the New English Bible: The First Book of Samuel.* Cambridge: Cambridge University Press, 1971. p. 211.

[33] Harris, R. Laird, ed. *Theological Wordbook of the Old Testament Vol. 1.* Chicago: Moody Press, 1980. p. 16.

[34] Strong, James. *The New Strong's Complete Dictionary of Bible Words.* Nashville, TN: Thomas Nelson Publishers, 1996. p. 385.

a knowing one, specifically a conjurer.[35]

The Theological Wordbook of the Old Testament explains that:

> As the Hebrew word [יִדְּעֹנִי] *yiddônî* is related to knowledge, so the English word "Wizard" is related to wisdom.[36]

*The Oxford English Dictionary* concurs, defining the word *wizard* as:

> A philosopher, sage = wise man.[37]

The same connection between wise man and wizard exists with the word *witch*. *The Oxford English Dictionary* indicates that the word *witch* is derived from the word *wicca*.[38] The *Encyclopedia of Occultism & Parapsychology* explains that:

> Wicca [is] believed to be an old term for Witchcraft or "Wisecraft," dating from Anglo-Saxon times... The word witch or "wise woman"...[39]

Bible translators failed in their attempt to cast the medium of Endor in a negative light. By labeling the woman a witch, they were actually complementing her by stating that she was a wise woman. She was wise because she understood and utilized psychic science. She knew how to penetrate the veil that separates the two realms and to bring information from the world of Spirit into our world. In ancient and Biblical times, people who had this knowledge and ability were revered and considered wise.

Returning our attention to 1 Samuel 28:3, we discover that from two Hebrew words, we end up with a list of 30 expressions for הָאֹבוֹת (*haovos*), and 28 expressions for הַיִּדְּעִים (*hayid'onim*).

| 30 | Bible | Date | הָאֹבוֹת = *trance/ trumpet mediums* |
|----|-------|------|-------------------------------------|
| 1 | WBC | 1983 | (images of) ancestral spirits |
| 2 | BELL | 1818 | basilisks |
| 3 | THOM | 1808 | belly speakers |

| 28 | Bible | Date | הַיִּדְּעִים = *clairvoyants* |
|----|-------|------|------------------------------|
| 1 | JSOC | 1960 | a familiar spirit |
|  | SON | 1977 | a familiar spirit |
| 2 | CJB | 1998 | a demonic spirit |

---

[35]Strong, James. *The New Strong's Complete Dictionary of Bible Words*. Nashville, TN: Thomas Nelson Publishers, 1996. p. 385.

[36]Harris, R. Laird, ed. *Theological Wordbook of the Old Testament Vol. 1*. Chicago: Moody Press, 1980. p. 848.

[37] *The Oxford English Dictionary*. Vol. 20. NY: Oxford University Press, 1989. p. 471.

[38] *The Oxford English Dictionary*. Vol. 20. NY: Oxford University Press, 1989. p. 437.

[39] *Encyclopedia of Occultism & Parapsychology*. 3rd Edition. Vol. 2. Detroit, MI: Gale Research Co., 1978. p. 1808.

| | | | | | | | | |
|---|---|---|---|---|---|---|---|---|
| | SEPT | 1954 | belly speakers | | 3 | JBPR | 1984 | divine with the Jidoa bone |
| 4 | CJB | 1998 | communicating with the dead | | 4 | TFFR | 1986 | divined by spirits |
| 5 | ABBR | 1971 | converse with the spirits of the dead | | 5 | THOM | 1808 | diviners |
| 6 | OGD | 1950 | control of spirits | | | KNOX | 1944 | diviners |
| 7 | JSOC | 1960 | divined by a ghost | | | SEPT | 1954 | diviners |
| 8 | EWYC | 1384 | diviners | | 6 | COV | 1535 | expounders of tokens |
| | LAMSA | 1933 | diviners | | 7 | LWYC | 1395 | false diviners, charmers of devils in womb |
| 9 | BREN | 1844 | divining spirits | | 6 | TANK | 1985 | familiar spirits |
| | SEPZ | 1970 | divining spirits | | 7 | NAB | 1970 | fortune-tellers |
| 10 | PUR | 1764 | familiar Spirits | | | EB | 1987 | fortune-tellers |
| | KJV | 1611 | familiar spirits | | | ETR | 1987 | fortune-tellers |
| | FRY | 1812 | familiar spirits | | | NCV | 1991 | fortune-tellers |
| | WEBR | 1841 | familiar spirits | | | MODL | 1945 | fortunetellers |
| | LEES | 1856 | familiar spirits | | | CCB | 1995 | fortunetellers |
| | YNG | 1863 | familiar spirits | | 10 | WBC | 1983 | ghosts |
| | BEN | 1864 | familiar spirits | | 11 | EWYC | 1384 | keepers of devils, charmers of devils in womb |
| | SMITH | 1867 | familiar spirits | | 12 | OGD | 1950 | made use of secret arts |
| | ERV | 1885 | familiar spirits | | 13 | RAY | 1799 | magicians |
| | CAMB | 1889 | familiar spirits | | 14 | WMF | 1975 | mediums |
| | SPUR | 1885 | familiar spirits | | | TEV | 1976 | mediums |
| | WORD | 1885 | familiar spirits | | | ANCR | 1980 | mediums |
| | ROTH | 1897 | familiar spirits | | 15 | ARATJ | 1987 | necromantic apparitions |
| | YLT | 1898 | familiar spirits | | 16 | NIrV | 1996 | people who talk to the spirits of the dead |
| | GRANT | 1899 | familiar spirits | | 17 | WMF | 1975 | people using ESP |
| | ASV | 1901 | familiar spirits | | 18 | NWT | 1961 | professional foretellers of events |
| | CENT | 1905 | familiar spirits | | 19 | BOTR | 1824 | prognosticators |
| | MORD | 1912 | familiar spirits | | | BELL | 1818 | prognosticators |
| | HARK | 1928 | familiar spirits | | 20 | GODWD | 1995 | psychics |
| | DART | 1950 | familiar spirits | | | NTL | 1996 | psychics |
| | MKJV | 1962 | familiar spirits | | 21 | GRT | 1540 | soothsayers |
| | KJ21 | 1994 | familiar spirits | | | GEN | 1560 | soothsayers |
| | WEB | 1997 | familiar spirits | | | BISH | 1568 | soothsayers |
| 11 | WMF | 1975 | fortune tellers | | | DOU | 1609 | soothsayers |

| | | | | | | | | |
|---|---|---|---|---|---|---|---|---|
| | TEV | 1976 | fortunetellers | | | CHAN | 1750 | soothsayers |
| 12 | SON | 1977 | ghost | | | CLEM | 1790 | soothsayers |
| | TANK | 1985 | ghosts | | | GEDD | 1792 | soothsayers |
| 13 | ARATJ | 1987 | lying oracles | | | KEN | 1860 | soothsayers |
| 14 | DOU | 1609 | magicians | | | DARBY | 1920 | soothsayers |
| | CHAN | 1750 | magicians | | | FENT | 1922 | soothsayers |
| | CLEM | 1790 | magicians | | | WEST | 1958 | soothsayers |
| | KEN | 1860 | magicians | | | CONF | 1965 | soothsayers |
| | WEST | 1958 | magicians | | 22 | PUR | 1764 | Sorcerers |
| | CONF | 1965 | magicians | | | TYND | 1537 | sorcerers |
| 15 | MOFF | 1922 | mediums | | | TAV | 1539 | sorcerers |
| | SMGO | 1939 | mediums | | | MATT | 1549 | sorcerers |
| | MODL | 1945 | mediums | | 23 | NASB | 1960 | spiritists |
| | RSV | 1952 | mediums | | | NIV | 1978 | spiritists |
| | NASB | 1960 | mediums | | | NKJV | 1982 | spiritists |
| | AMP | 1965 | mediums | | | GLT | 1993 | spiritists |
| | NAB | 1970 | mediums | | 24 | NEB | 1976 | spirits |
| | LIV | 1971 | mediums | | | REB | 1989 | spirits |
| | BECK | 1976 | mediums | | 25 | ROTH | 1897 | them who were oracles |
| | FRISH | 1977 | mediums | | 26 | KJV | 1611 | wizards |
| | NIV | 1978 | mediums | | | HAAK | 1657 | wizards |
| | NKJV | 1982 | mediums | | | FRY | 1812 | wizards |
| | EB | 1987 | mediums | | | WEBR | 1841 | wizards |
| | ETR | 1987 | mediums | | | BREN | 1844 | wizards |
| | NRSV | 1990 | mediums | | | LEES | 1856 | wizards |
| | NCV | 1991 | mediums | | | WELL | 1861 | wizards |
| | GLT | 1993 | mediums | | | YNG | 1863 | wizards |
| | GODWD | 1995 | mediums | | | BEN | 1864 | wizards |
| | NTL | 1996 | mediums | | | SMITH | 1867 | wizards |
| 16 | GEDD | 1792 | necromancers | | | JUSMI | 1876 | wizards |
| | BOTR | 1824 | necromancers | | | ERV | 1885 | wizards |
| | WELL | 1861 | necromancers | | | SPUR | 1885 | wizards |
| | JUSMI | 1876 | necromancers | | | WORD | 1885 | wizards |
| | DARBY | 1920 | necromancers | | | CAMB | 1889 | wizards |
| | JER | 1966 | necromancers | | | SHAR | 1892 | wizards |
| | ANCR | 1980 | necromancers | | | YLT | 1898 | wizards |
| | JBPR | 1984 | necromancers | | | GRANT | 1899 | wizards |
| | NJER | 1985 | necromancers | | | ASV | 1901 | wizards |
| | STONE | 1996 | necromancers | | | CENT | 1905 | wizards |
| 17 | RAY | 1799 | necromancers speakers from belly | | | MORD | 1912 | wizards |
| 18 | LIVT | 1994 | ovoth | | | MOFF | 1922 | wizards |
| 19 | NIrV | 1996 | people who get messages from those who have died | | | HARK | 1928 | wizards |
| 20 | HAAK | 1657 | sooth-sayers | | | LAMSA | 1933 | wizards |

| | | | | | | | | |
|---|---|---|---|---|---|---|---|---|
| | COV | 1535 | soothsayers | | | SMGO | 1939 | wizards |
| | KNOX | 1944 | soothsayers | | | DART | 1950 | wizards |
| 21 | GEN | 1560 | sorcerers | | | RSV | 1952 | wizards |
| | BISH | 1568 | sorcerers | | | MKJV | 1962 | wizards |
| 22 | SHAR | 1892 | speaking bottles [of ventriloquists] | | | AMP | 1965 | wizards |
| 23 | NWT | 1961 | spirit mediums | | | JER | 1966 | wizards |
| | BYIN | 1972 | spirit-mediums of different kinds | | | SEPZ | 1970 | wizards |
| 24 | FENT | 1922 | spirit-raisers | | | KJ21 | 1994 | wizards |
| 25 | GRT | 1540 | spirits of prophecy | | | LIV | 1971 | wizards |
| | TAV | 1539 | spirits of prophesy | | | BECK | 1976 | wizards |
| | MATT | 1549 | spirits of prophesy | | | FRISH | 1977 | wizards |
| | TYND | 1537 | spirits of prophecy | | | NJER | 1985 | wizards |
| 26 | CCB | 1995 | spirits of the dead and | | | NRSV | 1990 | wizards |
| 27 | CEV | 1995 | spoke with spirits of dead. | | | WEB | 1997 | wizards |
| 28 | NEB | 1976 | trafficked with ghosts | | 27 | STONE | 1996 | Yidoni-diviners |
| | REB | 1989 | trafficked with ghosts | | 28 | LIVT | 1994 | yidonim |
| 29 | LWYC | 1395 | witches | | | ABBR | 1971 | Not Translated |
| | WMF | 1975 | witches | | | BYIN | 1972 | Not Translated |
| 30 | TFFR | 1986 | wizards | | | RDB | 1982 | Not Translated |
| | RDB | 1982 | Not Translated | | | BBC | 1993 | Not Translated |
| | BBC | 1993 | Not Translated | | | CEV | 1995 | Not translated |
| | FOX | 1995 | Not Translated | | | FOX | 1995 | Not Translated |

Were there no scholars able to reliably translate two simple Hebrew words into English? If there is so much diversity in the translation of two words, how accurate can the translations of the other thousands of words from the original Hebrew text into English be?

What is even more shocking, from the author's point of view, is that Hebrew scholars also avoid translating הָאֹבוֹת (*haovos*) and הַיִּדְעֹים (*hayid'onim*)! LIVT is so uncomfortable by these two phrases that it leaves the words in their original Hebrew. In STONE I discovered that הָאֹבוֹת (*haovos*) is translated as *necromancers*, and הַיִּדְעֹים (*hayid'onim*) is translated *Yidoni-diviners*. Yet STONE refuses to translate אֹבוֹת (*ovos*) or *yid'onim*/יִדְעֹים in *Leviticus* 20:6, [note *ha*/הַ before a word means *the*] leaving them in the original Hebrew.

> **And the person who shall turn to the sorcery of the Ovos and the Yid'onim to stray after them. . .**[40]

> To continue along those lines, הָאֹבוֹ (*haovos*) is also found in 1 Chronicles 10:13-14.

---

[40] Leviticus 20:6 [STONE].
[41] Leviticus 20:6 [STONE].

> **So Saul died for his transgression which he committed against the LORD, even against the word of the LORD, which he kept not, and also for asking counsel of one that had a familiar spirit, to enquire of it. And enquired not of the LORD....**

What is fascinating is that 30 Bibles translate הָאֹבוֹת (*haovos*) differently in *1 Samuel* 28:3 and *1 Chronicles* 10:13. Why would הָאֹבוֹת (*haovos*) have one meaning in one chapter and a totally different meaning in another when both chapters are describing the same event? These 30 inconsistently translated Bibles make up 34% of the 88 Old Testament versions that contain *both* of these verses. This startling statistic makes one wonder how many other discrepancies exist in Bible translation? As one examines this chart, one begins to question how much the translator's theology manifests in his work.

| | Bible | Date | הָאֹבוֹת *in 1 Samuel 28:3* | הָאֹבוֹת *in 1 Chronicles 10:13* |
|---|---|---|---|---|
| 1 | EWYC | 1384 | charming ghost | witch and hopid not in the Lord. |
| 2 | TYND | 1537 | mistress of a spirit of prophecy | woman that wrought with a spirit, and asked not of the Lord. |
| 3 | TAV | 1539 | spirit of prophecy | woman that wrought with a spirit, and asked not of the Lord. |
| 4 | GRT | 1540 | spirit of prophecy | woman that wrought with a spirit, and asked not of the Lord. |
| 5 | MATT | 1549 | mistress of a spirit of prophecy | woman that wrought with a spirit, and asked not of the Lord. |
| 6 | BISH | 1568 | familiar spirit | woman that wrought with a spirit: And asked not of the Lord. |
| 7 | CHAL | 1750 | divining spirit | witch, And trusted not in the Lord. |
| 8 | CLEM | 1790 | divining spirit | witch, And trusted not in the Lord. |
| 9 | BREN | 1844 | divining spirit | wizard to seek counsel and Samuel the prophet answered him, and he sought not the Lord. |
| 10 | KEN | 1860 | divining spirit | witch, and trusted not in the Lord. |
| 11 | JUSMI | 1876 | mistress of necromancy | sorcerer to seek out; And not seeking to Jehovah. |
| 12 | ROTH | 1897 | familiar spirit | necromancy when he desired to enquire; and enquired not of Yahweh. |
| 13 | FENT | 1922 | divining spirit | a Spirit-raiser, instead of going to the Lord. |
| 14 | MOFF | 1922 | witch | medium, resorting to a medium and not to the Eternal. |
| 15 | SMGO | 1939 | divining talisman | medium, resorting to it and not to the Lord. |
| 16 | KNOX | 1944 | an enchantress | witch, too, instead of trusting in the Lord. |
| 17 | MODL | 1945 | contacts spirits | medium's seance. He did not look to the Lord. |
| 18 | OGD | 1950 | control of a spirit | directions to one who had an evil spirit, And not to the Lord. |

---

[42] 1 Chronicles 10:13-14 [KJV].

| 19 | WEST | 1958 | divining spirit | witch, And trusted not in the Lord. |
|----|------|------|-----------------|-------------------------------------|
| 20 | CONF | 1965 | divining spirit | witch, and trusted not in the Lord. |
| 21 | NAB | 1970 | medium | necromancer, and had not rather inquired of the Lord. |
| 22 | SEPZ | 1970 | woman who has in her a divining spirit. | wizard to seek counsel and Samuel the prophet answered him, and he sought not the Lord. |
| 23 | NEB | 1976 | familiar spirit | ghosts for guidance. He had not sought guidance of the Lord. |
| 24 | TEV | 1976 | medium | spirits of the dead instead of consulting the Lord. |
| 25 | ANCR | 1980 | ghostwife | necromancer for guidance. Because he did not consult Yahweh. |
| 26 | JBPR | 1981 | necromanceress | dead spirit. And he did not inquire of the Lord. |
| 27 | WBC | 1983 | a woman dealing with ancestral spirits | necromancer. He did not seek Yahweh. |
| 28 | REB | 1989 | familiar spirit | ghosts for guidance. He had not sought guidance of the Lord. |
| 29 | GLT | 1993 | familiar spirit [a medium], | a medium, to inquire; and did not inquire of Jehovah. |
| 30 | GODWD | 1995 | woman who conjures up the dead | medium to request information from a dead person. He didn't request information from the Lord. |

What proves to be even more fascinating is that **CHAL, CLEM, KEN, KNOX, WEST,** and **CONF,** all Catholic Bibles, translate הָאֹבוֹת (*haovos*) as *witch* in *1 Chronicles* 10:13, but not in *1 Samuel* 28:3. It is ironic how this mimics what happened in the Middle Ages. Catholic theologians saw witches everywhere, which gave them an excuse to torture and burn thousands of innocent women. **MOFF** did an about face and abandoned the word *witch* in *1 Samuel* 28:3 and chose to use *medium* in *1 Chronicles* 10:13.

The more closely one examines the work of these translators, the more it becomes apparent that their translations are full of inaccuracies and inconsistencies. As the concept that "the Bible is the exact, unaltered word of God" begins to erode word by word, one is left with a disturbing mistrust of the accuracy of the holy text. Awan's statement that the Bible had been changed through the years was clearly demonstrated. My error had been in believing my religious teachers with blind faith. Now that I have examined the facts for myself, I can only agree with Awan.

There is more evidence that reveals to what length translators and theologians have gone to obscure the fact that Saul talked to Samuel though a genuine medium. **JBPR** has translated הַיִּדְעֹים (*hayid'onim*) as *divine with a Jidoa bone.* The translator then goes on to describe how this was done.

> **They would take the bone of an animal known as Jidoa, and place it in their mouth, whence it would speak. This beast had a human form in both its face and body. It had a cord protruding from its**

---

[43] 1 Chronicles 10:13-14 [KJV].

navel, which was rooted to the ground. The Jidoa was very fierce and would prey on all who came within the radius of its root.[44]

A. J. Rosenberg, the author of **JBPR**, provides Jewish sources for this account of the Jidoa.[45] However, I could not find any dictionary,[46] Bible dictionary,[47] Jewish encyclopedia,[48] animal encyclopedia,[49] or even a book about Biblical animals,[50] that mentioned the Jidoa. If God created this animal, why isn't it known to anyone except Jewish theologians?

It becomes evident that the theologians who continually retranslated the Bible wanted to obscure the fact that countless stories of psychic phenomena are present in the Bible. Theologians have concentrated on this chapter because it proves, beyond a shadow of doubt, that there is value in consulting a medium. Saul was desperate to learn his destiny. Would he be successful against the Philistine army? As was customary in his time, he went to consult a prophet. He ran into a problem though, since he himself had banished all the people who had the Gifts of the Spirit.

No matter what word a theologian uses, he cannot change the fact that King Saul had a conversation with the Spirit of Samuel. Despite the fact that **REB** calls it *the fictitious Samuel,* it was the Spirit of Samuel that spoke with Saul. The Bible provides confirmation of this fact in the *Apocrypha* (inspired books that were *not* included in the Bible):

> And after he [Samuel] fell asleep [died] he prophesied again,
> warning the king of his death; he lifted up his voice from the earth
> in prophecy, to blot out the wickedness of the people.[51]

Mediumship is the only method for a deceased person to speak with a physical person living on the earth plane. After Samuel had died, his soul left his physical body to live in a timeless realm. It was easy for him to see the future, and to tell Saul that he and his son Jonathan would die in battle the very next day.

---

[44]A. J. Rosenberg, ed. *Samuel I : A New English Translation of the Text and Rashi, with a Commentary Digest.* NY: Judaica Press, 1980. p. 229.

[45] Sefer Mitzvoth Gadol, quoted by Sifthei Hachamim, *Commentary on the Mishnah.* See footnote #7.

[46] *Oxford English Dictionary 2nd edition.* Oxford, England: Clarendon Press, 1989.

*Webster's Third New International Dictionary of the English Language, Unabridged.* Springfield, MA: G. & C. Merriam Co., 1961.

[47] *Roget's Thesaurus of the Bible.* HarperSanFrancisco, 1992.

Kitto, John. *A Cycloaedia of Biblical Literature. Vol. 2.* Philadelphia, PA: J. B. Lippincott and Co., 1866.

[48] *Encyclopaedia Judica. Vol. 10.* NY: Macmillian, 1971.

[49] Drimmer, Frederick. *The Animal Kingdom. 3 Vols.* NY: Greystone Press, 1954.

Walker, Ernest P. *Mammals of the World. 3rd edition.* Baltimore, MD: John Hopkins University Press, 1975.

Farrand, John Jr., Ed. *The Audubon Society Encyclopedia of Animal Life.* NY: Potter, Inc. 1982.

[50] Wood, John George. *Wood's Bible Animals: A Description of the Habits, Structure and Uses of Every Living Creature Mentioned in the Scriptures.* Philadelphia, PA: Bradley, Garretson & Co. 1875.

[51] Ecclesiasticus. 46:20 [JER].

If this were not genuine mediumship, do you think the woman of Endor would have risked her life? The woman of Endor recognized that King Saul had come to her for a reading. If she were going to fake mediumship, why would she give the king a disastrous message? Why not tell the king he would be victorious over the Philistines, which after all is what King Saul really wanted to hear. Why not tell the king what he wanted to hear, the same way a group of prophets did to King Ahab and Jeroboam?[52] Genuine mediums don't fake their gifts. The medium of Endor went into deep trance, allowing Samuel's Spirit to speak to Saul and reveal the bad news. As you can see, this book of the Bible presented many problems for priests and church theologians.

As much as translators have twisted the text of the Bible for centuries, they still have not managed to extract all of the psychic truth from these verses. They have tried and tried, but the facts still remain. The woman went into deep trance, and Samuel prophesied Saul's death. The fact that the séance occurred in a **cave**, where mediums often did their work, was omitted from the story. (It was no accident that the Lord spoke to Elijah as he was hiding from Ahab in a cave.[53]) Translators also stripped the medium of her identity. Why remove her name from the Bible? The translators purposely depersonalized the woman—Witch Miriam or Witch Ruth would sound much too sympathetic. Translators want to make this woman as scary and evil as possible. So they removed her name and called her the *Witch* of Endor.

After many centuries, let us restore some dignity to this psychically gifted woman. Mr. Ginzberg, in his book entitled *The Legends of the Jews*, provides us with a fact that other theologians took great pains to hide. In the footnotes to his book, Ginzberg states:

> In PRE [פרקי רבי אליעזר Pirke Rabbi Eliezer] the name of the witch is Zephaniah = "the hidden one."[54]

It is ironic that the medium's name means *the hidden one*, since theologians have depersonalized her by removing and hiding her name from the text of the Bible.

Some people recognize the name Zephaniah. A prophet in the Bible named Zephaniah has his own book. I discussed this with an Israeli friend of mine who speaks Hebrew fluently. He said that Zephaniah can be a man's or a woman's name. There is a more literal translation of Zephaniah—*the hidden God*. My mind flashed to my conversation with Awan: He told me that Jesus taught that people could find God by going within and that theologians sought to cover this truth up. How ironic that the name of this medium means *the hidden God*, while her name and its meaning, have been hidden from humanity for centuries.

What has not been hidden is the disdain translators felt for this story. In the **MOFF** [Moffatt Bible], verse 7 reveals the translator's feelings toward mediumship:

---

[52] 1 Kings 22:5-18.

[53] 1 Kings 19: 9-10.

[54] Ginzberg, Louis. *The Legends of the Jews Vol. 6*. Philadelphia. PA: The Jewish Publication Society of America, 1968. p. 236. Footnote no. 74. [פרקי רבי אליעזר Amsterdam 1709 or Warsaw 1852].

**Then Saul said to his courtiers, "Find me a *witch* that I may go and consult her."[55]**

The Moffatt translation is a deliberate, malicious misrepresentation of the truth and deceives its readers. When I studied verse 7 in *The Interlinear Hebrew English Old Testament*,[56] I found the Hebrew phrase בַּעֲלַת אוֹב (*ba aals ôwb*). I used *The Englishman's Hebrew and Chaldee Concordance*[57] and looked up the word *witch*. I discovered that the Hebrew word for *witch* is כַּשָּׁף (*kashshâph*). Anyone, even someone who cannot read a word of Hebrew, can recognize that בַּעֲלַת אוֹב (*ba aals ôwb*) and כַּשָּׁף (*kashshâph*) are not the same. *The Interlinear Hebrew English Old Testament* translated בַּעֲלַת אוֹב (*ba aals ôwb*) as *mistress of medium*. Why is Mr. Moffatt inserting the word *witch*, with all its negative connotation into this passage? An unbiased, literal translation of the Hebrew word would not support the word *witch* in this text. Therefore, I conclude his only motivation would be his disdain of mediumship.

Stobart discusses the use of the word *witch* in her book *The Open Secret*.

> **The word 'witch' does not occur. The medium to whom King Saul went for advice, when troubled at the thought of his coming conflict with the army of the Philistines, is called the *woman* of Endor, the same word used (in Hebrew) when applied to the mother of Jesus.[58]**

Stobart is referring to the following verse, which describes Jesus' reunion with his mother before the wedding at Canna:

> **And when they wanted wine, the mother of Jesus saith unto him, They have no wine. Jesus saith unto her, *Woman*, what have I to do with thee? Mine hour is not yet come.[59]**

Moffatt translated the same verse as follows:

> **As the wine ran short, the mother of Jesus said to him, "They have no wine." "*Woman*," said Jesus, "What have you to do with me?"[60]**

---

[55] 1 Samuel 28:7 [MOFF].

[56] Kohlenberger, John R., III. *The NIV Interlinear Hebrew-English Old Testament*. Vol. 2. Grand Rapids, MI: Zondervan, 1980. p. 241.

[57] *The Englishman's Hebrew and Chaldee Concordance of the Old Testament* Vol. 2. London: Walton and Maberrly, 1866. p. 621.

[58] Stobart, Mabel Annie Boulton. *The Open Secret*. London: Psychic Press Limited, 1947. p. 94.

[59] John 2:3-4 [KJV].

[60] John 2:3-4 [MOFF].

What horror would rip through the soul of an orthodox Christian if Moffatt were consistent in his translations and used the word, *witch* to describe Mary? Would that have raised the eyebrows of devout Christians? Would they be ranting and raving, screaming from their pulpits of the wickedness of this translator? Yet, no one complained when Moffatt called the woman of Endor a witch in 1 Samuel 28:7.

Stobart provides us with another irony:

> **And it is at least interesting to realize that in the Hebrew the word 'Endor' means 'possessing rare qualities'—of a supernormal nature.**[61]

After digging through piles of slanderous language, we have arrived at the truth. Zephaniah of Endor channeled Samuel, one of the greatest seers of all time. After Zephaniah awoke from her deep trance, she found Saul very distraught. Samuel had given Saul his death sentence. Saul was terrified, which Zephaniah recognized. Exhausted from the séance, she managed to prepare food for Saul and his servants. Surely, this was an act of human kindness, not the act of a malevolent witch.

Others agree, Zephaniah should not be considered a witch.

> **Yet at no point is the work of the seer associated with the diabolical; on the contrary, it is indirectly God who is speaking through the voice of Samuel, as relayed by the medium. The medium of Endor is the equivalent of the sibyls of pagan antiquity: She is the mouthpiece of God.**[62]

During one of my many conversations with Awan, he discussed the medium of Endor.

Zephaniah was a great medium who channeled the Spirit of Samuel. She lived in what was, in those days, a very modern home. Zephaniah was quite famous. People travelled great distances to seek her advice, just as people travel from distant countries to seek the advice of this medium [Carl Hewitt]. The people who went to her protected her. She never went without food or shelter, because she was so loved.

*I later discovered this quotation which supported Awan's assertion that Zephaniah was a famous medium:*

> **In disguise, and accompanied by two trusted men-servants, he [King Saul] sought out a woman at Endor who was a famous medium.**[63]

---

[61] Stobart, Mabel Annie Boulton. *The Open Secret*. London: Psychic Press Limited, 1947. p. 94.

[62] Messadié, Gerald. *A History of the Devil*. Translated by Mare Romano. NY: Kodansha International, 1996. p. 236.

[63] Comay, Joan. *"Saul." Who's Who in the Old Testament Together with the Apocrypha*. NY: Holt, Rinehart and Winston,

The Religions in your world have had more trouble with Zephaniah than any other person in your Bible. Theologians do not know what to do with this story. They wish they could rip the pages out of the Holy Bible. This medium [Carl] once compared the witch of Endor to Jesus. People who heard this lecture were irritated by this comparison. Some contemplate killing this medium [Carl] because he dared make such a comparison. I had to protect him from these enraged people.

One should realize that this is a correct comparison. Both Jesus and Zephaniah were mediums, channeling information from my realm to the people living in yours. Jesus was a far greater medium than Zephaniah, they both demonstrated the Gifts of the Spirit. Theologians maligned Zephaniah and described her as a witch because priests wanted to camouflage her mediumship.

*End of conversation fragment*

I find it interesting that Zephaniah and Jesus delivered the same message. Unfortunately, one has to be able to read the Bible in the original Hebrew to discover this. The message I am referring to is found in verse 13, when King Saul asks Zephaniah what she sees:

> **And the king said unto her, Be not afraid: for what sawest thou? And the woman said unto Saul, I saw *gods* ascending out of the earth.[64]**

Contrast that with the NIV Bible:

> **The woman said, "I see *a spirit* coming up out of the ground."[65]**

*The Interlinear Hebrew English Old Testament* has these two Hebrew words רָאִיתִי (*râ âhsee*) meaning *I see* and אֱלֹהִים (*Elohim*) meaning *Spirits*.[66] Because I am Jewish, I have said the Hebrew word אֱלֹהִים (*Elohim*) thousands of times. אֱלֹהִים (*Elohim*) appears in the Bible thousands of times too, yet it is usually not translated as *Spirits*. Usually the word אֱלֹהִים (*Elohim*) is translated as *God*, as in the very first verse of the Bible.

---

1971. p. 342.

[64] 1 Samuel 28:13 [KJV].

[65] 1 Samuel 28:13 [NIV].

[66] Kohlenberger, John R., III. *The NIV Interlinear Hebrew-English Old Testament*. *Vol. 2*. Grand Rapids, MI: Zondervan, 1980. p. 242.

בְּרֵאשִׁית בָּרָא אֱלֹהִים אֵת הַשָּׁמַיִם וְאֵת הָאָרֶץ[67]
**In the beginning *God* created the heavens and the earth.**[68]

In fact, Ackroyd states:

**'Elohim' [אֱלֹהִים] a word most often used for God.**[69]

If the translators of the NIV Bible were consistent in their translation, they would have said: "In the beginning *Spirits* created the heavens and the earth." Ironically, translators have done us a favor this time, as this was the message Jesus gave to the woman at the well:

**God is spirit, and those who worship him must worship in spirit and truth.**[70]

As Awan said, because theologians didn't know how to interpret this story, they did their best to extract the psychic truth, including translating אֱלֹהִים (*Elohim*) as *Spirits* instead of *God*. Examine the 25 different phrases translators have created for the word אֱלֹהִים (*Elohim*), which is usually translated as *God*.

| 25 | Bible | Date | אֱלֹהִים |
|----|-------|------|----------|
| 1 | BOTR | 1824 | a chief |
| 2 | SPUR | 1885 | a dignitary rising |
| 3 | LEES | 1856 | a divine being |
| 4 | JER | 1966 | a ghost |
| 6 | NEB | 1976 | a ghostly form |
| 7 | TYND | 1537 | a god |
|   | AMP | 1965 | a god [terrorizing superhuman being] ! |
| 8 | GEDD | 1792 | a god-like figure |
| 9 | JSOC | 1960 | a godlike being |
| 10 | MODL | 1945 | a godlike form |
| 11 | FRISH | 1977 | a godlike man |
| 12 | STONE | 1996 | a great man |
| 13 | RAY | 1799 | a magistrate |
| 14 | TFFR | 1986 | an old man |
| 15 | KEN | 1860 | a personage |

| 16 | NAB | 1970 | a preternatural being rising |
|----|-------|------|----------|
| 17 | LIV | 1971 | a specter |
| 18 | TEV | 1976 | a spirit |
| 19 | BELL | 1818 | a supreme |
| 20 | JBPR | 1984 | angels |
| 21 | FENT | 1922 | divine messengers |
| 22 | KJV | 1611 | gods |
| 23 | ARATJ | 1987 | the angel of the Lord |
| 24 | SMITH | 1867 | the words of Samuel |
| 25 | WMF | 1975 | various forms and one of them is an old man, and he is covered with the robe of a prophet. |

---

[67] Kohlenberger, John R., III. *The NIV Interlinear Hebrew-English Old Testament. Vol. 1.* Grand Rapids, MI: Zondervan, 1979. p. 1.

[68] Genesis 1:1 [NIV].

[69] Ackroyd, Peter R. *The Cambridge Bible Commentary on the New English Bible: The First Book of Samuel.* Cambridge: Cambridge University Press, 1971. p. 214.

[70] John 4:24 [RSV].

Joseph Smith, the founder of the Mormon Church, wrote the **SMITH** Bible. Even he didn't know how to deal with this Bible story. He translated this verse as:

**I saw the *words of Samuel* ascending out of the earth.**

Samuel's words did not come out of the ground, but out of the mouth of the entranced medium, Zephaniah.

It was difficult for me to give up the beliefs I had learned as a child and to come to a new understanding. Each time I picked up a new edition of the Bible, I would turn to the story of the Medium of Endor and study its wording. At times, I would smile in agreement with the translations but often, I was outraged. As I typed each of the Bible verses into my database, I would take one step away from imposed beliefs and one step toward creating my own.

# EIGHT

## The English Bible

For millions of people, the Bible is the unaltered word of God, which came directly from the lips of God to the pen of man. It arrives in our hands without a comma missing, or a word changed. (If this were in fact the truth, this method of transmission is, in its own way, a form of mediumship!) For today's Christians, the King James Bible reigns supreme—it recorded the law of God exactly as dictated by God.

It is a comforting conviction. Moral dilemmas are easily reduced to black and white. There are no mitigating circumstances, no gray areas. Life would be grand if it were really like that. Rarely is it that simple.

The Bible is not that simple. Most people don't realize that the Bible is a collection of diaries. Different authors with drastically different points of view wrote it, over the course of a 1000 years.[71]

I have come to believe that the Old Testament of the Bible is more like a work of Congress than a work of God. When Congress passes a bill, it goes through different committees. Opposing sides debate the differing points, and eventually a compromise is reached. Often the bill that goes before the president has been so radically changed, the writers of the original bill wouldn't recognize it.

The Pentateuch, the first five books of the Bible, (Genesis-Deuteronomy) was compiled the same way Congress passes a bill. Groups with opposing views had to compromise. Each group had to allow other groups to enter their ideas into the text of the Holy Scriptures. Each of these different groups had their own written documents. Unfortunately, they were lost over time, and we have evidence for this only within the Bible itself. That's why there are so many disagreeing accounts in the Bible. They come from different sources. For example there are two accounts of the creation of man and woman[72] and the naming of Isaac.[73] Each of these groups had a different view of God. The first group, **J**, thought that *Jehovah* and/or *Yahweh* were God. The second group, **E**, considered *Elohim* was God. The third group, **D**, is only found in the book of **Deuteronomy**. The fourth group, **P**, represented the *Priests*. **P**

---

[71] Barclay, William. *Introducing the Bible*. Nashville, TN: Abingdon, 1972. p. 20.

[72] Genesis 1:27 and Genesis 2:7, 21-23.

[73] Genesis 18:9-15 and Genesis 21:1-7.

was the largest group and "concentrated a great deal on matters having to do with priests."[74]

When we compare different accounts of the creation of man, we discover two completely different stories using different names for God. In Genesis 2:7 we discover that God's name is *Eloheim Yahweh* (יְהוָה אֱלֹהִים), a combination of the two names *Eloheim* (אֱלֹהִים) and *Yahweh* (יְהוָה) *Eloheim Yahweh* (יְהוָה אֱלֹהִים) created man by taking dust and forming Adam's body.

| Genesis 1:27 | אֵת אֱלֹהִים וַיִּבְרָא |
| --- | --- |
| | ** God So he created |
| | אֱלֹהִים בְּצֶלֶם בְּצַלְמוֹ הָאָדָם |
| | God in-image in-image the man[75] |
| Genesis 2:7 | אֵת אֱלֹהִים יְהוָה וַיִּיצֶר |
| | ** God Yahweh And he formed |
| | הָאֲדָמָה מִן עָפָר הָאָדָם |
| | the ground from dust the man[76] |

In the seventeenth chapter of Genesis, Yahweh (יְהוָה) is talking to Abraham. A few verses later it is Eloheim (אֱלֹהִים). These accounts come from different sources who had differing opinions on the name of God.

| Genesis 17:1 | אַבְרָם אֶל יְהוָה וַיֵּרָא |
| --- | --- |
| | Abram to Yahweh And he appeared[77] |
| Genesis 17:9 | אַבְרָהָם אֶל אֱלֹהִים וַיֹּאמֶר |
| | Abraham to God Then he said[78] |

A full discussion of these groups is beyond the scope of this book. However, all readers of the Bible, especially of the Old Testament, should keep in mind that the traditional concept—that Moses was the author of the first five books of Moses—is historically inaccurate. It is also important to remember that **priests** wrote all the

---

[74] Friedman, Richard Elliot, *Who Wrote the Bible?* NY: Summit Books, 1987. p. 22.

[75] Genesis 1:27. Kohlenberger, John R., III. *The NIV Interlinear Hebrew-English Old Testament. Vol. 1.* Grand Rapids, MI: Zondervan, 1979. p. 3.

[76] Genesis 2:7. Kohlenberger, John R., III. *The NIV Interlinear Hebrew-English Old Testament. Vol. 1.* Grand Rapids, MI: Zondervan, 1979. p. 5.

[77] Genesis 17:1. Kohlenberger, John R., III. *The NIV Interlinear Hebrew-English Old Testament. Vol. 1.* Grand Rapids, MI: Zondervan, 1979. p. 36.

[78] Genesis 17:9. Kohlenberger, John R., III. *The NIV Interlinear Hebrew-English Old Testament. Vol. 1.* Grand Rapids, MI: Zondervan, 1979. p. 36.

laws concerning the priests: the rituals of sacrifice, and the customs and ceremonies of temple worship.

There are many versions of the Bible besides the King James Version. When I began my research of the Bible nearly 20 year ago, I never dreamed I would be studying over 160 different versions. These versions can be grouped in various ways. One way might be along religious lines. The Jewish, Catholic, Protestant, Mormon, Jehovah Witness, and Coptic religions each have their own version of the Bible.

Another grouping might be special texts. There are several Septuagint versions of the Bible. These are translations of the Greek manuscripts of the Old Testament instead of the Hebrew manuscripts. Then there are the modern paraphrase Bibles. These Bibles do not attempt to stay faithful to the true meaning of the ancient Hebrew and Greek texts. They use modern language, with modern phraseology and idioms. Sometimes these are easier to understand than the more literal translations.

Another grouping could deal more with the business of selling Bibles than with scholarship. Many Bibles are reprints of older editions. The names are changed and usually (but not always) the commentary. It's the same old version with a new cover and title. For example: *The Way, The Book, The Year, Vietnam Veterans' Bible, Parents' Resource Bible,* and *The Small Group Study Bible,* are all *The Living Bible* with different covers. It is true that some of the commentary is different in these variations, but the **text** of the Bible remains the same. The **CAMB** and **CENT** are the **KJV** and **ERV** with new covers and new commentary.

In recent years there has been an explosion of new Bibles. The newest market is for children's Bibles. Special editions, new translations, utilizing simpler language have been written especially for young people.

The group of Bibles I find most intriguing are those new translations, which, based on knowledge gained from recent archeological findings, strive to make the language clearer and to provide new insight. This group may help to change perceptions of psychic phenomena.

As I collected and compared various Bible verses, I began to see a pattern emerge. Some chapters in different versions were identical except for a few minor variations such as: *to* might be used instead of *unto,* or *speak* instead of *spake.* However, as soon as psychic phenomena are discussed, there is a sudden myriad of differences. The translators couldn't agree on which words to use. 1 Kings 19 is an excellent example. All the Bibles used similar language to tell the story of Elijah, who is hiding in a cave from King Ahab. However, when discussing the clairaudient voice heard by Elijah, (**KJV**'s *a still small voice*), translations vary greatly as illustrated in the following chart.

## 1 KINGS CHAPTER 19 VERSE 12

| KJV | 1611 | And after the fire, *a still small voice.* |
|-----|------|------|
| EWYC | 1384 | And after the fire *whistlynge of a thin blast*; there the Lord. |
| LWYC | 1395 | And after the fire is the *hissing of thin wind*; there is the Lord. |
| COV | 1535 | And after the fire, came there a *still soft hissing.* |
| GEN | 1560 | And after the fire came a *still and soft voice.* |
| DOU | 1609 | And after the fire a *whistling of a gentle wind.* |
| HAAK | 1657 | And after the fire a *low noise of a soft calm.* |
| CHAL | 1750 | And after the fire *a whistling of gentle air.* |
| PUR | 1764 | And after the Fire there was a *small Voice in Silence.* |
| GEDD | 1792 | But, after the lightning, there will be heard a *calm, gentle voice.* |
| RAY | 1799 | And after that a *quiet small voice.* |
| THOM | 1808 | And after the fire, there was a *sound of a gentle breeze.* |
| BREN | 1844 | And after the fire, the *voice of a gentle breeze.* |
| LEES | 1856 | And after the fire was the *sound of a soft whisper.* |
| BEN | 1864 | And after the fire *a voice—a soft whisper.* |
| JUSMI | 1876 | And after the fire, a *voice of light stillness.* |
| ROTH | 1897 | And after the fire the *voice of a gentle whisper.* |
| DARBY | 1920 | And after the fire, *a soft gentle voice.* |
| MOFF | 1922 | And after the fire the *breath of a light whisper.* |
| SMGO | 1939 | And after the fire the *sound of a gentle whisper.* |
| KNOX | 1944 | And after the fire, the *whisper of a gentle breeze.* |
| MODL | 1945 | After the fire came the *sound of a light whisper.* |
| OGD | 1950 | And after the fire, the *sound of a soft breath.* |
| NASB | 1960 | And after the fire a *sound of a gentle blowing.* |
| NWT | 1961 | And after the fire there came a *calm, low voice.* |
| NAB | 1970 | And after the fire there was a *tiny whispering sound.* |
| ABBR | 1971 | After this, there was a *gentle voice.* |
| BYIN | 1972 | And after the fire a *sound of soft whispering.* |
| WMF | 1975 | there came *a voice* again saying. |
| BECK | 1976 | And after the fire there was a *gentle, quiet Voice.* |
| NEB | 1976 | And after the fire a *low murmuring sound.* |
| TEV | 1976 | And after the fire there was the *soft whisper of a voice.* |
| NIV | 1978 | And after the fire came a *gentle whisper.* |
| NJER | 1985 | And after the fire, a *light murmuring sound.* |
| TANK | 1985 | And after the fire—*a soft murmuring sound.* |
| WBC | 1985 | And after the fire came a *gentle little breeze.* |
| ARATJ | 1987 | And after the army of the angels of the fire was the *voice of those who were praising softly.* |
| EB | 1987 | After the fire, there was a *quiet, gentle voice.* |
| HIRS | 1989 | And after the fire—the *sound of the deepest silence.* |
| REB | 1989 | And after the fire a *faint murmuring sound.* |
| NRSV | 1990 | And after the fire a *sound of sheer silence.* |
| NCV | 1991 | After the fire, there was a *quiet, gentle sound.* |
| CCB | 1995 | After the fire, the *murmur of a gentle breeze.* |

| CEV | 1995 | Finally, there was a *gentle breeze.* |
| GODWD | 1995 | And after the fire there was a *quiet, whispering voice.* |
| STONE | 1996 | After the fire came a *still, thin sound.* |
| CBJ | 1998 | And after the fire came a *quiet, subdued voice.* |

# 47 Differing Translations

As I said before, it appeared to me that the oldest translations of the Bible were often more accurate than the newer ones. It wasn't until the 74,433 verses I had collected were entered into a data-base that I was able to sort them into groups. It was then that the magnitude of evidence supporting this theory began to emerge. Let us briefly examine the history of the English Bible.

> The story of the translation of the Bible into English is an important part of the struggle of democracy against autocracy and liberty against dictatorship both in the field of politics and in the field of religion.[79]

This quote is significant. Theologians didn't want to give up control of the Bible. John Wycliffe made the first attempt to translate the Bible into English. The Catholic Church was furious. As long as the Bible remained in Latin, the people could not understand it. This allowed the Church freedom. Priests were free to read and translate to the members of their churches the portions *they chose*. This made it easy to avoid the "sticky problems" that are contained in the Bible. For centuries, people didn't know there were contradictions and inconsistencies in the text of the Bible. Jewish people, because they read and understood Hebrew, and studied the Hebrew texts, knew more of these inconsistencies. They enjoyed debating differing interpretations of the text. This was contrary to Christian doctrine which mandated only *one* interpretation of the Bible, the one the church chose. Is it any wonder that Christians (Catholics before the Reformation) were so anti-Semitic.

John Wycliffe translated the New Testament in 1384. Margaret T. Hills describes the Wycliffe Bible in her booklet entitled *A Ready Reference History of the English Bible*, as:

> ...A very stiff, literal translation from inferior Vulgate texts..."[80]

Church officials wanted to stop this new trend of translating the Latin Bible into the vernacular languages. Margaret Hills explains:

> In 1408 a constitution adopted by the provincial council at Oxford read in part: "The Holy Scripture is not to be translated into the

---

[79] May, Herbert Gordon: *Our English Bible in the Making: The Words of Life in Living Language.* Philadelphia, PA: The Westminster Press, 1952. p. 7-8.

[80] Hills, Margaret T. *A Ready Reference History of the English Bible.* NY: American Bible Society, 1980. p. 8.

**vulgar tongue, nor a translation to be expounded, until it shall
have been duly examined, under pain of excommunication and
the stigma of heresy.**[81]

The church became so infuriated by John Wycliffe's English translation of the
Bible that they exhumed his body.

**Twenty years later [after his death], by order of the Council of
Constance, Wycliffe's body was even disinterred and burned, and
his ashes cast into the River Swift.**[82]

During the several years since my first conversation with Awan, my opinions on
the Bible were transformed. Awan was correct. Not only had the Bible undergone
changes, but translators had continually tampered with the Bible's wording since its
first translation into English in 1381. Sometimes the wording was made more
accurate, but more often, the Bible's words were changed, creating confusing or
inaccurate images. In these cases translators weren't concerned with the original
Hebrew or Greek texts, but had hidden agendas to promote. All too often those
agendas were to disguise psychic events in the Bible.

It is difficult to accept that the facts one learned as a child from religious
teachers are inaccurate. I began to question many of my religious beliefs. Learning
that the Bible had been changed was the first step in the transformation of my
beliefs. The second was an understanding of psychic phenomena and how it worked.
I was fortunate to be exploring both subjects at the same time.

At the end of one of Carl's classes, he pulled me aside. "I have a message for
you, Sidney. Awan wishes to speak with you again. Would it be possible for you to
come back here on Saturday?"

My heart skipped a beat, and my stomach turned. All I could think of was how
much turmoil the first conversation with Awan had created in my life. Was I ready
for a second dose? "Do you know what he wants to talk about?" I asked.

"No," Carl replied. "All I know is that he is quite anxious to talk to you."

"Well if it's that important, I suppose I can be here," I replied.

Carl smiled, "Good. I'll see you on Saturday at 10:00 A. M."

---

[81] Hills, Margaret T. *A Ready Reference History of the English Bible.* NY: American Bible Society, 1980. p. 8.

[82] Hills, Margaret T. *A Ready Reference History of the English Bible.* NY: American Bible Society, 1980. p. 8.

# NINE

## You Must Write a Book!

For the second time, I was summoned to Carl's office because Awan wished to speak to me. I was nervous—would Awan shake up my world again, as he had in our first conversation?

As in the previous deep trance session, Carl said the prayer, closed his eyes, and became very quiet. After a minute or two his body began to spasm. This time the spasms were milder than the first session. It appeared that Awan was mastering his technique of entering Carl's body.

 My greetings to you.

 Greetings, Awan.

 I have watched your search for the truth. Tell me, what have you discovered?

 Well, I must admit, Awan, I really thought you were mistaken about the Bible being changed. But after reading many different editions of the Bible I agree with you. The Bible has been changed many times.

 That is correct. You have only begun to scratch the surface. You were able to compare the changes that took place within the English Bible. However, you still have no idea how many changes are now invisible—changes made to alter the theology of the Bible. It is impossible to find those changes, since the original copies of the Bible no longer exist. These originals were destroyed, so that a researcher like you couldn't compare the documents and discover the many changes. In time, you will come to understand this.

Actually, I didn't invite you here today to discuss the Bible. I would like to talk with you about a matter I feel you don't fully understand. I have watched you, as you participated in my medium's psychic development classes. I am pleased with the progress you are making.

 Thank you, Awan, but I don't feel any more psychic then when I started.

That is not the point, my friend. You are not here to learn to become a medium.

 Then what was the purpose of my being here?

 Do you know what the Hebrew word מַלְאָךְ (*mal âk*) means?

 I think that מַלְאָךְ (*mal âk*) means angel.

 That is correct. Do you know what the exact definition of an angel is?

 No Awan, I don't.

 The literal translation of מַלְאָךְ (*mal âk*) is messenger. The same is true for αγγελοδ, the Greek word for *angel*. Both מַלְאָךְ (*mal âk*) and αγγελοδ mean *messenger*. Angels are God's messengers. And now it is time for me to give you this title.

 What do you mean?

 You are to be my messenger.

 How am I to do that?

 I am offering you the keys to the vaults of hidden knowledge. What I am about to teach you was once recorded in great books, scrolls, and tablets. These precious records were in a great and wonderful library on the shores of the Mediterranean Sea, in a city called Alexandria. A deliberately set fire destroyed the library. The people who ignited the fire wanted that knowledge reduced to ashes. I am about to resurrect this knowledge. I have special plans for you. You are to be an instrument of the Spirit, but not in the same manner as this instrument that we are using. You will have another mission. You are to be my messenger. You are to write down my teachings in the form of books that will help people raise their consciousness.

Awan, you must be joking! Me, a writer!? I can't put two sentences together and have them make sense. Besides, writing is an extremely painful process for me. I hate it.

You lack confidence in yourself and are placing mental road blocks in the way, inhibiting your writing. In time your confidence will grow, and you will be able to carry out our work.

What would I write about?

I want to talk to you about the history of your own people. The Jewish lineage was rich with information about psychic phenomena. Your Bible is basically a book of psychic history. Every major character in the Bible used some phase of psychic phenomena. In fact, if you took all the psychic events out of the Bible, you would be left with twenty or thirty pages of man-made laws created by priests to rule people.

Are you saying that all the commandments that God instructs through Moses did not come from God, but were put there by priests?

Yes. I will see to it that the right information is placed in your hands, and, in time, you will understand just how much the Bible has been changed. It is very important that you *not* simply accept every word I say, but research it on your own. That is why we saw to it that you studied to become a librarian, though at first you were not happy with the idea.

That's true, Awan. I hated it! In time, however, I learned to enjoy the work. Now I'm glad that I'm a librarian.

This is not the first time that you worked in a library, my friend. In a previous life you worked in the great library of Alexandria, which we'll need another session to explore. You have the skills to find information. I am asking that you investigate for yourself before you come to any conclusions.

OK Awan, I will do that.

As I said before, the Bible is a book of psychic history. Most people are ignorant of the Gifts of the Spirit, so they don't recognize them in the Bible.

What sort of evidence are you talking about?

 When Noah, Abraham, Isaac, Jacob, Joseph, Moses, Samuel, and all the other prophets heard God's voice, it was because they had the gift of clairaudience. The Gifts of the Spirit reside in a now dormant part of the brain. When these cells function, one is endowed with a psychic gift. Since these cells were functioning in these Biblical people, they were able to hear God's voice.

 I think I am beginning to understand.

 Remember that when I say *God*, I mean the voice of a Spirit person. Remember that when a person spoke to a spiritual being, he addressed that being as *the Lord*, as a sign of respect.

 Yes, the medium explained that to me during my first reading.

 The man you know as Jesus was the greatest medium that ever lived.

 Jesus was a medium?

 He certainly was. He was the only person in the Bible who had all the Gifts of the Spirit. His entire brain was functioning. People whose brain is totally functioning are able to do phenomenal things.

 Most people think Jesus is God, or the Son of God, not a medium.

 My friend, we are all the sons and daughters of God. If you will read The New Testament carefully, you will discover that Jesus never claimed to be God. He said he was the Son of God, the same as you are.

 I've never read The New Testament, but I think it's time.

 What the Bible terms *a miracle* is simply a demonstration of the Gifts of the Spirit. Ask my medium, when he returns to his waking state, to teach you more about each of these spiritual gifts. Jesus used the gift of *apports* when he multiplied food to feed 5,000 people. He used the gift of *levitation* when he walked on the water. I will not use this valuable energy to list all of them for you. Discuss them with my medium.

 I will.

 Do you know another Biblical person who could multiply food?

 Elijah multiplied oil and meal for a widow he was staying with.[83]

 That is correct! Then you know that Elijah also raised the dead, like Jesus did?[84]

 Yes, the widow's son had died, and Elijah brought him back to life.

 And what do you call Elijah? What title do the Jewish people give him?

 Elijah was a prophet.

 And you understand that the word *prophet* is another word for *medium*? Think about this: Both Elijah and Jesus multiplied food and raised the dead. Correct?

 Yes, that is correct.

 Then why do Jews call Elijah a prophet and the Christians call Jesus a God? Why don't Christians call Elijah a God, too?

 I don't know.

 Jesus didn't go to your realm to become a God. He did not come to start a religion. Jesus came to bring truth to the people. The Jewish people had had a long line of prophets who professed the true nature of God. However, Jews became entrenched in laws that were created by priests. The priests designed many laws and rituals to maintain their role as intermediary between the people and God. Jesus came to your world to teach that God was within. You didn't need a priest to

---

[83] 1 Kings 17:10-16.

[84] 1 Kings 17:17-24.

communicate with God. Early Christians employed the Gifts of the Spirit on a regular basis. Eventually, their priests succeeded in removing the Gifts of the Spirit from the church, and Christianity changed course. Today, very little of what Jesus came to share with the world is being taught in church.

That's sad.

It is, but the time is approaching when all that will change. Your writing will help wake people up. Don't worry about what others will say. Be proud of your heritage. Many great teachers have come from the Jewish faith. Unfortunately, Jewish people have been tortured and murdered for centuries. So-called Christians have butchered, beheaded, shot, and burned Jews at the stake and in ovens. To this day, Jews don't have a peaceful place to call home.

The Catholic Church possesses the largest collection of paintings and artifacts the world has ever known. Only the high priests and cardinals know about this collection. A major portion of these treasures came from people of the Jewish race.

You must write a book to educate people about the Gifts of the Spirit and the massive cover-up of truth. This is your mission. We ask you to go forward, and from this moment on, do not look back. Do not let the teachings of your past effect you. Put your focus on the task you have been given and you will accomplish your goal.

I will try to fulfill your wishes, Awan.

*Carl's body gave a sudden jerk, and he began coughing. I helped him with a glass of water, which he eagerly drank. Carl seemed quite tired, and went to nap. Several hours later we had the first of many discussions about the **Gifts of the Spirit**.*

# TEN

## What Are the Gifts of the Spirit?

**Now concerning spiritual gifts, brethren, I would not have you ignorant.**[85]

Saint Paul's opening statement in chapter twelve of the first book of Corinthians, clearly states his message. While traveling to Damascus, Paul heard Jesus' voice through the psychic gift of clairaudience.[86] This personal experience altered his life, and inspired Paul to continue Jesus' mission of teaching the Gifts of the Spirit to the masses.

Deplorably, the religion, which Paul helped to create, ignored these important words. The hierarchy of the Catholic Church drove the practice of the Gifts of the Spirit underground, making it *occult* (hidden). The Church did this to gain control over its followers and to stifle independent, inquiring thought. It led its parishioners blindly down the narrow path of faith, threatening an eternity of hell's damnation to anyone who left the fold.

Saint Paul wanted to emancipate humanity from such ignorant superstition. He taught people that the Gifts of the Spirit would enrich their lives. He wanted men and women to be in communication with the living God, not enslaved by a lifeless book entitled the Holy Bible.

Why did Saint Paul promote an understanding of psychic phenomena? The answer lies within the etymology of the word *psychic*. Psychic comes from the Greek word *psychikos* that means *soul*, or *mind*. No one could dispute that Saint Paul was interested in the human soul or mind. Therefore, by definition he was interested in the psychic realm. In 1 Corinthians 12:8-11, Saint Paul describes the many different abilities that can be demonstrated by the power of the soul, through the Spirit of God.

**To one through the Spirit is given the utterance of wisdom; and to another the utterance of knowledge, according to the same Spirit; to another faith, in the same Spirit; to another the gift of healing,**

---

[85] 1 Corinthians 12:1 [CONF].

[86] Acts 9: 3-5.

> **in the one Spirit; to another the working of miracles; to another prophecy; to another the distinguishing of spirits; to another various kinds of tongues; to another the interpretation of tongues. But, all these things are the work of one and the same Spirit, who allots to everyone according as he will.**[87]

Saint Paul was describing, in first century terms, psychic gifts that are still performed today. The "utterance of wisdom" and "utterance of knowledge" are today called *clairvoyance, clairaudience,* and *prophecy.*

You will notice that Saint Paul states that these spiritual gifts are the result of Spirit, not the devil, which reinforces the idea that people have been misinformed. The Holy Bible is humanity's most comprehensive record of psychic events in ancient times. The events recorded within its pages are descriptions of people demonstrating the Gifts of the Spirit.

Sir Oliver Lodge, an eminent 19th century physicist, was knighted in 1902 for his contributions to science.[88] He states:

> **Ignorance of what are often called psychic, or more accurately metapsychic, phenomena is so thorough and wide-spread, that people can fail to perceive that the Bible, which they are so familiar with and regard with such reverence, is saturated with metapsychic or mediumistic phenomena of every kind.**[89]

Laurence Tunstall Heron states in his book entitled *ESP in the Bible* that:

> **Indeed, the Old Testament constitutes mainly a record of how a people received its guidance by ESP through prophets and seers—whose language and message were especially comprehensible to solitary shepherds and lonely travelers, a large proportion of whom likewise were proficient in receptive meditation.**[90]

> **The pervasive historical truth is that the Scriptures recount a continuous chain of psychic events, from the call of Abraham (Gen. 12:1-3) in the Bronze-Age to the book of Revelations, which consists of the psychic visions of a seer, in the steely era of Imperial Rome. To a Christian or a Jew, therefore, the study of psychic phenomena constitutes an additional aid to the understanding of his religion and its Scriptures; affords one more**

---

[87] 1 Corinthians 12:8-11 [CONF].

[88] "Lodge, Sir Oliver Joseph." *Biographical Dictionary of Parapsychology.* N.Y.: Helix Press 1964, p. 189.

[89] Stobart, Mabel Annie Boulton. *Ancient Lights: or the Bible, the Church, and Psychic Science.* London: Kegan Paul, Trench, Trubner & Co., Ltd., 1923. p. xix.

[90] Heron, Laurence Tunstall. *ESP in the Bible.* Garden City, NY: Doubleday & Company, Inc., 1974. p. 20.

means of applying the teaching of Jesus and the prophets more confidently and more effectively.[91]

Experts agree that as one understands psychic science, it deepens and enriches one's understanding and respect for the Bible. No longer does one consider the Bible as a book of fairy tales with fantastic miracles that could never have happened. Instead, the Bible becomes a history book of mediumship; one that records how psychic phenomena was demonstrated centuries ago.

The reader should realize that the laws of psychic science have not changed since Biblical times. What happened in the days of Abraham, Moses, Elijah, and Jesus, can, and still does, happen today. All the major personalities of the Bible were mediums and demonstrated some of the Gifts of the Spirit. There has been only one person in all of history, Jesus of Nazareth, who used and demonstrated every one of the Gifts of the Spirit. As each of the Gifts of the Spirit that Paul mentions in the Bible is discussed, I will point out the specific instances where each gift was demonstrated, and the medium that demonstrated it.

## *Clairaudience*

Clairaudience is the most commonly found Gift of the Spirit in the Bible. People who are clairaudient can hear clearly within their minds, sounds that cannot be heard by others around them. What are heard are sounds, which come from the Spirit World. These sounds might be words from a person who is living in the Spirit World, or might be music.

Most of the famous Biblical characters, as well as some of the minor ones mentioned in the Old Testament, were clairaudient. Many Old Testament chapters opened with phrases such as these:

> "And God spake unto Noah, saying"[92]
> "And the Lord spake unto Moses saying"[93]
> "Then the Lord called Samuel, Samuel"[94]
> "This is the message which the Lord spoke to Jeremiah."[95]

Each of these is an example of a message coming from God, through the psychic gift of clairaudience. Unfortunately, the English speaking readers of the Bible are deprived of this information. Because the original texts were in Hebrew and Greek, it was necessary for the holy text to be filtered through translators, who were blinded by their preconceived ideas and dogmas.

---

[91] Heron, Laurence Tunstall. *ESP in the Bible*. Garden City, NY: Doubleday & Company, Inc., 1974. p. 49.

[92] Genesis 8:15 [KJV].

[93] Numbers 8:1 [KJV].

[94] 1 Samuel 3:4 [RSV].

[95] Jeremiah 46:13 [NASB].

I wouldn't want my English-speaking surgeon performing a French doctor's new technique, if the instructions were translated by someone ignorant of medical science. The chance for error would be great simply because the translator would be interpreting words without understanding the concepts behind them. It follows suit that a person ignorant of the Gifts of the Spirit, who would translate the Bible, which is a history of psychic events, might misinterpret valuable information. To further illustrate this point, let's consult *Webster's Dictionary* for its second definition *oracle*:

**The revelation or response of a medium or priest.[96]**

Now let's translate *oracle* into Hebrew by consulting *The Englishman's Hebrew and Chaldee Concordance of the Old Testament*, a book used to translate words from Hebrew into English. It lists the locations of particular Hebrew words within the Hebrew text of the Bible. We find two Hebrew words under the word *oracle*. One is the word דְבִיר (*debir*) and the other is the word דָבָר (*dâbâr*).[97]

Every Hebrew word has a three letter consonant root. If you notice, both words for *oracle* have the same letters ר (*Rash*) ב (*Vuv*), and ד (*Dalad*). The small dots and dashes underneath the letters are called vowels. Many different words can have the same root letters, it is *the vowels that create the difference between words*, thereby changing their meaning. One should also be aware that, in ancient times, the scribes *did not* write the vowels in the Biblical text, thereby creating further ambiguity as to the exact meaning of some passages in the Bible.

*The Englishman's Hebrew and Chaldee Concordance of the Old Testament* indicates that דְבִיר (*debir*) is a noun,[98] which means 'the place where oracles were given.' The *Theological Wordbook of the Old Testament* explains that דְבִיר (*debir*)

> **... refers to the holy of holies and is translated sixteen times in KJV and ASV as "oracle."[99]**

דָבָר (*Dâbâr*) is also a noun that can mean *oracle*. The *Theological Wordbook of the Old Testament* explains that דָבָר (*dâbâr*)

> **"... is translated eighty-five different ways in KJV! ... [דָבָר]** *dâbâr* **basically means what God said or says.[100]**

---

[96] *Webster's New World Dictionary of the American Language. College edition.* Cleveland, OH: The World Publishing Company, 1964. p. 1030.

[97] *The Englishman's Hebrew and Chaldee Concordance of the Old Testament.* Vol. 2. London: Walton and Maberrly, 1866. p. 1593.

[98] *The Englishman's Hebrew and Chaldee Concordance of the Old Testament.* Vol. 1. London: Walton and Maberrly, 1866. p. 318.

[99] Harris, R. Laird, ed. *Theological Wordbook of the Old Testament. Vol. 1.* Chicago: Moody Press, 1980. p. 181.

[100] Harris, R. Laird, ed. *Theological Wordbook of the Old Testament. Vol. 1.* Chicago: Moody Press, 1980. p. 180.

דָבָר (*Dâbâr*) is used over fourteen hundred times in the Old Testament. Some examples are:

> **And Moses told Aaron all** *the words of* (*dâbâr*) **the Lord...**[101]
> **And God spake** *all these words* (*dâbâr*), **saying...**[102]
> **a man had enquired at** *the oracle* (*dâbâr*) **of God...**[103]
> **and see what** *answer* (*dâbâr*) **I shall return to him...**[104]
> **according to the** *saying* (*dâbâr*) **of Elisha which he spake...**[105]

The consonant roots (in this case ר-דבר (*Rash*) ב (*Vuv*), and ד (*Dalad*)) link words together in families. There is another Hebrew word that has the same root as the words for *oracle* (דְבִיר (*debir*) and דָבָר (*dâbâr*)). This Hebrew word דָבַר (*dâbar*) is a verb.[106] The *Theological Wordbook of the Old Testament* explains that דָבַר (*dâbar*):

> **is probably a denominate verb from [**דָבָר**]** (*dâbâr*).[107]

*The New Strong's Complete Dictionary of Bible Words* concurs that דְבִיר (*debir* (noun)), דָבָר (*dâbâr* (noun)) and דָבַר (*dâbar* (verb)) all share the same root and are related words.[108] What makes this so fascinating is that **the English language has no verb meaning "oracle,"** yet it d exists in Hebrew. Where is it used in the Bible? The verb form of *oracle* דָבַר (*dâbar*) is used some eleven hundred times in the Old Testament. Some examples would include:

> **As the Lord had** *spoken* (*dâbar*) **unto him...**[109]
> **And the Lord** *spake* (*dâbar*) **unto Moses...**[110]
> **As the Lord** *spake* (*dâbar*) **unto David...**[111]
> **The angel of the Lord** *said* (*dâbar*) **to Elijah...**[112]
> **For the mouth of the Lord** *hath spoken* (*dâbar*) **it.**[113]

---

[101] Exodus 4:28.

[102] Exodus 20:1 (The Ten Commandments).

[103] 2 Samuel 16:23.

[104] 2 Samuel 24:13.

[105] 2 Kings 2:22.

[106] *The Englishman's Hebrew and Chaldee Concordance of the Old Testament. Vol. 1.* London: Walton and Maberrly, 1866. p. 318.

[107] Harris, R. Laird, ed. *Theological Wordbook of the Old Testament. Vol. 1.* Chicago: Moody Press, 1980. p. 178.

[108] Strong, James. *The New Strong's Complete Dictionary of Bible Words.* Nashville, TN: Thomas Nelson Publishers, 1996. p. 344-345.

[109] Genesis 12:4 [KJV].

[110] Exodus 33:11 [KJV].

[111] 1 Kings 5:5 [KJV].

[112] 2 Kings 1:3 [KJV].

[113] Isaiah 1:20 [KJV].

> **The Lord God of Israel** *hath spoken* **(dâbar) it.**[114]
> **Jeremiah the prophet** *spake* **(dâbar) ...**[115]

This is just one of many examples where the psychic connotation of a Hebrew word was lost in the translation from Hebrew to English. Readers of the English Bible are left unaware that every time God spoke, it was to a medium who possessed the gift of clairaudience.

With this newly gained insight into the Hebrew language, we can now become Bible translators who are educated in the Gifts of the Spirit (a rather unique distinction in the six hundred fifteen year history of the Bible's translation into the English language). The phrase: *"And the Lord spake unto Moses"* would become *"And Spirit oracularly spoke to Moses."* However, using a 21st century understanding of psychic science, this phrase would metamorphose into: *"And Spirit clairaudiently spoke to Moses."*

In The New Testament, Jesus demonstrated the Gift of Clairaudience when he delivered the Sermon on the Mount. The Bible uses the words:

> **And he opened his mouth and taught them saying...**[116]

Jesus heard Spirit clairaudiently and repeated the words to the people.

## *Clairvoyance*

Clairvoyance is the ability to see images beyond the range of normal vision. Everyone has had experience using their psychic third eye. It is the screen on which we view our dreams. Spirit projects pictures to clairvoyants on this same screen.

The Bible is full of examples of mediums demonstrating clairvoyance. When Abraham saw God,[117] and Moses saw the burning bush,[118] both were using clairvoyant vision. Amos,[119] Jeremiah,[120] and Ezekiel[121] are just a few of the prophets who had clairvoyant visions, recorded in the Bible. Jesus chose his disciples using his clairvoyant vision to study their auras, the light given off by their spiritual bodies. This was implied when the Bible says that Jesus "watched Peter and Andrew," and "caught sight of James and John."[122]

---

[114] Isaiah 21:17 [KJV].

[115] Jeremiah 45:1 [KJV].

[116] Matthew 5:1-2 [RSV].

[117] Genesis 12:7.

[118] Exodus 3:2-6.

[119] Amos 1:2.

[120] Jeremiah 1:11-14.

[121] Ezekiel 37:1-14.

[122] Matthew 4:18-22 [NAB].

The "utterance of wisdom" and "utterance of knowledge" (clairaudience and clairvoyance) that Saint Paul was teaching about 2000 years ago is still used today. The Catholic Church, and many of the other Christian religions, have forbidden mediumship, and the demonstration of these gifts within their churches.

## *Healing*

Saint Paul mentions healing in 1 Corinthians 15, which is the most important Gift of the Spirit. Healing occurs when a person becomes a receiver and transmitter of healing energy. The person who is the instrument for healing can receive healing energy from doctors and teachers in the Spirit World. A spiritually attuned healer goes into a meditative state. Healing takes place when the energy flows from Spirit, through the medium, into the patient's body. The healer transmits the energy he is receiving by placing his or her hands on the patient's body. This is known as "laying on of the hands."

The most famous Biblical healer was Jesus, though he wasn't the only medium in the Bible to heal. In fact, not only did both Elijah[123] and Elisha[124] demonstrate the ability to heal, they raised people from the dead.

Saint Paul also mentions "the working of miracles." There is evidence found in the Bible that links psychic phenomena and miracles. Jesus was described as a *prophet* and a *miracle worker*. Obviously you cannot prophesy unless you can demonstrate a psychic gift.

> **He was a prophet, who did incredible miracles and was a mighty teacher, highly regarded by both God and man.**[125]

It is interesting to note here that Jesus was not called God, nor the son of God, merely a *teacher* and *prophet*. It is also interesting to note that the term *miracles* in this verse is directly related to the actions of the *prophet*. (He *did* perform incredible miracles, or psychic feats.)

There are many Gifts of the Spirit that would come under Saint Paul's "miracle" category. They include: *materialization, direct voice, apports, levitation, automatic writing, dowsing.*

## *Materialization*

Materialization occurs when Spirit draws *ectoplasm* from the cells of the body of the medium, and sculpts it into a form. *The American Illustrated Medical Dictionary* explains that ectoplasm is:

---

[123] 1 Kings 17 :17-24.
[124] 2 Kings 4 :32-36.
[125] Luke 24:19 [LIV].

**The outer stiffer portion or region of the cytoplasm of a cell which may be differentiated in texture from the inner portion...[126]**

Under the right conditions, Spirit can draw the ectoplasm from the cells of the medium's body and use the energy that emanates from the ectoplasm. The energy found in ectoplasm is life force energy.

Most people are familiar with photographic film, and know that if light were to touch the surface of the film, it would destroy any recorded images. Ectoplasm reacts similarly. In order for Spirit to draw the ectoplasm from the body, the medium must sit in a completely darkened room. If the lights were turned on, the energy would be destroyed, and all communication ended. This sudden jolt could be hazardous to the medium, even fatal. Under special conditions determined by Spirit, ectoplasm may be produced in daylight, but this is extremely rare. In daylight, ectoplasm has the appearance of fire. In darkness, it appears as a cloud of smoke.

In the Old Testament, there are several instances where Spirit drew ectoplasm from the Hebrews to form a cloud to lead them through the desert. God was in a pillar of cloud, which looked like fire during the day. The Hebrews would only travel when the cloud traveled.[127]

More often materialization occurs when Spirit molds the ectoplasm into a human form. Using energy from ectoplasm, Spirit can speak through this ectoplasmic body. The Bible describes a materialization in the Meeting tent, when *"the Lord spoke to Moses face to face, as a man speaks to his friend."*[128] Jesus demonstrated materialization during the transfiguration, when Moses and Elijah came to talk with him.[129] (Photographs of actual materializations are included in Chapter 12.)

## *Direct Voice*

Direct Voice occurs when people in the Spirit World and people in the physical world can communicate directly. The use of a medium is required, but his voice isn't used. The Spirit People extract ectoplasm from the medium's body and mold it to form a voice box, which is then used to speak.

There are two forms of direct voice. The first is called *trumpet mediumship*. A trumpet is a conical device, similar to a megaphone. Spirit places the ectoplasmic voice box inside the trumpet, which is used to amplify the voice. The second is called *independent voice*. This is when the voice is heard without the use of the trumpet.

Moses demonstrated Direct Voice in Exodus 9:9, 19.

**And the LORD said unto Moses, Lo I come unto thee in a thick**

---

[126] Doland, W. A. Newman, *The American Illustrated Medical Dictionary.* Philadelphia: W. B. Saunders Co., 1951. p. 474.

[127] Exodus 40:34-38.

[128] Exodus 33:8-11 [NKJV].

[129] Luke 9:28-36.

cloud, that the people may hear when I speak with thee, and may believe thee forever.[130]

And when the *voice of the trumpet* sounded long, and waxed louder and louder, Moses spake, and God answered him by a *voice*.[131]

The cloud was ectoplasm which can look like clouds, or smoke. Ectoplasm is needed for trumpet mediumship to occur. Jesus demonstrated independent direct voice during his baptism when the "voice from heaven" declared that Jesus was his son.[132]

## Apports

An apport is a type of materialization by which physical objects appear where they did not previously exist. When conditions are right, Spirit can make this phenomena happen. Spirit can dematerialize objects from the Spirit World, and materialize them in our physical world. When the object materializes, it is very hot, just as an object that enters our atmosphere from outer space becomes hot. When both Elijah[133] and Jesus[134] multiplied food, they were demonstrating apports.

## Levitation

Levitation happens when Spirit creates a type of energy that can lift people or objects off the ground, defying the laws of gravity. When levitation is demonstrated, tables, furniture, and even people can rise in the air without any visible means of support.

Elisha applied the Gift of Levitation when he made the axhead float from the bottom of the Jordan River to the surface.[135] When Jesus walked on water, he was levitating.[136]

## Automatic Writing

Automatic writing happens when a medium allows Spirit to use his or her hand to produce a written message or to draw a picture. The medium needs to put himself

---

[130] Exodus 19:9 [KJV].

[131] Exodus 19:19 [KJV].

[132] Mark 1:11.

[133] 1 Kings 17: 8-16.

[134] Matthew 14:14-21.

[135] 2 Kings 6:1-7.

[136] Matthew 14:22-28.

in a relaxed, meditative state, erasing all conscious thought from his mind. Spirit then places his hand over the medium's hand, and begins to write. It is identical to the way a kindergarten teacher places her hand over her student's hand to help form a letter correctly. The medium has no conscious knowledge of what is being written or drawn, and the speed of the writing or drawing can be incredibly fast.

Automatic writing is described in the Old Testament when the Ten Commandments were written by "the Finger of God." Moses was the channel.[137] Jesus performed automatic writing during the episode with the adulteress. He stooped down to write something on the ground. Seeking guidance from Spirit on how to handle this matter, Jesus received the guidance through automatic writing.[138]

# Dowsing

Dowsing is the ability to find water under the surface of the ground, by using a divining rod. The dowser begins walking with the divining rod pointing toward the sky. This divining rod can be a forked stick, however, some dowsers use wire rods. As the dowser steps over the underground source of water, the divining rod immediately swings down, pointing to the ground. Often the dowser will intuitively know how deep one would have to dig into the ground to get to the water source. Some dowsers are able to locate mineral deposits of oil.

In the Old Testament, Moses was dowsing when he struck the rock with his rod and water gushed out.[139] Jesus performed dowsing without using a rod. For "the miraculous catch of fish," Jesus told his disciples where and when to cast their nets into the sea.[140]

# Prophecy

Saint Paul also mentions the Gift of Prophecy on his list of the Gifts of Spirit. Prophecy occurs when the prophet or medium receives a vision from Spirit regarding another time period. Spirit is not bound by time and can relay to the prophet information about the future. This information can come in the form of pictures or verbal messages.

A complete list of Biblical prophecies would require quoting most of the Bible. Today, many ministers are examining the Bible for prophecies that were predicted about the present time. To cite two examples: Ezekiel prophesied the Holocaust of World War II preceding the re-establishment of the State of Israel when he described

---

[137] Exodus 32:15-16.

[138] John 8:2-11.

[139] Exodus 17:5 –6.

[140] Luke 5:1-6.

his vision of the dry bones.[141] Jesus prophesied about his own death and resurrection.[142]

## Dreams

Many people have had precognitive dreams, meaning they have dreamt about an event before it happens. Scientists have determined that everyone dreams, but not everyone has recall of their dreams. Not all dreams would be considered a Gift of the Spirit, but many are. When a person is asleep, the physical body is in a relaxed state. During this quiet state Spirit can project an image, or vision to the subconscious mind. We call these visions "dreams." When the dream experiences spill over from the subconscious mind into our conscious mind, we have recall, and can remember what we have dreamt.

Dreams are the easiest way for Spirit to communicate with people on the physical plane. Everyone has dreams. The sleep state prevents the conscious mind from blocking out communication from Spirit.

The Bible records many instances where mediums dreamt; Jacob dreamt of a ladder where angels were ascending and descending to earth.[143] Joseph dreamt that he would rule over his brothers. This dream was precognitive, a prophesy that came true.[144] The Pharaoh of Egypt dreamt of a drought, and Joseph interpreted the Pharaoh's dream.[145] In the Gospels, Joseph, Jesus' father receives the warning to flee into Egypt for his family's safety from Spirit through a dream.[146]

## Psychometry

Psychometry is the ability to detect the vibrations of an object. When a person holds an object or wears it, much of the owner's pattern of life is recorded in the object's vibrations. *Everything* on the earth plane has a vibration. When a person who is sensitive to vibrations holds an object that belongs to another person, he or she can pick up the vibrations of the owner's past, present, and future. Since future events can sometimes be "seen" by a medium, psychometry is often linked to prophecy.

There are no examples of psychometry recorded within the pages of the Old Testament. Jesus was the only Biblical medium to use psychometry. This event

---

[141] Ezekiel 37:1-14.

[142] Matthew 12:38-40.

[143] Genesis 28:10-15.

[144] Genesis 37:9-11.

[145] Genesis 41:15-31.

[146] Matthew 2:13-14.

occurred when Jesus held the water jar of a Samaritan woman and began discussing events in her life.[147]

## *Trance*

Talking in Tongues is the last of the Gifts of the Spirit that Saint Paul wishes us to be educated about. The medium goes into trance and the Spirit speaks a foreign language. This gift is the best evidence of trance and clearly illustrates this Bible verse:

> **And the Spirit of the Lord will come upon thee, and thou shalt prophesy with them, and shalt be turned into another man.[148]**

Talking in Tongues is a specific application of trance. Deep trance happens when a medium allows his spiritual body to temporarily leave his physical body. During this time, the medium's physical body is in a state similar to deep sleep, and is controlled and guarded by a Spirit. Spirit controls can bring the medium into different levels of trance, depending on the amount, or type of work the medium is to do.

For example, if the medium is to present a lesson, lecture, medical diagnosis, or personal reading, the Spirit guide would bring the medium into a higher level of trance. During deep trance, the Spirit body of the medium leaves his physical body, and the Spirit guide allows another Spirit to enter the body to speak through the medium.

If a master teacher were to enter the medium's body, a philosophical lecture might be given. If a Spirit doctor uses the medium, he might diagnose a person's illness. During a personal reading, the Spirit of a family member who had passed on might use the medium to convey a message of some importance to the listener.

Trance was demonstrated in the Old Testament when the woman of Endor informed King Saul of his impending death.[149] In the New Testament, Jesus' disciples were in a trance state up on the Mount of Transfiguration.[150]

Knowledge of psychic science will open new vistas in a person's life. One's spiritual horizons will expand and a greater understanding of the Bible unfolds. No longer will the Bible be a dusty book on the shelf, filled with morality plays, and inconceivable miracles. Knowledge of psychic phenomena rejuvenates the Bible. It becomes very alive and real. As one realizes that the psychic phenomena that happened in Biblical times is still practiced today, one's perception of God begins to change. No longer is God an old man sitting on a throne in a divine palace in the sky, judging our every move or reflecting on whether or not to answer our prayers. God

---

[147] John 4:7-26.

[148] 1 Samuel 10:6 [KJV].

[149] 1 Samuel 28:7-19.

[150] Luke 9:28-36.

becomes a tangible source, able to help us and guide us through the tribulations of our lives.

Saint Paul called the Gifts of the Spirit tools for communicating with God. Can you imagine what the world would be like today if the church had honored and taught these precious Gifts of the Spirit?

# ELEVEN

## The Death of My Father and Grandmother

Early in February of 1981, my father took sick and went to a doctor who ordered a battery of tests. My father had bone cancer. He chose not to have chemotherapy, but took medications. The doctor said he should live comfortably for about two years. When I explained the situation to Carl, he advised me to make the arrangements for his funeral. Although that sounds morbid, I was glad I listened to this advice, because it was not a simple matter. The area where my parents lived was almost totally Christian. There were no Jewish funeral homes in the area. To further complicate matters, my father's family plot was in a cemetery in Long Island, almost three hours from my parent's home.

I decided to make the arrangements at a nearby funeral home in New Jersey. It was difficult to do, yet, comforting to know that all these complicated preparations were complete. A funeral home in the next town would bring my father's body to New Jersey, where they would prepare the body for burial. Then they would transport us to Long Island for the funeral. I went home and told my mother of the arrangements I had made. She seemed relieved that I had taken care of all the complicated details. Luckily we didn't need these plans for another year and a half.

One morning I received a phone call from Carl. "Spirit has given me a message to give to you. I see two coffins draped in black cloths. Do Jewish people drape black cloths over coffins?"

" I don't know," I answered. "I've never been to a Jewish funeral before."

"Well, I see two coffins draped in black cloths. I see your father passing first. The flowers on his grave will barely have time to whither before your grandmother's funeral takes place. I see a period of three attached to it."

On May 2, 1983, my grandmother suffered a major stroke. I had spoken to her that morning—we were making plans for Mother's day. That was the last time she spoke — the stroke left her totally paralyzed and speechless. I called Carl and asked him what was happening, as he had seen my father dying first. He said, "Sometimes I see a negative image. Perhaps your grandmother will go first. I still see them passing one after the other."

I felt helpless, for I couldn't do anything to help my grandmother or my father. I knew the Spirit World was preparing for them. Carl had helped me understand "afterlife." A few months earlier, Carl had invited several of his students up to his house for dinner. We sat down to this scrumptious meal. Carl wanted to say grace, so everyone around the table joined hands, expecting Carl to bless the food. Suddenly we heard a strange voice:

> **We would like to inform you at this time of the meaning of Jacob's ladder. The true message of Jacob's dream is that there are many levels in the Spirit World; levels of spiritual progression, advancement and growth. This was represented through the symbol of the ladder. Just as one climbs a ladder from the ground upwards, so does one climb the ladder of spirituality, stepping higher, advancing further to a state of more perfect being.**

Abruptly Carl looked up and asked, "What happened?" We told him that he went into trance for a couple of minutes. I have never seen Carl do that before or since. Usually when he enters a trance state, he needs to sit quietly and adjust his vibration. I didn't know that someone could snap into a trance state and just as suddenly snap out of it. Carl spent the whole of dinner discussing Jacob's ladder.

After this experience, I began to compare the Spirit World to a staircase, instead of a ladder. You naturally gravitate to the position on the staircase that you deserve to be on, based on how you've lived your life on earth. There will be Spirits higher on the staircase and lower. The lower levels are where the less enlightened reside. The ones on the very bottom of the staircase are in hellish regions. The people that are on your level are like-minded. I believe that, in the Spirit World, we end up living in an environment that we create. Each level in the Spirit World has a different vibration. The different frequencies separate the evolved masters from the unenlightened criminals.

The end of the school year is an extremely hectic time for a teacher. Somehow I did everything that I needed to do, and when school closed, I moved back to my parents' house to spend time with my father. One day my mother and I were sitting in my father's hospital room. She began talking to my father.

"Why do you always have to interrupt?" he asked, with a slightly annoyed edge in his voice.

"What do you mean?" my mother asked. No one had been talking.

"You always interrupt. I was talking to Rubinstein, and you started talking and interrupted him."

I looked at my mother, and she looked back at me with an understanding look in her eyes. She understood what had just transpired—it was her worst fear. My father was in conversation with a Spirit. Rubinstein had been a neighbor of my father when he was growing up and had been the first one in the neighborhood to buy a car. The car was a brand-new invention back then and had fascinated my father.

My mother and I realized that Dad's conversation with Rubinstein meant he would soon make the transition into the Spirit World. Before a person dies, he becomes clairvoyant and clairaudient. This usually happens during the last ten days or so of the person's life. Just as before a baby is born, the family is busy preparing for the new arrival, at the time of death, the same process happens, but in reverse. Spirits who preceded my father into the Spirit World his parents, relatives, and friends were preparing to greet the soul of my father as he passed over. Apparently Rubinstein was one of the people helping my father to make that transition.

This same process happened in Biblical times. Abraham's ancestors meet him in the Spirit World when he died.

> **Then Abraham gave up the spirit and died in a good old age, an old man and full of years, and was gathered to his people.**[151]

The phrase *was gathered to his people* describes the Spirits of Abraham's family coming to greet him, as he entered the Spirit World. Why would Abraham be gathered? The phrase would not make sense if it referred to Isaac and Ishmael and their families.

Spirits also visited Jesus before he died. We can find a record of that encounter in Luke 9:28-36, which describes the Transfiguration of Jesus. Moses, who had been dead for 1482 years, and Elijah, who had been dead for 928 years,[152] came back to help prepare Jesus for his torturous death. Elijah and Moses came to talk with Jesus because they had assisted him during his life. Regardless of how a person dies, relatives and friends come to greet the newly arrived soul.

No matter how well prepared you are for a loved one's passing it always comes as a shock, even if it is after a prolonged illness. Fortunately my father enjoyed his life until the last month when the pain starting getting the better of him. It seemed like a long vigil. One evening the nurses came looking for me. My father's time had come. As he crossed into the Spirit World, I held one of his hands and my mother held the other. He seemed to slowly drift away.

My father's funeral was a simple graveside service. Afterward, my mother and I went back to my apartment to sit *Shiva*, a long list of prescribed mourning rituals that last for seven days after a Jewish funeral. During that time we had to remain in our own house, sitting on low boxes. We draped and covered all the mirrors with cloth. This was a difficult period for me as I didn't accept these rituals. My mother needed to go through them, so for her sake, I did my best to follow the traditions.

Carl came to visit my mother and me as we sat *Shiva* for my father. He told us that Dad had crossed over without any trouble, and was now adjusting to his new environment. These were words of comfort for us.

I desperately wanted to visit my grandmother. Her stroke had left her completely incapacitated. Before my father died, my uncle and mother had decided to have her brought to her home, with 24-hour nursing care. Obviously my mother couldn't be with her mother and husband at the same time, so my uncle took care of overseeing the care of my grandmother. I had not seen her since she had come home. After the *Shiva* was over, we both went to my grandmother's house to visit. I don't know if she knew we were there or not. My mother was having a very difficult time with

---

[151] Genesis 25:8 [KJ21].

[152] Sprague, E. W. Rev. *All the Spiritualism of the Christian Bible and the Scripture Directly Opposing it.* Detroit, MI: (self-published), 1922. p. 249.

seeing her mother completely paralyzed. "Why?" she kept asking. "Why did this have to happen to my mother?"

It came time for us to leave. It was the last time I saw my grandmother alive. I drove my mother back to her house, and decided to stay for a few days. One night about 1:30 A.M. the phone rang. I knew what it had to be. My uncle was on the phone, informing us that my grandmother had just passed away. Her funeral was to be the next morning. In the Jewish religion, funerals take place as quickly as possible, then are followed by the week-long *Shiva*.

During the *Shiva*, many of my grandmother's friends came to express their condolences to us. My mother kept asking each of them, "Why did my mother have such a devastating stroke? What could she have done to deserve this? She kept a kosher home, and followed all the Jewish laws and traditions? Why did this happen to her?"

All of these people, attended my grandmother's orthodox synagogue, and had an identical response. "You are not supposed to question God."

Perhaps this kind of response can comfort some people, but it did not work for me. I did not have an exact answer, but I knew my grandmother's stoke happened for a reason. Perhaps she needed the experience of helplessness, to grow in understanding from it.

I felt fortunate for all the knowledge I had gained during the previous eight years. It protected me, like a knight's armor, from total devastation at such a tragic time. Loosing loved ones is always painful no matter what philosophy you hold. I was comforted in knowing that my father and grandmother were living, pain-free, in the Spirit World. Deep in my heart, I knew I would again communicate with them through a medium. It was these thoughts that got me through those painful nineteen days in July 1983.

I had promised myself that I would continue to attend High Holiday services for as long as my grandmother lived even though I found the experience hollow and detested my grandmother's synagogue. My father and grandmother died in July. As September approached, we all faced the first Jewish High Holidays without them. The double loss took a heavy toll on my mother. She had enough emotional turmoil to deal with without my adding to it by not attending services. I decided I would attend the synagogue for one more year. Perhaps, I could find a different synagogue with services more to my liking. Perhaps I could relive those awe-inspiring experiences I had had when I was a child.

At the time, I was living in Fort Lee, New Jersey. I found a small orthodox synagogue a mile from my house. I knew my mother would not want to ride in a car on the holidays, which was the orthodox custom. Because it was an orthodox service, my mother and I could not sit together. So I sat with the men, and my mother sat with the women in a curtained area. Little did I know that I would find these services exceedingly more offensive than the ones I had experienced at my grandmother's synagogue.

Without going into all the details, this synagogue was much more modern and the sermons were in English. Much to my surprise, three out of the four sermons that the rabbi gave during these holiday services, had psychic themes. I wasn't sure if the rabbi knew that he was discussing psychic topics. Sadly, during two of those three sermons, the rabbi delivered psychically incorrect information. The event that totally infuriated me, to the point of almost loosing self-control, occurred at the *Yiskor* service. Four times a year, the *Yiskor* service is held in the synagogue. These are special prayers that a person says for a dead relative. It is customary to say these prayers after your relative has been dead for over a year. You say *Yiskor* prayers for parents, spouses, brothers, and sisters. If you don't have any relatives who are deceased, you leave the synagogue while these prayers are being said. This rabbi asked that if you had someone who had died less then a year ago, you remain to say these prayers. Following his instructions, I stayed for this service.

Before the *Yiskor* service began, the rabbi told a story. It had to do with a woman interred in a concentration camp during World War II. This woman began feeling ill. She had an inner feeling that if she could get to the top of the hill in the camp, she would survive. It took all her strength to pull herself to the top of this hill, because she was so weak. But she managed to reach her goal. Once on the top of the hill, she collapsed and went unconscious. She was found there the next day by the liberators of the camp. She later discovered that the hill she had climbed was a mass grave and the bones of her father were in this grave. It was quite a moving story.

The rabbi next explained the meaning of the *Yiskor* prayers. He went on to say, "The only way a Jewish person can communicate with a dead relative is through the *Yiskor* service."

I couldn't believe my ears! What utter nonsense! Many of my dead relatives—my grandmother's sisters who had died in the holocaust in Europe, and here in America during the late 1940's—had spoken to me through Carl's mediumship. I certainly did not say *Yiskor* prayers before I had a reading in Carl's office. I was seething! However, the worst was yet to come.

The rabbi continued, "The way to have a stronger communication with your deceased relatives is to give a donation to the synagogue." The rabbi then enumerated the types of donations that were available in the forms of plaques and such, and their prices. He said, "I will start the *Yiskor* service in five minutes. You have five minutes to pledge your contribution to make your communication stronger with your dead relatives." The rabbi then sat down, and the president of the synagogue got up and began to take the pledges.

I was so infuriated, I was shaking like a leaf. I was ready to explode, but I knew that if I did, I would start screaming at the top of my lungs about this outrage. What lies this rabbi was telling people. He was literally selling people a "bill of goods." This is Judaism's most holy day, one should not be spending money, one was supposed to be atoning for one's sins.

I kept thinking of my mother sitting behind the curtained area. How would she react if she heard my screaming voice calling the rabbi an ignorant liar? This religion, like so many others, is a big business. Their interest is in gathering money, not worshipping or serving God. This was the most hypocritical, unethical experience I had had in a synagogue. If I wanted to watch people giving pledges, I would watch the Jerry Lewis muscular dystrophy telethon during labor day weekend!

Using every bit of restraint I could muster, I managed to keep my mouth shut—but only for my mother's sake. I could not, however, keep it shut when I saw my mother during the afternoon recess of the services. I bitterly complained to her that this was 10,000 times worse than my grandmother's synagogue.

That was the last time I attended a High Holiday service. I could not make myself a witness to such hypocrisy again. To this day, my absence from the synagogue greatly disturbs my mother. She feels that I overreact in these situations. "The synagogue has to raise money," she says. That may be true, but why hold these auctions on your most holy of days when it is expressly forbidden to use money. Why not hold flea markets, raffles, and other fund raising activities during the year when it is not a holiday?

I was distressed by the deception about communicating with one's relatives on the other side. Communication between this world and the next depends on mediumistic abilities, not how much one empties one's purse or wallet. And if one lacks the psychic abilities to communicate with people on the other side, then communication can easily be accomplished in the presence of a genuine medium, just as Saul was able to communicate with the deceased seer, Samuel, through the medium of Endor.[153]

---

[153] 1 Samuel 28:7-14.

# TWELVE

## The Significance of the Cabinet

As my studies progressed, I became more and more fascinated by the world of psychic phenomena. I considered myself very fortunate to be in Carl's classes. He made his lectures so interesting, and the information that came through him when he was in a deep trance state was "out of this world."

One evening, our lecture was about materialization. This is quite rare today. Unfortunately, I have not yet had the privilege of attending a materialization séance where Spirit withdraws ectoplasm from a medium's body and mold it as an artist would mold clay. If there is sufficient ectoplasm, Spirit may form the whole body of a person, then inhabit that ectoplasmic body, and speak to the people present. If there is not enough ectoplasm Spirit forms a body part, like a hand or head.

To demonstrate materialization the medium needs a cabinet, which is an enclosed space, such as a small closet that has a curtain hanging in front of it. The cabinet creates a small area of total darkness. When the medium sits in the cabinet, he or she can condense enough of the psychic energy needed to have the ectoplasm withdrawn from his or her body.

An analogy to this would be taking a pot of water, placing it on the stove and turning on the burner. In seven or eight minutes the water would begin to boil and steam would begin rising from the pot. If we let it boil for an hour, all the water will evaporate, because it has changed into steam. The result is that there is no water left in the pot. Let's take a plate that was refrigerated, and hold it over the pot of boiling water. The steam collects on the cold plate, the water vapor begins to cool, and water droplets form on the plate. Eventually, the water droplets would fall back into the pot. Could we keep this up indefinitely? No. Too much of the steam escapes, and eventually all the water would boil out anyway.

Ectoplasm is like the water. The cabinet, like the plate, traps the energy of the ectoplasm and allows it to build up. Spiritual energy from the ethereal world mixes with the energy of the medium to form ectoplasm. The ectoplasm can then be molded by Spirit to look like the body of someone who once lived on earth.

Over the years, many scientists have studied mediumship. These scientists conclude that materialization is the most difficult type of mediumship, because it is the most taxing, and tiring for the medium. As the séance is ending, and the materialized form begins to unravel, the ectoplasm returns into the cells of the medium's body. However, not all the ectoplasm returns, since much of it, rich in psychic energy, was used during the séance. When a materialization séance is over, the medium is completely exhausted and often needs to rest so that his or her body can regenerate.

First let's examine some Bible verses that involve a materialization and required a cabinet. Then we'll examine a materialization séance that happened during the 20th century. The laws of psychic science are unchangeable. What was true in Biblical times is true today.

God told Moses to build the tabernacle,[154] a tent where the Hebrews could assemble, and instructed him to build a cabinet within it.

> **And you shall hang the veil from the clasps. Then you shall bring the ark of the Testimony in there, behind the veil. The veil shall be a divider for you between the holy place and the Most Holy.[155]**

The same instructions in **NAB** use different words, and will help us to prove these were instructions for creating a medium's cabinet.

> **Hang the veil from clasps. The ark of the commandments you shall bring inside, behind this veil which divides the holy place from the holy of holies.[156]**

Centuries later, King Solomon built his temple in Jerusalem. In 1 Kings 6:16 in **THOM**, we read that Solomon built *the holy of holies,* within his temple. [See chart] The Hebrew word for *holy of holies* is דְּבִיר (*debir*), which is translated as *oracle.* Analyzing different Bibles, we find the older versions describe *the holy of holies,* keeping its psychic nature intact. **EWYC**, first published in 1384, precisely translates דְּבִיר (*debir*) as *heavenly answering place.* The דְּבִיר (*debir*), or *holy of holies* was the cabinet where the medium would sit to go into deep trance.

---

154 Exodus Chapter 26.

155 Exodus 26:33 [NKJV].

156 Exodus 26:33 [NAB].

# 1 KINGS CHAPTER 6 VERSE 16

| KJV | 1611 | And he built twenty cubits on the sides of the house, both the floor, and the walls with boards of Cedar: he even built them for it within, even for *the Oracle*, even for the most holy place. |
|-----|------|---|
| EWYC | 1384 | And he made an innermore house of the *heavenly answering place*, into the holy of halewis. |
| LWYC | 1395 | And he made the inner house of *God's answering place*, in to the holy of holy things. |
| COV | 1535 | And there on the inside builded he the *quere* for the most holy. |
| TAV | 1539 | And dressed it within to be the *choir* and place most holy. |
| GRT | 1540 | And dressed it within the *secret place* of the temple, even in the most holy. |
| DOU | 1609 | And he made the *inner house of the oracle to be Sanctum Sanctorum* |
| THOM | 1808 | And made of that *the dabir—the Holy of Holies*. |
| WELL | 1861 | And he built it within, for *a sanctuary*, even for the most holy place. |
| ROTH | 1897 | And he built it within for *a shrine*, even for the holy of holies. |
| FENT | 1922 | He built it for himself, as *a Lecture Hall* to discuss Philosophy with Philosophers. |
| MOFF | 1922 | At the far end of the temple he built of a space of thirty feet as an inner shrine, *the most sacred interior.* |
| SMGO | 1939 | And he built for himself within, *an inner room*, for the most sacred place. |
| OGD | 1950 | And at the back of the house a further space of twenty cubits was shut in with boards of cedar-wood, for *the inmost room.* |
| RSV | 1952 | And he built this within as *an inner sanctuary,* as the most holy place. |
| CONF | 1965 | And made the *inner house of the oracle to* be the holy of holies. |
| WBC | 1985 | And he constructed the interior as *an adytum* (a holy of holies). |
| ARATJ | 1987 | And he built for it a house inside, for a *house of atonements, for a holy of holies.* |
| NIrV | 1996 | That formed *a room* inside the temple. It was the Most Holy Room. |
| STONE | 1996 | And he prepared this area inside *the Partition* to be the Holy of Holies. |
| CJB | 1998 | And reserved this part of the house to be a *sanctuary, the Especially Holy Place.* |

## 21 Differing Translations

As we analyze the chart for 1 Kings 6:6, notice how all mention of *heavenly answering place* or *oracle* fades out. The truth about the oracle fades from this verse. Notice the 1996 NIrV uses the word *room*. Surprisingly, the **THOM, LEES, HARK, JER,** and **NJER** do not attempt to translate the word דְּבִיר (*debir*) at all. These versions leave the word in the original Hebrew. I find this peculiar. These writers translated many thousands of words from Hebrew into English to create their versions of the Bible. Why skip the word דְּבִיר (*debir*) LEES and HARK are *JEWISH* editions of the Bible. Surely these writers could translate Hebrew. Was the meaning that difficult to find? That is hardly the case. I'm not a professional Bible translator, nor do I speak Hebrew, but I can read it. Even I found the meaning of

דְּבִיר (*debir*) in *The Everyman's Hebrew and Chaldee Concordance*: דְּבִיר (*debir*) means "an oracle (n), a place where Spirit will prophesy the future."[157]

Perhaps the most interesting translation is **WBC**: *And he constructed the interior as an adytum (a holy of holies)*. The Oracle of Delphi sat in the *Adytum* (the name of her cabinet), when she prophesied. Obviously the translator of **WBC** had some knowledge of psychic science to correctly make this comparison.

**FENT** provides us with a very unique translation of this verse:

> **He built it for himself, as a Lecture Hall to discuss Philosophy with Philosophers.**

This translation is correct. However, it is misleading to the Bible reader ignorant of the Gifts of the Spirit. This uneducated reader would interpret *the Lecture Hall* to be similar to one that he or she might have experienced in college. Most lecture halls would hold anywhere from 100-700 people. The דְּבִיר (*debir*) cabinet would be extremely small, just big enough for one person to sit in. The medium would go into deep trance and probably lecture the people sitting on the other side of the curtain (or veil). I have had the immense pleasure of attending hundreds of deep trance séances. Often participants asked philosophical questions, which Spirit answered. Awan has provided most of the information for this book, while Carl was in deep trance. The same Spirits, living in a timeless realm, can discuss historical and philosophical subjects easily. Often if the Spirit speaking through the medium doesn't have an answer to a particular question before the deep trance ends, another Spirit will research the answer. That second Spirit gives the answer to the first Spirit, who then relays the answer to us. It is a fascinating process.

Here is another Bible story that discusses the cabinet. King Jehoshaphat of Judah and King Ahab of Israel were debating whether to wage war against Ramoth Gilead.

> **But Jehoshaphat also said to the king of Israel, "First seek counsel of the Lord."[158]**

Ahab summoned his 400 prophets and they all said to him:

> **"Go," they answered, "for God will give it into the king's hand." But Jehoshaphat asked, "Is there not a prophet of the Lord here whom we can inquire of?"[159]**

We need to stop and analyze what is happening here before we continue. Ahab called his prophets together to get an answer from God. However, Jehoshaphat was

---

[157] *The Englishman's Hebrew and Chaldee Concordance of the Old Testament. Vol. 2.* London: Walton and Maberrly, 1866. p. 318.

[158] 2 Chronicles 18:4 [NIV].

[159] 2 Chronicles 18:5-6 [NIV].

not satisfied, he wanted an answer from the Lord. What is happening here? How many Gods are there?

The answer is complex. Remember the words of Jesus, **"God is Spirit."**[160] Within each of us is a spark of divine energy that is our soul. When death comes to our physical body, our soul continues to live in the Spirit World, which is timeless. After we arrive in the Spirit World, we can study the laws of communication. After we master these laws we can choose to become a guardian angel, or a teacher for someone back on the physical plane. As long as the physical person has the gift of clairvoyance or clairaudience, he or she can receive the messages sent from the Spirit World. During Biblical times, when a gifted person communicated with a Spirit, the medium referred to the Spirit as the *Lord*. Mediums do not use the same terminology today.

Ahab worshipped many gods.

> **Ahab erected an altar to Baal in the temple of Baal which he built in Samaria. Ahab also made an Asherah pole and did more to provoke the Lord, the God of Israel, to anger than did all the kings of Israel before him.**[161]

Ahab had summoned 400 mediums to ask their opinions. Some of the prophets were mediums for Spirits other than Jehovah. Imagine that you have two friends, Fred and Anthony. Fred is an expert car mechanic, Anthony an electrician. If you had a problem with you car you would seek Fred's advice. If you had an electrical problem, you would call Anthony. You would seek the guidance of the person who is an expert on the topic of your problem. It works exactly the same way in the Spirit World. Because someone dies and crosses into the other realm doesn't mean they become a saint or a sage. The soul enters the Spirit World with the same belief system, values, personality, and knowledge it had in this world, but because of the timeless factor, it can see into our future.

Jehoshaphat was having difficulty deciding whether to go to war. He wished to consult a Spirit he had consulted before, one that he could rely on. That Spirit's medium was Micaiah. Ahab didn't like Micaiah.

> **Then King Ahab said to Jehoshaphat, "There is still one man here. We can ask the Lord through him. But I hate this man, because he never has a good message from the Lord about Me. He always has bad messages for me. That man's name is Micaiah."**[162]

Micaiah agreed to channel his Spirit. He promised that he wouldn't change anything he saw to please King Ahab.

---

[160] John 4:24 [NASB].

[161] 1 Kings 16:32-33 [NIV].

[162] 2 Chronicles 18:7 [ETR].

**Micaiah replied, "By the life of Yahweh, I will speak just what my God tells me!"[163]**

Micaiah proceeded to tell the two kings that they would loose the battle. Ahab complained that Micaiah never prophesied anything good for him. Now there was a predicament, as two different Spirits had two different opinions. How often has this happened to you, when you've asked two different friends for advice on a matter. This contradiction didn't sit well with Zedekiah, one of Ahab's prophets.

> **Then Zedekiah the son of Chenaanah came near and struck Micaiah on the cheek, and said, "Which way did the Spirit of the Lord go from me to speak to you?" And Micaiah said, "Behold, you shall see on that day when you go into an inner chamber to hide yourself."[164]**

Unless one understands psychic phenomena, this question, *"Which way did the Spirit of the Lord go from me to speak to you?"* is confusing. This is an example of one medium who is jealous of another. Zedekiah wanted to be "the star," making himself feel important by being the instrument to channel *the Lord*. Zedekiah claimed that he was channeling the same Spirit as Micaiah. This was not the case. Since the kings were neither clairaudient nor clairvoyant, they couldn't prove nor disprove Zedekiah's claim. A Spirit can work with more than one medium, but not at the same time. Zedekiah was furious with Micaiah. His question, "Which way did the Spirit of the Lord go," implies that Zedekiah knew that Micaiah was clairvoyant and a deep trance medium.

Micaiah's answer is shrouded by poor translations. The phrase "hide yourself" is confusing, and even puzzled me for sometime. Why *hide* in a cabinet? The word "seclude" would have been a better choice. Only one of the hundred and seven Old Testaments comes close to a psychically correct interpretation of this verse.

> **And Micaiah said, Behold, thyself seeing on the same day when thou shalt come into an inner chamber to be *concealed*.[165]**

When a medium enters a cabinet, he does so alone. He sits in the dark with the curtain closed. Someone who is not familiar with this phenomenon might think that the medium is hiding himself. "Hide" and "seclude" have different nuances. By sitting in the darkness, the medium allows Spirit to withdraw the required ectoplasm, which enables materialization to take place. If people were to watch this process, it might be very frightening. That fear would prevent the phenomenon from continuing. This is why the medium must be alone in the dark cabinet.

---

[163] 2 Chronicles 18:13 [ANCR].

[164] 2 Chronicles 18:23-4 [RSV].

[165] 2 Chronicles 18:24 [BELL].

Even Jesus, the most powerful biblical medium, was unable to perform miracles when he was in the presence of people thinking negative thoughts.

**And they were offended in him. But Jesus said unto them, A Prophet is not without honor, save in his own country, and in his own house. And he did not many mighty works there, because of their unbelief.[166]**

Millions of Christians view Jesus as God, and believe Jesus could perform miracles because he **was** God. If Jesus were God, he would have had tremendous powers and could performe his miracles (psychic phenomena) no matter what people thought. Since Jesus was susceptible to people's negative thought, it demonstrates that Jesus was a human medium. Even Jesus could not change the laws of psychic science. It is interesting to study Bible translators' terminology describing the Jesus' psychic feats.

## MATTHEW CHAPTER 13 VERSE 58

| KJV | 1611 | And he did not many *mighty works* there, because of their unbelief. |
|-----|------|--------|
| EWYC | 1384 | And he did not there many *vertues*, for the unbelief of them. |
| TYND | 1534 | And he did not many *miracles* there, for their unbelief's sake. |
| GEN | 1560 | And he did not many *great works* there, for their unbelief's sake. |
| BISH | 1568 | And he did not many *mighty works* there, because of their unbelief. |
| PUR | 1764 | And he did not do many *powerful Things* there, by reason of their Unbelief. |
| MURD | 1851 | And he did not perform there many *works of power*, because of their unbelief. |
| JUSMI | 1876 | And he did not many *powers* there, because of their unbelief. |
| WEY | 1903 | And He performed but few *mighty deeds* there because of their want of faith. |
| FENT | 1922 | And He did not *display much power* there, because of their unbelief. |
| SMGO | 1939 | And he did not do many *wonders* there, because of their want of faith. |
| WILL | 1950 | And so He did not do many *wonder-works* there, because of their lack of faith. |
| RSV | 1952 | And he did not do many *deeds of power* there, because of their unbelief. |
| WMF | 1975 | Because of their lack of belief, Jesus did very few **good works** there, and he left soon. |
| ANCR | 1987 | And because of their unbelief he was unable to perform many *acts of power* there. |

## 14 Differing Translations

The phrases *works of power, powers, deeds of power, acts of power* are extremely interesting because it refers to the psychic energy required to perform the Gifts of the Spirit.

[166] Matthew 13:57-58 [KJV].

Another Bible story involving a cabinet concerned Elisha.

> **And it came to pass on the morrow, Elisha went and came to Shiloh, where was a wealthy woman; and she constrained him to eat food. So that whenever he passed by, he turned in there to eat food.**[167]

## 2 KINGS CHAPTER 4 VERSE 9

| KJV | 1611 | And she said unto her husband, Behold now, I perceive that this is **an holy man of God,** which passeth by us continually. |
|------|------|-----------------------------------------------------------------------------------------------------------|
| KNOX | 1944 | Til at last she said to her husband, I find him to be **a servant of God**, and a holy one, this man that passes our way so often. |
| LIV | 1971 | She said to her husband, "I'm sure this man who stops in from time to time is a **holy prophet.**" |
| ARATJ | 1987 | And she said to her husband: "Behold now I know that the **prophet of the Lord is holy.** He turns aside unto us always." |

## 4 Differing Translations

These four verses demonstrate that *a holy man of God*, a *servant of God*, and a *holy prophet* all have the same meaning. The woman knew that Elisha, a man possessing the Gifts of the Spirit was coming through town periodically. She wanted him to stay in her home as a guest. Notice what she tells her husband.

> **Let us make *a small, enclosed upper chamber* and place a bed, a table, a chair, and a lampstand there for him, so that he can stop there whenever he comes to us.**[168]

This story demonstrates how Hebrews in Biblical times understood psychic phenomena. The woman knew that this medium needed a cabinet to be the instrument between this world and the Spirit World. She wanted to provide Elisha with a comfortable place to stay. By building him a cabinet to work in, she knew that Elisha would stop by her house often.

The next description of the use of a cabinet the Bible occurs when Moses leads the Hebrews through the desert.

> **As for Moses, he proceeded to take his tent away and he pitched it outside the camp, far away from the camp; and he called it a tent of meeting. And it occurred that everyone inquiring of Jehovah would go out to the tent of meeting which was outside the**

---

[167] 2 Kings 4:8 [LAMSA].

[168] 2 Kings 4:10 [TANK].

camp.[169]

The second part of the verse clearly describes the purpose of the meeting tent. It was where people could go to ask questions of Spirit. Study the chart of this verse. Notice the different phrases used to explain what the tent was for. Notice that **COV**, the oldest version, is the clearest of the variations.

## EXODUS CHAPTER 33 VERSE 7B

| KJV | 1611 | And it came to pass, that every one which *sought the Lord*, went out unto the Tabernacle of the Congregation, which was without the camp. |
| COV | 1535 | And who so ever would *ask any question at the Lord* went out unto the Tabernacle of Witness. |
| GRT | 1540 | And so it came to pass, that everyone which would *pray unto the Lord*, went out unto the tabernacle of witness. |
| GEN | 1560 | And when any did *seek to the Lord*, he went out unto the Tabernacle of Congregation, which was without the hoste. |
| DOU | 1609 | And all the people that *had any question* went forth to the Tabernacle of the Covenant, without the camp. |
| RAY | 1799 | And every one that *sought to call on the Eternal* went out to it. |
| WELL | 1859 | And all who would *consult Jehovah* went out to the tent of meeting, which was without the camp. |
| JUSMI | 1876 | And it was every one *seeking Jehovah* went forth to the tent of appointment, which is from without the camp. |
| FENT | 1922 | So that all who wished to *inquire of the Ever-Living* were obliged to come to him in his Hall of Assembly that was outside the camp. |
| LAMSA | 1933 | And it came to pass that every one who sought to *inquire of the Lord* went out to the tabernacle of the congregation, which was outside the camp. |
| KNOX | 1944 | To this, all who *had disputes to settle* must betake themselves away from the camp. |
| OGD | 1950 | And everyone *desiring to make his prayer to the Lord* went to the Tent of Meeting outside the tent-circle. |
| ARATO | 1987 | Now, anyone *seeking instruction* from before the Lord would go out to the Tent of the Place of Instruction which is outside the camp. |

## 13 Differing Translations

It is interesting that in 1535 **COV** uses the phrase *had any question* while **OGD** uses the phrase *desiring to make his prayer to the Lord*. Clearly asking a question and praying are two totally different actions. Also, you can see how translators changed the words *cabinet* or *chamber* into *tabernacle* or *assembly hall*—one of the most distressing achievements of the Church in its cover-up of Biblical mediumship. Awan explained to me that the Roman Catholic Church replaced the prophets and cabinets with priests and confessional booths!

---

169 Exodus 33:7 [NWT].

As we continue, we discover Moses attended a materialization séance in the meeting tent.

> **As Moses went into the tent, the pillar of cloud would come down and stay at the entrance, while the Lord spoke with Moses.**[170]

The *pillar of cloud* the Bible speaks of is actually ectoplasm. *The Lord* materialized in front of the cabinet.

> **And all the people saw the pillar of cloud at the tent door, and all the people rose up and worshipped, every man at his tent door.**[171]

This verse is significant. It shows that all the people saw the ectoplasm. It shows that ancient Hebrews relied on psychic phenomena as a part of their lives. They didn't understand the science behind the phenomena, but they knew that ectoplasm (a pillar of cloud) always appeared in front of the cabinet before God spoke to them. This will be important when we examine the conflict between priests and mediums.

> **Yahweh would talk to Moses *face to face, as a man talks to his friend*, and afterwards he would come back to the camp, but the young man who was his servant, Joshua son of Nun, never left the inside of the Tent.**[172]

Now we come to the actual proof that materialization was happening in the Tabernacle. Joshua son of Nun was the medium. He sat in the dark cabinet and went into deep trance. Spirit extracted ectoplasm from Joshua's body. This pillar of cloud formed from the ground upward. Spirit then molded it into the likeness of Yahweh. Yahweh's Spirit entered the ectoplasmic body, and conversed with Moses *face to face, as a man talks to his friend*. When they finished their conversation, the materialized body would begin to disintegrate. The ectoplasm would lose the form of Yahweh's body, and would retract into Joshua's body, returning into Joshua's cells. By the end of this process Joshua was exhausted, depleted of all his energy, and so would remain in the tent for a long time. He probably slept the rest of the night inside the tabernacle. This is why the Bible states: *Joshua son of Nun, never left the inside of the Tent.*

A few verses further we find an event, which appears to contradict Moses' face to face dialogue with God, but if we have knowledge of psychic science, there is no contradiction.

> **Then Moses said [to God], "I pray Thee, show me Thy glory!" And He [God] said, "I Myself will make all My goodness pass before**

---

[170] Exodus 33:8 [NIV].

[171] Exodus 33:10 [AMP].

[172] Exodus 33:11 [NJER].

you, and will proclaim the name of the Lord before you; and I will be gracious to whom I will be gracious and will show compassion on whom I will show compassion." But He said, "You cannot see My face for no man can see Me and live!"[173]

This verse might raise questions in the mind of someone who is ignorant of the Gifts of the Spirit. Verse 11 of this chapter describes Moses talking to God, *face to face, as a man speaks to his friend.* How it is possible to talk to someone face to face, and yet not see that face? Verse 20 says that if Moses looks at the face of God, he will die.

To one educated in the Gifts of the Spirit, there is no contradiction. During the materialization, Moses looked at the materialized ectoplasmic face of Jehovah. When Moses asked to see God's glory, he was not asking to see God in a materialized ectoplasmic body, he wanted to see God's etheric body, or God's Spirit body. When God said, *You cannot see My face for no man can see Me and live!* God was telling Moses he could see God's spiritual body when he died. The only body Spirit has is the Spirit body we call the soul. The soul produces a light that we call the aura. God's aura would be so bright, it would have blinded and killed Moses.

The most famous materialization séance that ever took place is not in the Old Testament, but in the New Testament. Most Bibles label this incident the "Mount of Transfiguration." Let's examine this séance.

> **About eight days after saying this he took Peter, John, and James, and went up onto a mountain to pray. While he was praying, his face changed in appearance and his clothes became dazzling white. Suddenly two men were talking with him—Moses and Elijah. They appeared in glory and spoke of his passage, which he was about to fulfill in Jerusalem. Peter and those with him had fallen into a deep sleep; but awakening, they saw his glory and likewise saw the two men who were standing with him. When these were leaving, Peter said to Jesus: "Master, how good it is for us to be here. Let us set up three booths, one for you, one for Moses, and one for Elijah." (He did not really know what he was saying).[174]**

Jesus had taken his three most advanced students—Peter, John, and James—to witness this great psychic event. While they were praying on the mountaintop, Jesus went into a deep state of meditation. The Bible said that Jesus' *face changed in appearance and his clothes became a dazzling white.* This happens when a person spends time in the presence of Spirit. His face becomes filled with radiance. This also happened to Moses when he returned from Mount Sinai:

---

[173] Exodus 33:18-20 [NASB].

[174] Luke 9:28-36 [NAB].

> **At length Moses came down from Mount Sinai with the two stone tablets of the Testimony in his hands, and when he came down, he did not know that the skin of his face shone because he had been talking with the Lord.[175]**

Notice that Moses had had the same experience as Jesus. And now, 1482 years[176] since his death, the Spirit of Moses was returning to advise Jesus. Moses was one of Jesus' Spirit teachers.

Meanwhile the three disciples went into a deep state of meditation, which the Bible calls sleep. The gift of materialization was beginning. Spirit drew ectoplasm from the disciples' bodies. This gave Jesus, Moses, and Elijah enough energy to increase the density of their spiritual bodies. Then Moses and Elijah stepped into the pillar of cloud. It would be like slipping on a wet suit, this ectoplasm would be like an additional special layer of skin, which clung to their spiritual bodies, but would be visible to the disciples. The Bible described their materialized bodies as *a glowing dazzling white.*

Moses and Elijah gave Jesus instructions on how to conclude his ministry in Jerusalem. They assured Jesus that the agony he would experience is what Spirit wanted. Spirit wanted Jesus to show the world there is life after death—Jesus would resurrect his dead physical body.

Peter, John, and James were familiar with materialization. Peter said, "Let us set up three booths, one for you, one for Moses, and one for Elijah." He knew Moses and Elijah would need a cabinet.

You may ask, "How did Moses and Elijah materialize in the first place without a cabinet?" The answer may lie with the people who gathered for this event. Moses was the most powerful medium in the Old Testament. Excepting Jesus, Moses performed more of the Gifts of the Spirit than any other Biblical figure. Jesus himself was a phenomenal medium. As mentioned earlier, Jesus was the only person in all of history who has performed all the Gifts of the Spirit. Elijah certainly performed many Gifts of the Spirit during his lifetime. Elijah, like Jesus, raised the dead,[177] and multiplied food.[178] In all likelihood Elijah assisted Jesus from the Spirit World in performing these phenomena. Remember, Elijah taught his own student, Elisha, to perform these same gifts.[179] These three extremely powerful mediums could muster enough psychic energy to materialize without a cabinet, even in the daylight.

Now let us examine all the different names the Bible translators have used for the cabinet in this verse.

---

[175] Exodus 34:29 [REB].

[176] Sprague, E. W. Rev. *All the Spiritualism of the Christian Bible and the Scripture Directly Opposing it.* Detroit, MI: (self-published), 1992. p. 249.

[177] 1 Kings 17: 17-24.

[178] 1 Kings 17: 10-16.

[179] (Raising the dead) 2 Kings 4: 18-37, (multiplying food) 2 Kings 4: 42-44.

# LUKE CHAPTER 9 VERSE 33

| KJV | 1611 | And it came to pass, as they departed from him, Peter said unto Jesus, Master, it is good for us to be here; and let us make *three tabernacles*, one for thee, and one for Moses, and one for Elias: not knowing what he said. |
|-----|------|---|
| MACE | 1729 | Who were just departing from him, when Peter said to Jesus, master, it is best for us to stay here: let us build *three apartments*, one for you, one for Moses, and one for Elias: not knowing well what he said. |
| WYNNE | 1764 | And it came to pass as they were departing from him, Peter said to Jesus, Master, it is good for us to continue here! and let us set up *three tents,* one for Thee, and one for Moses, and one for Elijah; not knowing what he said. |
| THOM | 1808 | And as they were withdrawing from him, Peter said to Jesus, Master, it is well that we are here. Let us make *three booths*, one for thee, and one for Moses, and one for Elias, not knowing what he said. |
| FENT | 1922 | And as they were parting from Him, Peter said to Jesus, "Teacher, how delightful it is for us to be here! Let us make *three dwellings*; one for You, one for Moses, and one for Elijah," hardly knowing what he said. |
| LAMSA | 1933 | And when they began to leave him, Simon said to Jesus, Teacher, it is better for us to remain here; and let us make *three shelters*, one for you, one for Moses, and one for Elijah; but he did not know what he was saying. |
| SMGO | 1939 | Just as they were parting from him, Peter said to Jesus, "Master, how good it is that we are here! Let us put up *three huts*, one for you and one for Moses and one for Elijah!" For he did not know what he was saying. |
| KNOX | 1944 | And, just as these were parting from him, Peter said to Jesus, Master, it is well that we should be here; let us make *three arbors* in this place, one for thee, and one for Moses, and one for Elias. But he spoke at random. |
| NOR | 1962 | As they left Jesus, Peter said to Him, "How good it is for us to be here! Let us make *three shrines*, on for You, one for Moses, and one for Elijah." He did not realize what he was saying. |
| ABBR | 1971 | Peter said, "Master, it is good for us to be here. Shall we build *three churches*—one for you, one for Moses, and one for Elijah?" |
| WMF | 1975 | They also saw them disappear. "It is a great treat," said Peter, "for us to be here. Why don't we at least establish *three historical markers*, one for you, one for Moses, and one for Elijah." |
| NLFB | 1983 | As the two men went from Jesus, Peter said to Him, "Teacher, it is good for us to be here. Let us build *three altars*. One will be for You. One will be for Moses. One will be for Elijah." He did not know what he was saying. |
| ORIG | 1985 | Then as they were vanishing Peter said to Jesus, 'Chief, how fortunate we are to be here! Now let us put up *three bowers*, one for you, one for Moses, and one for Elijah,' not realizing what he was saying. |
| GNC | 1989 | Furthermore, as the time came for them to be parting company with him, Peter said to Jesus, "Master, how good is it to be here; let us build *three places of shelter,* one for Moses, one for Elijah, and one for you." (He did not know what he was saying.) |
| MESS | 1993 | When Moses and Elijah had left, Peter said to Jesus, "Master, this is a great moment! Let's build *three memorials*: one for you, one for Moses, and one for Elijah." He blurted this out without thinking. |

## 15 Differing Translations

This verse provides another excellent example of how the Bible can be mistranslated when the translator is ignorant of the Gifts of the Spirit, or is controlled by the religious hierarchy. If Mr. Peterson, (the sole translator of **MESS**), understood materialization, he would realize that a cabinet was needed for the phenomenon to take place. A *memorial*, which is another term for a tombstone, would serve *no* purpose at a materialization séance. Despite the religious overtone, **NLFB**'s *altars* and **ABBR**'s *churches* also are not needed for a Spirit to materialize. Furthermore, how could Peter say, "*Shall we build three churches?*" when churches were *not* yet created? Did the translator of **ABBR** forget that Jesus was Jewish? Jesus did *not* establish a new church—it was Peter and Paul who started Christianity after Jesus was crucified. **WMF**'s three *historical markers* adds more fuel to the fire which proves Awan's contention that the Bible has been changed.

The Bible has been translated over 160 times. Each translator twists the meanings according to his or her preconceived beliefs. Some paraphrased Bibles such as **WMF** have no concern for accuracy.[180] So which Bible speaks the real truth? How could the **KJV** be translated more accurately than **NASB**, **NIV**, or **NAB**, or any of the other 160 versions? None of the translators had any knowledge of psychic science. This ignorance caused these translators to misconstrue the psychic events the Bible records. All these errors cause the average reader to have a difficult time understanding the Bible.

Why did Moses and Elijah appear to Jesus on the Mount of Transfiguration? The answer is simple—Moses and Elijah were Jesus' teachers. They were constantly with him, guiding him through his entire ministry. Jesus said:

> **I am not alone: I have at my side the One who sent me [the Father].**[181]

Awan told me that Bible translators have changed this verse, that Jesus actually said:

> **I am not alone: *my Father* is beside me, within me and around me.**

In this verse, Jesus used the term *my Father*, when he was referring to his soul, the creative force within him. It is also the description of the aura, the light that has its origin in the soul, and shines through and around the flesh body. We all have the same creative force or soul, no matter who we are or what we do.

The séance on the Mount of Transfiguration reveals that the souls of Moses and Elijah were still alive, teaching from the other side. These two great Jewish leaders had died long before Jesus came to earth. Yet the souls of these great entities were in constant communication with Jesus. Because Jesus was himself clairvoyant and clairaudient, he didn't need a medium to converse with Moses and Elijah.

---

[180] Edington, Andrew. *The Word Made Fresh: Genesis-Kings.Vol. 1.* Atlanta, GA: John Knox Press, 1975. Foreward.

[181] John 8:16 [NAB].

As we continue reading about the events on the Mount of Transfiguration, we discover that a second psychic event happened:

> **But even as he was saying this, a bright cloud formed above them; and terror gripped them as it covered them. And a voice from the cloud said, This is my Son, my Chosen One; listen to him." "Then as the voice died away, Jesus was there alone with his disciples. They didn't tell anyone what they had seen until long afterwards.[182]**

The gift of *direct voice* occurred when the voice from the cloud said that Jesus was Spirit's chosen medium.

The use of the cabinet is essential for some forms of mediumship. We have seen that the Biblical Hebrews were familiar with mediumship, and understood the need for a cabinet for certain types of phenomena to happen.

When one develops a greater understanding of psychic phenomena, one's understanding of the Bible is enhanced. Unfortunately not all religions want the general public to understand psychic phenomena. That explains the following quotation in *The Harper Collins Encyclopedia of Catholicism:*

> **Numerous interpretations of the episode [Mount of Transfiguration] have been proposed.... Whatever its origin, the episode serves as a literary device to place Jesus on the same level as the Law and the Prophets.[183]**

This quotation clearly demonstrates how frightened the Catholic Church is of mediumship. By labeling the greatest séance in the Bible a literary device, it allows the Church to disguise the truth. This powerful séance proves several key points about psychic experience. It clearly demonstrates that life continues after death. It shows that the people living in the Spirit World can follow our lives and give us guidance. When conditions are correct, communication between the two realms is possible. The Catholic Church has attempted to turn these truths into a *literary device*, implying that the writers were not describing actual events but using allegory to show that Jesus was on the same level as the other prophets.

Modern day mediums still perform the same psychic phenomena as Biblical mediums. Ethel Post-Parrish was a medium who lived in the twentieth century. In 1927 she opened a church and established a psychic camp in Ephrata, Pennsylvania. She named the camp Silver Belle, after her Native American control. Ethel Post-Parrish cooperated with many doctors and scientists to prove to the world of science that psychic science is a genuine science. The following is a description of one experiment as told by Peggy Barnes in her book, *Lo, I Am with You Always.*

---

[182] Luke 9:34-6 [LIV].

[183] "Transfiguration." *The HarperCollins Encyclopedia of Catholicism:* San Francisco: HarperCollins Publishers Inc., 1995. p. 1264.

I had the privilege of being present at a test seance given by Ethel Post-Parrish in 1928. Two doctors—one from Birmingham, Alabama and the other from New York City, had asked Mrs. Parrish to sit for them that they might try an experiment. As they do not wish their names used, I will call them Doctor X and Doctor Z. Before the seance two weighing machines had been placed in the seance room. A large scale was placed in the cabinet and the medium's chair was placed upon it—the second was a small bathroom scale and it was placed about ten feet from the cabinet. After the seance had started Doctor X said —

"Silver Belle, do you think that you could materialize a heart and lungs in one of the spirit-forms?" Silver Belle laughed and said that she was not sure but she would try.

After several of the Spirit Teachers had manifested, a beautiful spirit came from the cabinet and identified herself as the sister of Doctor X. As she walked from the cabinet she showed the cord of ectoplasm connecting her body to that of the medium. The cord looked like a fleecy rope and seemed to be connected at the back of the ectoplasmic body between the shoulders and ran along the floor through the curtains of the cabinet, presumably to the body of the medium.

After exchanging greetings with his sister the Doctor asked her if she would assist him in an experiment. She replied that she would be glad to do so if he was sure that it would not harm the medium. Silver Belle spoke from the cabinet and assured her that the medium was protected and then she said to the Doctor—

"I tried to do what you asked me to but I am not sure that your sister can hold the body together for very long so you had better hurry up."

The doctor then asked his sister to come down the room and step upon the scale that he might see how much she weighed. She complied with his request and with the aid of a little phosphorous light he was able to see the scale—

"My goodness," he exclaimed, "You weigh thirty-five pounds. I did not expect that."

He then proceeded to take the pulse of the spirit and the respiration. He remarked that the pulse was very strong.

While this was going on Doctor Z had been permitted to enter the cabinet with the entranced medium and we heard him say—

"Silver Belle, where are you? I can hear you but I cannot see you."

Silver Belle assured him that she was there but had dematerialized as all the psychic force was needed for the experiment. Directed by Silver Belle, Doctor Z proceeded to take the weight of the medium and found that it had decreased nearly thirty-seven pounds from her original weight taken before the seance. He then took her pulse and respiration and with the aid of a tiny flashlight wrote them down upon a slip of paper. After this was over and the spirit-form back in the cabinet, Silver Belle said in a tone of authority—"That's all now. My medium cannot stand any more."

After the seance was over the doctors compared notes and found that the pulse and respiration of the spirit were entirely different from those of the medium.

Later I asked Dr. Banks why the medium had lost thirty-seven pounds when the spirit only weighed thirty-five and he said that the other two pounds were in the cord of ectoplasm connecting the spirit-form to that of the medium.[184]

In 1953, Jack Edwards, using a camera and infrared film, took these famous pictures (reprinted on the following pages) at a test materialization séance given by Ethel Post-Parrish. These photographs were taken at fifty-second intervals. Eighty one people attended this famous séance.[185] At the left of each picture you can see Ethel Post-Parrish sitting in the cabinet, the curtained enclosure. The other woman is holding the curtain open, allowing us to see the medium. On the right side of the picture is the "pillar of cloud," or ectoplasm. In each of the first five pictures you can see how Spirit molded the ectoplasm to form Silver Belle's body. She is taking the ectoplasm and molding it into an image of herself. By the fifth picture she is fully materialized. At this point she was speaking to the people at the séance. As stated previously, this ectoplasmic body of Silver Belle would have its own heartbeat and blood pressure distinct from the medium. After the fifth picture, Mr. Edwards had to change the film in his camera. That is why there is such a dramatic difference between the fifth and sixth pictures. By the sixth picture the energy level had dropped, and the ectoplasmic body of Silver Belle was disintegrating. The ectoplasm was beginning to retreat into the body of Ethel Post-Parrish.

As we have seen, the cabinet is an important feature of mediumship. It allows the holiest form of communication to happen. The cabinet allows people to have a direct face to face conversation with Spirit. There is no communion holier than this.

---

[184] Barnes, Peggy, *Lo, I Am With You Always.* Cassadaga, FL: National Spiritualist Association of Churches, n. d. p. 36-38.

[185] Stemman, Roy. *Spirits and Spirit Worlds: The Supernatural.* The Danbury Press, 1975. p. 82.

# Silver Belle Materialization Séance 1953

## Ethel Post-Parrish, Medium —Jack Edwards, Infra-Red Photographer

[These pictures of Silver Belle and the portrait of her medium, Ethel Post-Parrish, are published with permission of the Trustees of Camp Chesterfield, Chesterfield, Indiana.]

1. The white, smoky ectoplasm is being drawn from medium, sitting inside of the cabinet.

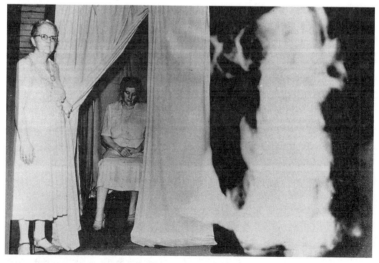

2. The Pillar of Cloud coming from the medium's body forms from the ground upwards.

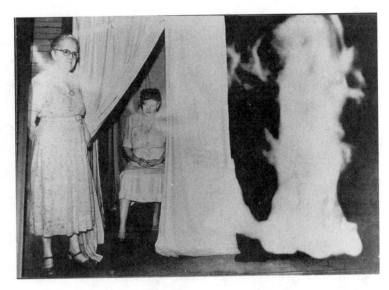

3. This type of phenomena is how Moses spoke to God face to face in Exodus 33:7-11.

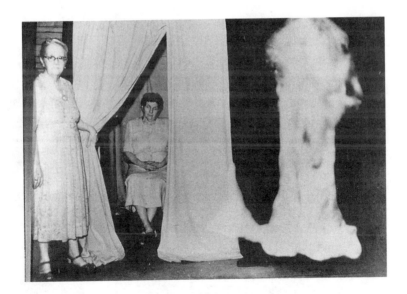

4. More of Silver Belle's features are formed in the column of ectoplasm.

5. The fully formed Silver Belle is now speaking to the people attending the séance.

6. Unfortunately, Mr. Edwards had to change film between pictures 5 & 6. At this point, Silver Belle is blessing the people. Her ectoplasmic form is beginning to break up. The ectoplasm will retract into the medium's body. However, not all of it will return, leaving the medium very exhausted.

In Numbers 10:2, Spirit instructs Moses to make silver trumpets. Mediums use these aluminum trumpets during trumpet séances. Spirit takes ectoplasm and forms a voice box, which is placed in the trumpet for amplification. God gave the Hebrews the Ten Commandments using trumpets such as these. The white bands are phosphorus tape. The medium "charges" the tape near a light bulb before the séance. This way you can watch the trumpets levitate in the pitch dark séance room.

Silver Belle's medium, Ethel Post-Parrish

Spirit produced these pictures at two of Bill English's precipitation séances. Each sitter received a piece of polyester cloth. The medium opened a bottle of India Ink, and left it on a table. I held the cloth during the séance, held in a dark room. At the end of the séance these portraits were on the cloth. Unfortunately, I did not recognize any of these faces. However other attendees did recognize the faces on their cloths.
(This is discussed in chapter 16).

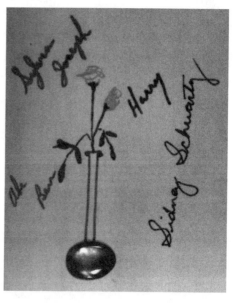

I received this card (right) during a card writing séance conducted by Bill English. Felt tip markers were placed in a basket, along with a sealed package of 3x5 cards. The basket was covered with a cloth. Next the medium went into trance, and announced a long list of names. The medium came out of trance. An assistant opened the still sealed package of cards. Abe and Ben were my uncles. Harry was my father. Sylvia and Joseph were my grandparents. Bill English did not know the names of my relatives. (This is discussed in chapter 16.)

# THIRTEEN

## Awan Discusses the Elimination of Mediums

T*he preparations for this deep trance session followed the usual procedure. Carl sat in his chair, and said the prayer with his eyes closed. It appeared that he had fallen asleep, since he began to snore softly. I was surprised when the snoring stopped, and I heard Awan's voice. Carl's body didn't spasm at all.*

 My profound greetings.

 Greetings, Awan.

 I see that you have been working very diligently to become more knowledgeable about the Gifts of the Spirit. For this I am very grateful. Mediumship has its drawbacks. It's not easy to be an instrument of the Spirit. The draining nature of this work is only the first of its challenges. When instruments adjust their frequencies to hear the voices coming from my realm, a great deal of physical and mental energy is required. This work exhausts the medium. It sometimes requires days for the medium to restore his energy.

 Yes, Awan, the instrument has frequently complained to me about that very issue.

 But what is even more difficult is that mediums are often despised.

 Awan, why would anyone despise a medium?

 Mediums are despised because they threatened established religions. Let's turn back the pages of time, to before the Catholic Church. Let's go back to before יְהוֹשֻׁעַ בֶּן יוֹסֵף (*Joshua ben Joseph*) came to the world.

Excuse me, Awan, who was *Joshua ben Joseph*?

 *Joshua ben Joseph* was the Hebrew name for the person you know as Jesus.

 Oh, I understand יְהוֹשֻׁעַ means *Joshua*, בֶּן means *son of*, and יוֹסֵף means *Joseph*. Of course, that is the way all Hebrew names are structured. יְהוֹשֻׁעַ בֶּן יוֹסֵף means *Joshua the son of Joseph* in English.

 As I was saying, before the Hebrews entered the land of Canaan, they went to see the *Gifted One*, or medium, when they wanted to communicate with God or Spirit. Since there were not many gifted ones in existence at the time, the reputation of a particularly gifted person spread far and wide. People travelled great distances to hear words of wisdom through an instrument of the Spirit. In those days, people understood that the psychically gifted person was the only means of communicating with individuals living in the higher realms.

When Jesus returned to his homeland as an adult, he began teaching what he had learned at the ancient school of the Essenes. The record of the knowledge he gained from the Essenes was removed from the Bible. That is why there are eighteen years of Jesus' life missing from the Bible.

Despite the fact that the Essenes were a group of Jewish people once held in high regard, many of your present-day orthodox Jewish sects do not hold them in high regard.

 That is true, Awan. I know a professor of Jewish history who thought the Essenes were—let us say, second class Jewish citizens. He didn't think highly of them. He called them Hellenized Jews, meaning they had adopted ideas from the Greeks. From the way he spoke, he implied the Greeks had polluted Judaism.

 Orthodox Jews didn't like the Essenes because they studied mediumship. The school provided exercises to develop psychic abilities, and brought these gifts to the surface in many students. Once their mediumship was fully developed, members of the Essene community would go out into the world and demonstrate the Gifts of the Spirit. Mediumship threatened the Jewish religion, as it later threatened the Christians.

 Why is that?

 I would like you to go to your libraries and read all you can about Christianity and Judaism. You will discover that originally priests were supposed to be psychically gifted people. The masses were persuaded that priests could communicate with people in my realm. However, most priests didn't possess the

Gifts of the Spirit. Only the prophets could communicate with Spirit. Since priests extracted their living from the work of the people, their livelihood was vulnerable to the prophets, who could, at any moment, expose them as frauds. Therefore, priests wished to silence the prophets by having them killed.

That is what happened to Jesus. He had studied with the Essenes, and then come back to his native land to demonstrate and teach the Gifts of the Spirit. The priests could not tolerate this. Jesus attracted large groups of people. His reputation quickly spread, far and wide, like a forest fire. His teachings threatened to devastate the religions of the time. Consequently, a group of priests from many different sects, not just the Jewish priests, set about having Jesus silenced. For centuries the Jewish priests have been blamed for conspiring against Jesus. In reality there were more religions in that part of the world than you could count. People didn't get along with each other—they hated each other. The hatred stemmed from each religious group's believing it had the most powerful God and the correct way to worship. This is still going on in that part of the world today.

 I understand what you mean, Awan.

These money-hungry priests wanted to preserve their luxurious life styles. People brought them the best food and gifts as *sacrifices*. When people began to follow Jesus, they no longer brought their sacrifices to these priests. These priests met to decide what they should do about Jesus. Too many people were asking questions. Jesus was teaching truths that those priests didn't understand. They decided to silence this great teacher by having him killed.

So Jesus was killed to stop him from teaching and performing the Gifts of the Spirit?

That is correct. This group of priests, who were behind Jesus' death, decided to create a religion using *Jesus* as their new God. These priests developed a belief system centered around the idea that Jesus lived out there in the sky somewhere. This was the foundation of Christianity. They decided to make Jesus the *God*, and forced people to convert to Christianity.

To accomplish this goal, they had to eliminate the gifted people. To convert everyone to Christianity, they said the oracles that had once been considered good and holy people were now possessed by an evil one (the devil). To rid the world of evil, and fight the devil, the priests declared that mediums and oracles must be burned at the stake.

While this didn't put an end to mediumship, it diminished mediumship's visibility. By denouncing mediumship the church forced these activities to become clandestine. People had to keep it shrouded in secrecy. They had to sneak off into the night for readings. This is how the word *occult*, became associated with mediumship.

In those days, it was not uncommon for people to seek out a gifted person for a reading to obtain spiritual guidance and advice. They went at night, so no one would see them. Many of these gifted people hid in caves, and wore robes with hoods over their heads, never allowing their faces to been seen. They wouldn't speak in crowds, so no one could recognize their voices. They were wanted as criminals. Priests offered very generous rewards to anyone who would help them capture these gifted people.

 This is fascinating, but also very tragic.

 That is true. If you read the history of the Catholic Church from its beginnings to this moment, you wouldn't believe what this *religion* has done to the people. You wouldn't believe what Popes have done nor how many people have died in the name of the Catholic Church. Catholic leaders butchered people who didn't conform to their beliefs because they wanted to rule the world. Today, the Vatican still attempts to control the world by amassing great sums of money and property.

 This sounds so cynical. Are you sure about this, Awan?

 Go, my brother, and research it for yourself. You have much work ahead of you. My peace be with you.

 Thank you, Awan. Peace to you, too.

*Carl returned into his body in the usual fashion, and was very thirsty. He drank three glasses of water. This time, however, his energy level after being in deep trance was unusually high, so he didn't take his customary nap.*

# FOURTEEN

## The Conflict Between
## the Priests and the Mediums

O nce again I answered Awan's challenge to do my own research to confirm the validity of his statements. Did orthodox religions, especially the Catholic Church, want to eliminate mediumship? Awan's reasoning was logical. People endowed with the Gifts of the Spirit could easily prove that priests were not intermediaries between people and those in the Spirit World. People might abandon the church to follow the prophet of the day. Then the priests' income would come to an abrupt halt.

After a year of research, I concluded that Awan was correct in his description of the conflict between priests and mediums. This chapter is a synthesis of what I learned.

Let's examine some examples where people in Biblical times sought the spiritual guidance of mediums. In the first example, Jehoshaphat, the King of Israel asked mediums to predict if going to war would be successful:

> So the king of Israel brought together the prophets—about four hundred men—and asked them, "Shall I go to war against Ramoth Gilead, or shall I refrain?" "Go," they answered, "for the Lord will give it into the king's hand."[186]

In the next quotation, Joash, the King of Israel, sought advice from Elisha. Joash was trying to decide if he should wage war. Elisha performed this act of mediumship from his deathbed.

> And he [Elisha] said, "Open the window eastward;" and he [Joash] opened it. Then Elisha said, "Shoot;" and he [Joash] shot. And he said "The Lord's arrow of victory, the arrow of victory over Syria!" For you shall fight the Syrians in Aphek until you have made an end of them."[187]

---

[186] 1 Kings 22:6 [NIV].
[187] 2 Kings 13:17 [RSV].

People also consulted mediums about droughts:

> **Elijah the Tishbite, from Tishbe in Gilead, said to Ahab: "As the Lord, the God of Israel, lives, whom I serve, during these years there shall be no dew or rain except at my word."[188]**

This is the first mention of Elijah in the Bible. We can only assume King Ahab summoned Elijah to the royal palace. Elijah predicted the onset of a drought.

The next quotation confirms that people concerned with health matters consulted mediums.

> **At that time Abijah the son of Jeroboam became sick. And Jeroboam said to his wife, "Arise now, and disguise yourself so that they may not know that you are the wife of Jeroboam, and go to Shiloh; behold, Ahijah the prophet is there, who spoke concerning me that I would be king over this people. And take ten loaves with you, some cakes and a jar of honey, and go to him, He will tell you what will happen to the boy."[189]**

King Jeroboam, worried about his son's health, sent his wife to the prophet to discover the boy's fate. It is important to note the third verse: *"And take ten loaves with you, some cakes and a jar of honey, and go to him."* It was customary to give the medium something of value as payment. We find confirmation of this custom in the following verses. *Man of God* is another term for *prophet*.

> **But the servant answered, "A man of God is in this town. People respect him. All the things he says come true. So let's go into this town. Maybe this man of God will tell us where we should go next." Saul said to his servant, "We can go into town. But what can we give the man? The food in our bags is gone. We have no gift to give the man of God. What do we have to give him?"[190]**

The custom of giving the medium a gift of food in exchange for spiritual guidance is **crucial** for understanding the animosity between the priests and mediums. This millenniums-old hostility has its origin in pre-Biblical times.

What did people expect when visiting a medium? The next two quotations provide the answer.

> **And all that would ask any question of the Lord went out unto the tabernacle of witness, which was without the hoste.[191]**

---

[188] 1 Kings 17:1 [NAB].

[189] 1 Kings 14:1-3 [NASB].

[190] 1 Samuel 9:6-7 [ETR].

[191] Exodus 33:7 [TAV].

**Before time in Israel when a man went to seek an answer of God, thus wise he spake, Come, let us go to the Seer: For he that is now called a *prophet*, was in the old time called a *Seer*.**[192]

These two verses create a clear picture of the ancient Hebrew's expectations of mediumship. People went to Moses' meeting tent to receive God's answers to their questions. There would be no reason to ask God a question, unless he could give an answer. In the second verse, people went to the prophet Samuel to obtain God's answers to their questions. Think about this. In Biblical times, it was commonplace for people to have a *two-way conversation with God*. People could ask God a question, and God responded. If God answered questions in Biblical times, why doesn't he answer them today? The laws of psychic science have not changed since Biblical times. The psychic phenomena that occurred in the Bible can happen today. So why can't we have a two-way conversation with God?

The answer is simple. Organized religions have made their priests the intermediaries between God and the people. Although the priests were supposed to have the Gifts of the Spirit, they did not. Only people endowed with the Gifts of the Spirit can deliver information from Spirit to us. When religions made ungifted priests the intermediaries, they severed the lines of communication with God.

## Who were the Priests?

Priests were supposed to have psychic gifts! The proof of this lies embedded in the Hebrew and Arabic languages.

**The Hebrew word for *'priest'* is כֹּהֵן (*kôhen*), and the corresponding Arabic word (*kâhin*) means *'a soothsayer'*—more exactly, as we learn from the Arabic lexicographers, *one who has a familiar spirit* to tell him things otherwise unknown.**[193]

By definition, *priests* and *prophets* were mirror images of each other! They shared one function—to be *soothsayers, mediums, prophets, seers,* and *instruments of the Spirit.* Unfortunately, the priests of the church were not endowed with the Gifts of the Spirit. Religious and political rulers chose these priests. The term *priest* came to mean something far removed from *prophet* or *seer.*

The Bible tells us that God wanted to create a class of priests to serve him. They would perform all the rituals that God himself explained.

**Have Aaron your brother brought to you from among the**

---

[192] 1 Samuel 9:9 [BISH].

[193] Smith, Henry Preserved. "Priest, Priesthood (Hebrew)," *Encyclopædia of Religion and Ethics,* edited by Hastings, James. Volume X. NY: Charles Scribner's Sons, 1920. p. 307.

**Israelites, along with his sons Nedab and Abihu, Eleazar and Ithamar, so they may serve me as priests.**[194]

This passage insured that Aaron's descendants would be priests. The priesthood was hereditary, passed from one generation to the next. This system was established because the Gifts of the Spirit run in families. One generation genetically passes these gifts to the next generation. We discover proof of this in our next verse. Miriam and Aaron (Moses' sister and brother) were also mediums. They became jealous of Moses' esteemed position among the Hebrews. Moses was leader of the Hebrews because through him, God guided the Hebrews.

**Miriam and Aaron attacked Moses asking, "Has the Eternal spoken to Moses alone? Has he not spoken to us as well?"**[195]

Once the class of priests was established, God gave them special privileges. One was a new wardrobe. When comparing various versions of the Bible, conflicting reasons arise as to why God wanted the priests to wear ornate clothing.

**Make sacred garments for your brother Aaron, to give him dignity and honor.**[196]

**For the glorious adornment of your brother Aaron you shall have sacred vestments made.**[197]

**And you shall make holy garments for Aaron your brother, for glory and for beauty.**[198]

**Make special clothes for your brother Aaron. These clothes will give him honor and respect.**[199]

Unfortunately, the glorious adornment of the priests made them more attractive, but didn't afford a direct link to the Spirit World.

Next, God "hires" the best designers to create a prestigious image for the priesthood:

**Therefore, to the various expert workmen whom I have endowed with skill, you shall give instruction to make such vestments for Aaron as will set him apart for his sacred service as my priest.**

---

[194] Exodus 28:1 [NIV] [P].

[195] Numbers 12:1-2 [MOFF] [E].

[196] Exodus 28:2 [NIV] [P].

[197] Exodus 28:2 [NAB] [P].

[198] Exodus 28:2 [RSV] [P].

[199] Exodus 28:2 [ETR] [P].

> These are the vestments they shall make: a breastpiece, an ephod, a robe, a brocade tunic, a miter and a sash... They shall use gold, violet, purple and scarlet yarn and fine linen.[200]

Priests received an endless supply of the best available food. However, not wanting to appear too greedy, they received their free food in an underhanded way. They inserted long lists of sins into the Bible. If one committed a sin, the only way to receive forgiveness was to provide an animal to sacrifice to God.

> Do not sacrifice to the Lord your God an ox or a sheep that has any defect or flaw in it, for that would be detestable to him.[201]

> If anyone of the common people sins unintentionally by doing something against any of the commandments of the Lord in anything which ought not to be done, and is guilty, or if his sin which he has sinned comes to his knowledge, then he shall bring as his offering a kid of the goats, a female without blemish, for his sin which he has sinned.[202]

> So the priest shall make atonement for him, and it shall be forgiven him.[203]

Priests sacrificed the animal. This act of butchery entitled them to special respect.

> Honor him as sacred who offers up the food of your God; treat him as sacred, because I, the Lord, who have consecrated him, am sacred.[204]

A sacrificial lamb brought to the priests would absolve many sins.

> If a person sins because he does not speak up when he hears a public charge to testify regarding something he has seen or learned about...[205]

> Or if a person touches anything ceremonially unclean...[206]
> Or if he touches human uncleanness...[207]

---

[200] Exodus 28:3-5 [NAB] [P].

[201] Deuteronomy 17:1 [NIV] [D].

[202] Leviticus 4:27 [NKJV] [P].

[203] Leviticus 4:31 [NKJV] [P].

[204] Leviticus 21:8 NAB [P].

[205] Leviticus 5:1 [NIV] [P].

[206] Leviticus 5:2 [NIV] [P].

> Or if a person thoughtlessly takes an oath to do anything, whether good or evil...[208]

> When anyone is guilty in any of these ways, he must confess in what way he has sinned and, as a penalty for the sin he has committed, he must bring to the Lord a female lamb or goat.... [209]

> If he cannot afford a lamb, he is to bring two doves or two young pigeons to the Lord as a penalty for his sin...[210]

> If, however, he cannot afford two doves or two young pigeons, he is to bring as an offering for his sin a tenth of an ephah of fine flour for a sin offering....[211]

Why was this system of sacrifice needed? Did you need to bribe God to forgive your sins? This continuous flow of fresh meat was not for God—**it was to feed the priests.**

> Speak to Aaron and to his sons, saying 'This is the law of the sin offering: in the place where the burnt offering is slain the sin offing shall be slain before the Lord; it is most holy. *The priest who offers it for sin shall eat it.* It shall be eaten in a holy place, in the court of that tent of meeting.[212]

> Every male among the priests may eat of it; it is most holy.[213]

> You must eat the whole animal that same day and not leave any of the meat for the next morning. I am the Lord. [214]

> And whatever is over Aaron and his sons may have for their food, taking it without leaven in a holy place; in the open space of the Tent of meeting they may take a meal of it. [215]

---

[207] Leviticus 5:3 [NIV] [P].

[208] Leviticus 5:4 [NIV] [P].

[209] Leviticus 5:5-6 [NIV] [P].

[210] Leviticus 5:7 [NIV] [P].

[211] Leviticus 5:11 [NIV] [P].

[212] Leviticus 6:25-26 [NASB] [P].

[213] Leviticus 6:29 [NASB] [P].

[214] Leviticus 22:30 [NCV] [P].

[215] Leviticus 6:16 [OGD] [P].

These verses demonstrate how the sacrifices intended for God provided the priests with free meals. Every time a common person sinned, he supplied a barbecue for a priest. (The more *sins* the priests could come up with for people to be guilty of, the more sacrificial food to hoard.) Priests were not the only people who enjoyed the sacrificial meat. Members of the priests' families also ate in great measure. The poor sinners were not entitled to a single bite of the sacrificial food.

> *No-one* outside a priest's family may eat the sacred offering, nor may the guest of a priest or his hired worker eat it.

> But if a priest *buys a slave with money*, or if a slave is born in his household, that slave *may* eat his food.

> If a priest's daughter marries anyone other than a priest, she may not eat any of the sacred contributions.

> But if a priest's daughter becomes a widow or is divorced, yet has no children, and she returns to live in her father's house as in her youth, she may eat of her father's food. No unauthorized person, however, may eat any of it.[216]

Priests and their families ate the sacrificial meat. However, it must have been monotonous to eat meat at every meal. Not even the priests and their families would enjoy a filet mignon for breakfast every day. So laws were written to provide some variety in the priests' diet.

> While the remainder of the cereal-offering is to go to Aaron and his sons as being the most sacred part of the Lord's sacrifices.[217]

> Speak unto the children of Israel, and say unto them, When ye become into the land which I give unto you, and shall reap the harvest thereof, then ye shall bring a sheaf of the firstfruit of your harvest unto the priests.[218]

The following description summarizes the privileges, given to the priests.

> Priests received twenty-four priestly privileges which included the meat of various sacrifices, flour and oil from the meal-offerings, the shewbread, the first ripe fruits, the heave-offering, hallah, the first wool from the sheep shearing, *and being thus freed from the worry of earning a livelihood* were able to devote themselves to primary

---

[216] Leviticus 22:10-13 [NIV] [P].

[217] Leviticus 2:10 [SMGO] [P].

[218] Leviticus 23:10 [KJV] [P].

**tasks of teaching and officiating at the temple service.**[219]

Some readers may be skeptical, and think that since the Bible is the word of God, he commanded this. People who believe this do not understand how the Bible was written. The Bible, (even the first five books of Moses), was *not* written in the time of Moses. The Rev. Harold B. Hunting, in his book, *The Story of Our Bible*, agrees that the priests, a class of elite rulers, invented many of the laws written into the Bible. It was not God who commanded people to obey these laws.

> **The earliest Bible of the Hebrews, that is, the earliest writings which were regarded as divinely inspired and sacred, were written laws and legal decisions of the priests. Half-civilized nations always put their laws under the direct sanction of the Gods, in order that evil-doers may be restrained by fear of supernatural vengeance. When the revised book of Deuteronomy was adopted by King Josiah and his people, in 622 B. C., it was regarded with special reverence on account of the wonderful impressiveness with which the laws were therein explained and enjoined upon the nation. In the course of the next two centuries, Deuteronomy was combined with earlier laws and also with an elaborate system of later priestly regulations.**[220]

Deuteronomy, not Genesis, was the first book of the Bible to be written down. Within Bible text, priests cleverly disguised their shrewd system of extorting food from the people. Priests claimed God wanted the sacrifices, so they could attend to their "priestly chores." They dressed in the finest clothes and enjoyed a lifestyle of leisure. They didn't engage in hard manual labor as the common person did. They didn't plant fields, or tend flocks. Common people did that work for them. Priests set themselves up as intermediaries between God and the people. There was one slight problem—they didn't have the Gifts of the Spirit. They couldn't conduct a two-way conversation between God and a person seeking counsel, as a medium could. A gift of food to a medium was food out of the mouth of a hungry priest! However, this conflict goes deeper than that.

Richard Elliott Friedman provides evidence that priests wrote laws into the Bible. In his book, *Who Wrote the Bible?*, we find that the entire book of Leviticus, with the exception of Leviticus 23:39-43 and 26:39-45, was written by priests.[221] All but one of the quotations I cited in this discussion about animal sacrifices were from the Book of Leviticus, *written by priests*. Priests claimed this elaborate system of sacrifices came from "God's mouth." This system supplied them with a fantastic living, and the best food and clothing available.

---

[219] Werblowsky, R. J. Zwi and Wigoder, Geoffrey. "Priestly Privileges," *The Encyclopedia of the Jewish Religion*. New York: Holt, Rinehart and Winston, Inc. 1965. p. 308.

[220] Rev. Harold B. Hunting. *The Story of Our Bible*. New York: Charles Scribner's Sons, 1915. p. 219.

[221] Friedman, Richard Elliot, *Who Wrote the Bible?* NY: Summit Books, 1987. p. 225.

## The Prophets Confront the Priests about Sacrifices

The system of sacrifices, became an institution in early Hebrew society. Sacrifices became the priests' primary focus as they became dependent on the endless supply of food.

> Then the Lord spoke to Moses, saying, "Command the sons of Israel and say to them, 'You shall be careful to present My offering, My food for My offerings by fire, of a soothing aroma to Me, *at their appointed time.*'"[222]

God spoke through several prophets, protesting this corrupt system.

> The spirit of the Lord hath spoken by me, and the utterance thereof is done thorough my tongue.[223]

Several prophets boldly confronted the priests, and decried the corruptness of the sacrificial system. God wanted these animal sacrifices to stop. The prophet Isaiah declared that God detested the sacrifices:

> "What care I for all your lavish sacrifices?" the Eternal asks; "I am sick of slaughtered rams, of fat from fatted beasts; the blood of bullocks and of goats is no delight to me."[224]

The prophet Hosea delivered a powerful message when he reprimanded the priests. Hosea warned that God would severely punish them for their disobedience. Not only did God express that priests were "growing fat" from the "sins" of the people, but that they were neglecting their duty. Priests were entrusted to teach people about God. Awan told me that God has always wanted all people to be educated in the Gifts of the Spirit. Priests ignored this.

> My people are destroyed for lack of knowledge: because thou hast rejected knowledge, I will also reject thee, that thou shalt be no priest to me. As they were increased, so they sinned against me: therefore will I change their glory into shame. They eat up the sin of my people, and they set their heart on their iniquity. And there shall be, like people, like priest: and I will punish them for their ways, and reward them their doings.[225]

---

[222] Numbers 28:1 [NASB].

[223] 2 Samuel 23:2 [COV].

[224] Isaiah 1:11 [MOFF].

[225] Hosea 4:6-9 [KJV].

Again Hosea presented God's wishes to the priests. God wanted people to live a righteous life, being kind to their neighbors, and understanding the Gifts of the Spirit.

**For I desired mercy, and not sacrifice; and the knowledge of God more than burnt offerings.[226]**

The prophet Amos also brought this message to the priests' ears. God wanted people to live a righteous life, not to be concerned with animal sacrifices.

**I hate, I despise your festivals, and I take no delight in your solemn assemblies. Even though you offer me your burnt offerings and grain offerings, I will not accept them, and the offerings of well-being of your fatted animals I will not look upon. Take away from me the noise of your songs; I will not listen to the melody of your harps. But let justice roll down like waters, and righteousness like an ever-flowing stream.[227]**

When the psychically gifted prophets delivered God's words, they publicly accused priests of neglecting their job. Priests weren't teaching people about God, nor were they a link between the two realms. Is it any wonder that the priests began to hate the prophets? A prophet could expose the priests' lack of psychic ability to the people.

Despite the outcry from the prophets Isaiah, Hosea, and Amos, God's words fell on deaf ears. The reform God wanted did not occur. Animal sacrifices lasted several more centuries, and still occurred during Jesus' lifetime.

**And on the first day of Unleavened Bread, when the Passover** *lamb* **was being sacrificed...[228]**

We can examine how the conflict between priests and mediums existed during the life of Jesus of Nazareth. Jesus was the greatest medium who ever lived. When Jesus performed his "miracles," he drew people's attention away from the priests. People were spiritually hungry and preferred to learn new knowledge from Jesus than perform the time worn ritual of animal sacrifice at the Temple. The priests had two choices. They could find a new job, or silence Jesus by killing him. They chose the latter, convincing the Romans that Jesus was a threat to the Roman government.

When Jesus was murdered, he had only begun educating people about psychic phenomena. His mission was incomplete, therefore, he decided to continue his teachings. This time he would not reincarnate into the physical world. This time he would work from the Spirit World. Jesus appeared as a Spirit to Paul on the road to

---

[226] Hosea 6:6 [KJV].

[227] Amos 5:21-24 [NRSV].

[228] Mark 14:12 [NASB].

Damascus.[229] Jesus chose Paul, because Paul had the latent gifts of clairvoyance and clairaudience. Through mediumship, Jesus taught Paul about the Gifts of the Spirit. Paul then enthusiastically taught all who would listen.

Three hundred years later, Christianity (Roman Catholicism) became the official religion of the Roman Empire. By this time, the Church no longer considered Jesus a phenomenal medium. Priests now wanted people to believe that Jesus was their savior-God. They wanted the masses to beg Jesus to come to their rescue in order to reach salvation and enter Heaven. In this new religion, the priest was needed as the "medium," to communicate with Jesus.

If the priests had been truthful, they would have taught the philosophy of the great teacher Jesus.

> **In solemn truth I tell you, anyone believing in me shall do the same miracles I have done, and even greater ones.[230]**

Jesus didn't die to absolve the sins of humanity. This is nothing but a centuries-old myth created by priests. Even today, some preachers shout this myth from the pulpits and broadcast it over radio and television.

The people who lived in Biblical times were more familiar with the Gifts of the Spirit than people living in the 21st century.

## Bible Verses that Forbid Mediumship

Priests inserted laws into the Bible that banned the Hebrews from seeking spiritual guidance from a medium. These laws camouflaged the fact that priests weren't able to perform the Gifts of the Spirit. These laws protected their luxurious lifestyle. Priests rewrote the Bible to make it appear that these laws were God's and brought to the people through Moses.

> **And Jehovah went on speaking to Moses saying:[231]**

This opening phrase of Leviticus 20:1 enabled priests to claim that God enjoined all the laws contained in the chapter. This "Divine legislation directly from Jehovah's mouth" commanded that people with familiar Spirits must be killed.

> **A man also or a woman that hath a familiar spirit, or that is a wizard, shall surely be put to death: they shall stone them with stones: their blood shall be upon them.[232]**

---

[229] Acts 9: 3-6.

[230] John 14:12 [LIV].

[231] Leviticus 20:1 [NWT] [P].

[232] Leviticus 20:27 [KJV] [P].

When one kills off one's competition, one's own business improves. Fewer mediums meant more people bringing their animal sacrifices to the priests. The next step in eradicating mediumship was to criminalize it. Mediumship became an abominable crime punishable by death.

> **And the soul that turneth after such as have familiar spirits, and after wizards, to go a whoring after them, I will even set my face against that soul, and will cut him off from among his people.**[233]

By definition, a כֹּהֵן (*kôhen*) is a priest, as well as a medium, or one who has a familiar spirit. Therefore, according to Mosaic Law as written by priests, consulting *a medium or a priest* was a crime punishable by death. The world might be in better shape if this had been the case. Unfortunately, that's not what happened. This priest-written law sought to eliminate the mediumistic threat to the priests' endless supply of free food. Let's examine one of the laws that prohibited mediumship.

> **There shall not be found among you any one that maketh his son, or his daughter to pass through the fire, or that useth divination, or an observer of times, or an enchanter, or a witch or a charmer, or a consulter with familiar spirits, or a wizard, or a Necromancer. For all that do these things are an abomination unto the Lord.**[234]

From reading these verses it is clear that *divination* suddenly became a crime, as it appears on God's abomination list. What exactly is the definition of *divination*?

> **This noun from the Latin words "Divinatio" and "Divino," to prophesy, to divine the future, means the foretelling of future events.**[235]

If God is the perfect, omnipresent, omnipotent being who created the world, he must be flawless. Therefore, it would seem he would be consistent with his viewpoints. If the Bible is the exact word of God, who is a perfect being, then the Bible should be letter perfect. There shouldn't be any inconsistencies within the Bible's text. There should be a clear and precise code of behavior that God wishes us to practice, and another describing what he forbids us to do. However, the very opposite is true. In the Book of Genesis chapter 44 we discover that Joseph practiced divination!

As you read this chart, notice that modern Bibles, published after 1944, don't make any mention of *divination*. Why do modern translators refuse to use the words *divine*, or *divination*, in their translations?

---

[233] Leviticus 20:6 [KJV] [P].

[234] Deuteronomy 18:10-12 [KJV].

[235] Manas, John H. *Divination: Ancient and Modern: An Historical, Archaeological and Philosophical Approach to Seership and Christian Religion.* NY: Pythagorean Society, 1947. p. 7.

# GENESIS CHAPTER 44 VERSE 5

| | | |
|---|---|---|
| KJV | 1611 | Is not this it, in which my lord drinketh? and whereby indeed he *divineth*? Ye have done evil in so doing. |
| EWYC | 1384 | The cup that you have stolen, it is in which my lord drinketh and in which he is *wonte to divine*; the most evil thing you han do. |
| COV | 1535 | Is not that it, that my lord drinketh out of: and that he *prophecieth withal*. It is evil done of you, that ye have done. |
| TAV | 1539 | Wherefore have ye rewarded evil for good? Is that not the cup of which my lord drinketh, and *doth he not prophecy therein*? Ye have evil done, that ye have done. |
| GEN | 1560 | Is that not the cup, wherein my lord drinketh? and in the which he *doth divine and prophecy*? Ye have done evil in so doing. |
| BISH | 1568 | Is not that the cup in the which my Lord drinketh and for the which *he consulteth with the propheciers:* Ye have evil done that ye have done. {He went not to the conjurers for any matter: but this is said by dissimulation to increase the crime.} |
| HAAK | 1657 | Is it not the same {Cup, namely} out of which my Lord drinketh? and whereby he *shall surely observe*. Ye have done ill that ye have done. |
| BOTR | 1824 | "Why have ye stolen my silver cup? Is it not that in which my lord drinketh, and for which, he indeed, *will make inquiry*? Ye have done evil in so doing." |
| BREN | 1844 | Why have ye stolen my silver cup? is it not this out of which my lord drinks? and he *divines augury* with it; ye have accomplished evil in that which ye have done. |
| YNG | 1863 | "Is not this that with which my lord drinketh? and he *observeth diligently* with it; ye have done evil in that which ye have done." |
| SPUR | 1885 | Wherefore have ye stolen my silver cup? Is not this that in which my lord drinketh? *Surely searching he will search for it!* This is a wicked thing that ye have done. |
| ROTH | 1897 | Is not this that in which my lord drinketh, and whereby he himself *doth divine*? |
| FENT | 1922 | 'Why have you returned evil for good? Where is that my lord drinks from? *He is very sharp-sighted.* He saw what you were doing?' |
| SMGO | 1939 | Is not this the one from which my lord drinks, which in fact he *uses for divination*? It is a wicked thing that you have done. |
| KNOX | 1944 | This is a poor return to make for the kindness you have received; you have stolen my master's cup, the one from which he drinks, *and takes omens*; you have done him a great wrong. |
| OGD | 1950 | Is not this the cup from which my lord takes wine and by which *he gets knowledge of the future*? Truly, you have done evil. |
| NWT | 1961 | Is not this the thing that my master drinks from and by means of which he *expertly reads omens*? It is a bad deed you have committed. |
| CONF | 1965 | "Why have you stolen the silver cup from me? It is the very one from which my master drinks. *He will certainly guess where it is*. This is an evil thing that you have done." |
| JER | 1966 | "Is this not the one my lord uses for drinking and also *for reading omens*? What you have done is wrong." |
| SEPZ | 1970 | Why have ye stolen my silver cup? Is it not this out of which my lord drinks? and he *divines augury* with it; Ye have accomplished evil in that which ye have done. |
| LIV | 1971 | Ask them, 'What do you mean by stealing my lord's personal silver drinking cup, which he *uses for fortune telling*? What a wicked thing you have done!' |

| BYIN | 1972 | 'This is what my master drinks in, and he *looks in it for signs*—it is a bad thing you have done.' |
| BECK | 1976 | "Isn't this the cup my lord drinks from and uses to *tell what is unknown*? You did wrong!" |
| FRISH | 1977 | Is not this that from which my lord drinks, and whereby indeed he *divines*? you have done evil in so doing. |
| NJER | 1985 | Is this not what my lord uses for drinking and also for *reading omens*? What you have done is wrong. |
| EB | 1987 | "The cup you have stolen is the one my master uses for drinking. And *he uses it for explaining dreams.* You have done a very wicked thing!" |
| ETR | 1987 | Why did you steal my master's silver cup? This is the cup that my master drinks from. This is the cup he uses *to ask God questions.* You have done wrong to steal his cup. |
| HIRSH | 1989 | Is it not just this one out of which my lord drinketh, and he *has a strong superstition about it.* Ye have don evil in that which you have done. |
| CEV | 1995 | "Not only does he drink from this cup, but he also uses it to *learn about the future.* You have done a terrible thing." |
| GODWD | 1995 | "Isn't this the cup that my master drinks from and that he uses for *telling the future*? What you have done is evil!" |
| NIrV | 1996 | "Isn't this the cup my master drinks from? Doesn't he also use it *to figure things out*? You have done an evil thing." |
| NLT | 1996 | "What do you mean by stealing my master's personal silver drinking cup, which he uses *to predict the future*: What a wicked thing you have done!" |

## 32 Differing Translations

If God hated divination and wanted diviners executed, why did he tolerate Joseph's divining and even facilitate Joseph's dream interpretation?

> **Joseph said to them, "Does not interpretations belong to God? Tell me your dreams."[236]**

Obviously, Joseph had the gift of interpreting dreams. He received the interpretations from Spirit. Therefore, Joseph was an instrument of the Spirit. The Bible tells us that God helped Joseph interpret Pharaoh's dreams.

> **He [Joseph] came in before Pharaoh, who said to him, "I have had a dream which no one can interpret. I have heard that you can interpret any dream you hear." Joseph answered, "Not I, but God, can give an answer which will reassure Pharaoh."[237]**

Pharaoh was so grateful to Joseph that he appointed him to an administrative post in his government. If God hated divination, you would think he would have abandoned Joseph as his medium. This was not the case. It seems that God was a bit fickle, and had difficulty forming an opinion on divination.

---

[236] Genesis 40:8 [NEB].

[237] Genesis 41:14-16 [REB].

If God thought divination was an abhorrent crime, as stated in Deuteronomy 18:10-12, he would have rejected Joseph. However, he didn't. We find proof of this in the next verse which are the last words of Joseph recorded in the Bible:

> **Upon which Joseph said to them, Fear not, for I am God's servant.**[238]

Deeper contradictions are revealed when we examine "God's" words about a system of divination for *priests* to use.

> **He [Joshua] will depend on Eleazar the priest, who will learn my will by using the Urim and Thummim.**[239]

I. Mendelsohn provides an explanation of Urim and Thummim:

> **Oracular media by which the will of God in relation to particular problems were ascertained. The initiator in this process of communication was man—he laid before God a question couched in precise words and expected an answer, or decision in like manner, usually in the form of "Yes" or "No."**[240]

Priests used the Urim and Thummim:

> **The functionary in charge of the *divinatory* implements was a priest, and inquires could be directed to any place where one carrying an ephod was present... Urim and Thummin were small objects, perhaps in the shape of dice, made of metal or precious stones and having some symbols impressed on them....The technique employed by the priest in handling the Urim and Thummim is not stated. Since they were kept in a pocket, the priest either shook them in the receptacle and then pulled one out, or used the same method as in the case of the lots—namely, he "cast" both of them on the ground or on any other surface...**[241]

God says in Deuteronomy 18:10-12 that divination is *an abomination to the Lord*. Why is it less abominable for priests to use divination? What allows priests to do something that God forbids? Why was there a need for priests to use Urim and Thummim to learn the will of God? If priests were clairaudient and clairvoyant, they wouldn't need props to talk with God. We have no account of Moses needing stones to have a discussion with God. He spoke with God *face to face* in a materialization

---

[238] Genesis 50:19 [SEPT].

[239] Numbers 27:21 [TEV].

[240] Mendelsohn, I. *The Interpreter's Dictionary of the Bible Vol. IV.* NY: Abington Press, 1962. p. 739.

[241] Mendelsohn, I. *The Interpreter's Dictionary of the Bible Vol. IV.* NY: Abington Press, 1962. p. 740.

séance,[242] or God spoke with him clairaudiently.[243] If priests were as gifted as Moses, they would be able to hear Spirit directly, as Aaron and Miriam had.[244] Priests were supposed to be *soothsayers*, or *mediums*, but they were not. There is only one reason priests needed external props to hear God—they didn't have the Gifts of the Spirit.

In Biblical times, Joseph used a cup for scrying, a form of divination. Despite the priest's ban against divination found in Deuteronomy 18:10-12, Jews living in the 21st century scry. Yet, Jews who performing this ritual are unaware that they are practicing a type of divination ritual.

> A specific form of divination—by means of the cup—is found in the history of Joseph. To judge from later parallels, the practice must have consisted in filling a cup with water or wine, and gazing intently on the surface, till the beholder saw all kinds of images. The method of diving by cups has not been entirely lost...[245]

> Traces of divination by the cup and by finger-nails have been preserved, though no longer understood, in the ceremonies connected with the cup of wine and the lighted candle used at the outgoing of the Sabbath at the service called *Habdalah*, or the division between Sabbath and the weekday, the beginning of the week being considered as a very propitious time. When the blessing is said over the wine-cup filled to overflowing, the man performing the ceremony at a certain moment shades the cup and looks into the wine; and when the blessing over the light is said, it is customary to let the light of the candle falls on finger-nails and to look at them intently. There is no doubt these are remnants of divination.[246]

The roots of psychic phenomena in religion run very deep. Vestiges of psychic practices are found in many of our religious rituals and customs. Because priests outlawed the practice of mediumship and psychic phenomena, most people do not realize the psychic meaning behind many of the rituals they practice today.

The mediums of gods other than Jehovah were an additional threat to the Hebrew priests. Most Jewish blessings begin as follows:

---

[242] Exodus 33:11.

[243] Exodus Chapters 3 and 4.

[244] Numbers 12:1-2.

[245] Gaster, M. "Divination (Jewish)," *Encyclopædia of Religion and Ethics*, edited by Hastings, James. Vol. IV. NY: Charles Scribner's Sons 1920. p. 807.

[246] Gaster, M. "Divination (Jewish)," *Encyclopædia of Religion and Ethics*, edited by Hastings, James. Vol. IV. NY: Charles Scribner's Sons 1920. p. 807.

בָּרוּךְ אַתָּה יְיָ אֱלֹהֵינוּ מֶלֶךְ הָעוֹלָם (*Blessed art thou, O Lord our God, King of the Universe.*)[247]

As a Jew, I have said this phrase in Hebrew hundreds of thousands of times. Therefore, it was automatic for me to believe there was one God, the ultimate being, creator of our world and universe. If that were really the truth, why does this verse appear in the Bible?

# EXODUS 34 VERSE 14

| KJV | 1611 | For thou shalt worship no other god: for the Lord, whose Name is *Jealous*, is a *Jealous* God. |
|-----|------|---|
| DOU | 1609 | Adore not a strange God. The Lord his name is jealous, God is an *emulator*. |
| PUR | 1764 | For thou shalt not bow down to another God; since the Lord whose Name is *zealous*, is a *zealous* God. |
| LEES | 1856 | For thou shalt worship no other god: for the Lord, whose name is *Watchful*, is a *watchful* God. |
| MODL | 1945 | For you shall not worship another god, because the Lord, whose name is *Ardent*, is a God who *brooks no rival.* |
| OGD | 1950 | For you are to be worshipers of no other god: for the Lord is a God *who will not give his honor to another.* |
| LIV | 1971 | For you must worship no other gods, but only Jehovah, for he is a god *who claims absolute loyalty and exclusive devotion.* |
| TEV | 1976 | Do not worship any other god, because I, the Lord, *tolerate no rivals.* |
| LIVT | 1981 | Do not bow down to any other god, for God is known as *one who demands exclusive worship*, and He does indeed demand it. |
| TANK | 1985 | For you must not worship any other god, because the Lord, whose name is *Impassioned*, is an *impassioned* God. |
| ETR | 1987 | Don't worship any other god. I am Yahweh Kanah—the jealous Lord. This is my name. I am *El Kanah*—the Jealous God. |
| CEV | 1995 | I demand your complete loyalty—you must not worship any other god! |
| GODWD | 1995 | Never worship any other god, because the Lord is a God who *does not tolerate rivals*. In fact, he is known for *not tolerating rivals*. |
| NLT | 1996 | You must worship no other gods, but only the Lord, for he is a God who is *passionate about his relationship with you.* |

# 14 Differing Translations

Why would God Almighty, the creator of the whole universe, be jealous of another god? If no other god had this power to create, why would people choose to worship weaker gods? People would want to worship the most powerful God. So why would God feel jealous?

If the Lord were more powerful, magnificent, and wondrous than Baal, Astarte, Asherah, and all the other gods found in Canaan, the Israelites wouldn't have tempted to worship another god. However, the truth is that Baal, Astarte, and

---

[247] Adler. *Service of the Synagogue: Day of Atonement.* NY: Hebrew Publishing Co., n. d. p. 14.

Asherah were equal to Jehovah. All these gods needed mediums to speak to the people. If God is a jealous God, he had reason to be. God who speaks in Exodus 34:14 is not the omnipotent creator of the universe, but a Spirit guide. God who spoke to Moses was the Spirit of a person, who had died, and was now guiding Moses from the Spirit World. There were many gods, just as there are many people on earth today. We must remember that God is Spirit,[248] which is another word for soul. Jesus taught us that we are all gods.

> **Jesus answered them, Is it not written in your Law, I said, Ye are gods?[249]**

When Jesus said, *"It is written in your law,"* he meant that the concept is recorded in the Book of Psalms 82:6. Jesus tried to teach us that we are all gods. One day, we will become as unlimited as a God should be.

The God we read about in Exodus was jealous of other Spirit guides, who spoke through mediums. We tend to think there is only one God who speaks through the various prophets in the Bible. That isn't true. God has many names; many different Spirits spoke to different people in the Bible. This might explain why there is more than one Hebrew name for God.

> **The simplest Hebrew name of God is *El;* it was a popular term for any deity and one widely used by the Israelites *and* their [non-Jewish] neighbors. In the Hebrew Bible, *El* is often modified by a second word. *El Shaddai,* for example means God Almighty, and *El Elyon* means God Most High. The most common name for God, however, is the plural term *Elohim,* suggesting that God in his majesty represents all aspects of divinity.[250]**

There were many other nations who had their own gods, with mediums to channel their knowledge. In the following Bible verse we see that Jehovah wanted to destroy the places where these mediums communicated with other gods.

---

[248] John 4:24.

[249] John 10:34 [KJV].

[250] *ABC's of the Bible: Intriguing Questions and Answers About the Greatest Book Ever Written.* Pleasantville, NY: The Reader's Digest Association, Inc., 1991. p. 39.

# EXODUS CHAPTER 34 VERSE 13

| KJV | 1611 | But ye shall destroy their altars, break their *images*, and cut down their *groves*. |
| LWYC | 1395 | But also destroy thou the alters of them, break the *images*, and cut down the *woods*. |
| COV | 1535 | But their altars shalt thou overthrow, and break down their *gods*, and rote out their *groves*: |
| TAV | 1539 | But overthrow their altars and break their *pillars* and cut down their *groves*, for thou shalt worship no strange God. |
| CHAN | 1750 | But destroy their altars, break their *statues*, and cut down their groves: |
| YNG | 1863 | But their altars shall ye break down, their *standing pillars* also shall ye shiver, and its *shrines* shall ye cut down; |
| BEN | 1864 | But ye shall pull down their altars, break their *monuments*, and cut down their groves: |
| ERV | 1885 | But ye shall break down their altars, and dash in pieces their pillars, and ye shall cut down their *Asherim*: for thou shalt worship no other God: |
| SHAR | 1892 | But ye shall destroy their altars, break their images, and cut down their *groves of Asherah*; for thou shalt worship no other god; |
| ROTH | 1897 | For their altars shall ye smash, and their pillars shall ye shiver,—and their *sacred stems* shall ye fell. |
| GRANT | 1899 | But ye shall break down their *altars*, and shatter their *pillars*, and cut down their *Ashera-images*. |
| ASV | 1901 | But ye shall break down their altars, and dash in pieces their pillars, and ye shall cut down their *Asherim*: |
| MOFF | 1922 | You must demolish their altars and break their *obelisks* and cut down their *sacred poles* (for you must never worship any other god: |
| LAMSA | 1933 | But you must destroy their altars, break their images, and cut down their *idols*. |
| KNOX | 1944 | Destroy their altars, break their images, cut down their *forest shrines*. |
| MODL | 1945 | Instead you must break down their altars, smash their images and cut down their *sacred trees*. |
| JER | 1966 | You are to tear down their altars, smash their *standing stones,* cut down their sacred poles. |
| LIV | 1971 | Instead, you must break down their heathen altars, smash the *obelisks* they worship, and cut down their *shameful idols*. |
| TEV | 1976 | Instead, tear down their altars, destroy their *sacred pillars*, and cut down their symbols of the *goddess Asherah*. |
| NIV | 1978 | Break down their altars, smash their *sacred stones* and cut down their Asherah poles. |
| LIVT | 1981 | You must shatter their altars, break down their sacred pillars, and cut down their *Asherah trees*. |
| NKJV | 1982 | But you shall destroy their altars, break their sacred pillars, and cut down their *wooden images*. |
| NJER | 1985 | You will tear down their altars, smash their *cultic stones* and cut down their sacred poles. |
| ARATN | 1987 | For you shall destroy their *objects of divination*, and you shall break their pillars, and you shall cut their Asherim. |
| EB | 1987 | But destroy their altars. Break their *stone pillars.* Cut down their *Asherah idols.* |
| ETR | 1987 | But destroy their altars. Break the *stones they worship*. Cut down their idols. |
| FOX | 1995 | Rather: their *slaughter-sites* you are to pull down, their *standing-pillars* you are to smash, their *tree-poles* you are to cut down. |

| NIrV | 1996 | Tear down their altars. Smash their **sacred stones**. Cut down the **poles they use to worship the goddess Asherah.** |
| NLT | 1996 | Instead, you must break down their **pagan altars**, smash the **sacred pillars** they worship, and cut down their **carved images**. |

# 29 Differing Translations

A frequent theme throughout the Bible is to label all competing religions as **"*pagan.*"** These pagan religions were always denigrated, and portrayed in the worst possible light. Negative images, such as prostitution and witchcraft, were always linked to these competing religions.

I once saw an exhibit at the National Archives in Washington D. C. of World War II posters. (A book entitled *Posters of World War II* contains many of these posters.[251]) It was astonishing to see the blatant hatred and stereotyping of the Japanese and Germans portrayed on those government sponsored posters. I'm not defending our enemies of World War II—especially given my family history. I'm simply pointing out one method used to increase patriotism in the United States was to villainize our enemies. Similarly, the ancient Israelites raised their nationalism by denigrating the neighboring religions, which were in competition with their own.

Let's examine two different versions of a verse to see how Jezebel, who worshipped Baal, was portrayed.

> But he said: "What peace could there be as long as there are the *fornications* of Jezebel your mother and her many *sorceries?*" [252]

> And he answered, "How can peace exist, as long as the *fornications* of your mother Jezebel and her *witchcrafts* are many?[253]

All people living in Canaan spoke the same language. Hebrews could enter a service for Baal, Asherah, or Astarte, and understand the service. These other religions had temples where the God resided in the *Holy of Holies*, or the cabinet. These other religions also practiced mediumship, and had rituals similar to the Hebrews. The primary difference was the god had a different name. If you went to worship Baal, you gave your sacrifice to the priests of Baal, not the Hebrew priests. Your visit to Baal meant an empty dinner plate for the priests of Jehovah. That is why Hebrew priests hated other religions, and claimed that Jehovah was jealous, demanding the destruction of these other gods. Hebrew priests wanted to eliminate their competition. These priests of the other gods had the Gifts of the Spirit. Both Hebrew prophets, and priests of competing religions, were threats to the psychically ungifted Hebrew priests.

---

[251] Gregory, G. H., ed. *Posters of World War II*. NY: Gramercy Books, 1993.

[252] 2 Kings 9:22 [NWT].

[253] 2 Kings 9:22 [AMP].

Hebrew priests used every conceivable ruse to cover their tracks. They inserted laws into the Bible that would eliminate their competition. They made it a sin to consult a medium, or to worship another God. They would even fake the Gifts of the Spirit to insure their continuous flow of "sacrificial" food and money.

## How Priests Mimicked the Prophets

The Hebrew priests were supposed to be the communication link between two realms. Since the priests didn't have the Gifts of the Spirit, they could only mimic what the mediums did. Priests hoped that the people would not notice the difference.

In our discussion of the cabinet, we found evidence that people understood that ectoplasm would be present.

> **And all the people saw the pillar of cloud at the tent door, and all the people rose up and worshipped, every man at his tent door.**[254]

Priests realized that people expected to see ectoplasm during a psychic demonstration. So this is what they wrote into the Bible:

> **You are to make an altar to make incense smoke. You are to make it of acacia lumber, a cubit in length and a cubit wide.** [255]

> **He put the golden altar [of incense] in the tent of meeting before the veil; He burned sweet incense [symbol of prayer] upon it; as the Lord commanded him. And he set up the hanging or screen at the door of the tabernacle. Moses put the altar of burnt offering at the door of the tabernacle of the tent of meeting, and offered on it the burnt offering and the cereal offering; as the Lord commanded him.**[256]

The Hebrews knew there was a smoky pillar of cloud near the cabinet when Moses held a séance. The pillar of cloud indicated the presence of God. Hebrews understood the only opportunity they had to ask God a question and receive an answer was when they saw the pillar of cloud. Priests were compelled to imitate the pillar of cloud. They hung the curtain as Moses had done. (See the Silver Belle pictures at the end of chapter 12.) Since the priests were not psychically gifted, they could not produce ectoplasm, so they burnt smoky incense instead. The incense, as **AMP** so kindly informs us, is to be a *symbol of prayer*. This is not just a theory—the Bible states it clearly. Compare these two verses:

---

[254] Exodus 33:10 [AMP] [E].

[255] Exodus 30:1 [WBC] [E].

[256] Exodus 40:26 [AMP] [P].

# LEVITICUS CHAPTER 16 VERSE 12-13

| NIV | 1978 | He is to take a censer full of burning coals from the altar before the Lord and two handfuls of finely ground fragrant incense and take them behind the curtain. He is to put the incense on the fire before the Lord, and the *smoke of the incense* will conceal the atonement cover above the Testimony, so that he will not die. |
|-----|------|------|
| NRSV | 1990 | He shall take a censer full of coals of fire from the altar before the Lord, and two handfuls of crushed sweet incense, and he shall bring it inside the curtain and put the incense on the fire before the Lord, that the *cloud of the incense* may cover the mercy seat that is upon the covenant, or he will die. |

It cannot be clear! Priests placed burning incense behind the curtain to produce a thick smoky cloud. This would duplicate ectoplasm coming from behind the curtain of a medium's cabinet. Hebrews expected to see this smoky substance. However, they were not sophisticated enough to notice the difference between the genuine ectoplasm and the priests' smoky incense. People were duped by the priests' imitation. Within twenty to thirty years, the new tradition became entrenched. A child would ask his father, "Why do priests burn incense inside the tabernacle?" The father, who did not remember seeing genuine psychic phenomena, says, "I don't know son, they've always done it that way." It only takes a decade or two to replace real mediumship with imitation.

The people outside a cabinet where authentic mediumship was being demonstrated often saw lights along the front curtain. Priests realized that if they wanted to delude people into believing they were talking to a real Spirit, they needed a light in front of the curtain. Hence, the priests wrote this verse into the Bible:

> **The Lord said to Moses, "Command the Israelites to bring you clear oil of pressed olives for the light so that the lamps may be kept burning continually. Outside the curtain of the Testimony in the Tent of Meeting, Aaron is to tend the lamps before the Lord from evening till morning, continually. This is to be a lasting ordinance for the generations to come.**[257]

The priesthood launched the most extensive deception ever perpetrated on humanity, when they disguised the fact that they did not have the Gifts of the Spirit. The priest-written book of Leviticus contains the evidence of this sham. The first aspect of this cover-up concerns death.

Carl has been present at the deathbeds of many people. His clairvoyance enabled him to watch the soul leave the body and make its passage into the Spirit World. Since Carl is also an ordained minister, he has handled many funerals. During these ceremonies, he has clairvoyantly seen the newly "departed soul" who remains invisible to most of the people attending the funeral. Carl can communicate

---

[257] Leviticus 24:1-3 [NIV] [P].

with the new member of the Spirit World, and comfort the people who remain behind in the physical world. In addition, Carl is able to tell these people that their loved one has successfully made the journey into a new realm. The person who suffered from an intensely painful disease in the physical world, is now liberated and living without pain in the Spirit realm.

One would think this would happen in all religions. Priests, ministers, and rabbis would comfort grieving families. However, we find evidence in the Bible that the opposite is true. Priests were forbidden to enter a cemetery, or to have anything to do with a person who has died!

> **Then the Lord said to Moses, "Speak to the priests, the sons of Aaron, and say to them: No one shall defile himself for a dead person among his people, except for his relatives who are nearest to him, his mother and his father and his son and his daughter and his brother, also for his virgin sister, who is near to him because she has had no husband; for her he may defile himself.**[258]

When priests wrote these verses, stating they were not to visit a cemetery, they were protecting themselves from being discovered. They didn't want people to realize they lacked the Gift of Clairvoyance. A priest was only permitted to "defile himself " for a member of his immediate family. These family members had a vested interest in protecting the priesthood. They were also eating from their father's, son's, or brother's plate. They would never reveal that their family member was not clairvoyant.

Chapter 21 of the book of Leviticus provides an escape clause for priests—one that excused them from officiating funerals. The prohibition—keeping priests away from dead bodies was imperative to protect their secret.

This next verse is even more mysterious. Priests were forbidden to preside over the funeral for the leader of the country. This was much too risky. Hundreds of people would want assurance that the prince of the country had made a safe transition. When you study the chart for this verse, notice that many Bibles change the subject, attempting to conceal the fact that a priest should *not* preside over the funeral of the nation's leader.

## LEVITICUS CHAPTER 21 VERSE 4

| KJV | 1611 | But he shall not defile himself being a **chief man** among his people, to profane himself. |
|-----|------|----|
| COV | 1535 | Moreover he shall not defile himself upon any **ruler** in his people to unhallow himself. |
| GRT | 1540 | But he shall not be defiled upon him that hath **authority** among his people, to pollute himself for him. |

---

[258] Leviticus 21:1-3 [NASB] [P].

| GEN | 1560 | He shall not lament for the *prince* among his people, to pollute himself. |
|---|---|---|
| HAAK | 1657 | He shall not defile himself (over) a *Chief (Or, Ruler, Governor)* |
| PUR | 1764 | A *Husband among his People* shall not be defiled, to profane himself. |
| BELL | 1818 | A *chief* among the people, shall not be unclean; or profane himself. |
| YLT | 1898 | A *master [priest]* doth not defile himself among his people--to pollute himself; |
| BYIN | 1972 | He shall not defile himself, *husband, among his kinsfolk,* to profane him. |
| BECK | 1976 | As the *head of his family* he should not get unclean making himself unholy. |
| GLT | 1993 | A *leader* shall not defile himself among his people, to pollute himself; |
| GODWD | 1995 | As the *head of your people*, you should never become unclean. |
| NLT | 1996 | As a *husband among his relatives*, he must not defile himself. |

# 13 Differing Translations

These other versions discuss completely different subjects! Fascinating, since all are translations of the same Hebrew text. Translators are so paranoid about this verse, they hide what the original Hebrew said. Would people question why God would forbid a priest to officiate at the funeral of the leader of a country?

| KJV | 1611 | But he shall not defile himself being a chief man among his people, to profane himself. |
|---|---|---|
| GEDD | 1792 | He shall not dishonor himself by incurring uncleanness on her account. |
| THOM | 1808 | He must not defile himself unexpectedly among his people, to occasion their defilement. |
| BOTR | 1824 | But if she have a husband, among his people, he shall not defile himself for her by any uncleanness. |
| BREN | 1844 | He shall not defile himself suddenly among his people, to profane himself. |
| YNG | 1863 | A master priest doth not defile himself among his people—to pollute himself. |
| FENT | 1922 | He shall not debase, or degrade himself with grief. |
| MOFF | 1922 | He must not defile himself by mourning among his kinsfolk, so as to profane himself. |
| SMGO | 1939 | He must not defile himself for those related to him by marriage by profaning himself. |
| MODL | 1945 | As a family man he shall not render himself unclean among the people so as to profane himself. |
| RSV | 1952 | He shall not defile himself as a husband among his people and so profane himself. |
| SEPT | 1954 | He must not defile himself unexpectedly among his people, to occasion their defilement. |
| NASB | 1960 | He shall not defile himself as a relative by marriage among his people, and so profane himself. |
| NWT | 1961 | He may not defile himself for a woman possessed by an owner among his people so as to make himself profane. |
| CONF | 1965 | But for a sister who has married out of his family he shall not make himself unclean; this would be a profanation. |
| JER | 1966 | If a husband, he must not make himself unclean for his family, in doing so he would profane himself. |
| NAB | 1970 | But for a sister who has married out of his family he shall not make himself unclean; this would be a profanation. |
| SEPZ | 1970 | He shall not defile himself suddenly among his people, to profane himself. |
| LIV | 1971 | For the priest is a leader among his people and he may not ceremonially defile himself as an ordinary person can. |

| NEB | 1976 | Nor shall he make himself unclean for any married woman among his father's kin, and so profane himself. |
|-----|------|---|
| TEV | 1976 | He shall not make himself unclean at the death of those related to him by marriage. |
| NIV | 1978 | He must not make himself unclean for the people related to him by marriage, and so defile himself. |
| LIVT | 1981 | [However,] a husband may not defile himself for his [dead] wife if she is legally unfit for him. |
| NJER | 1985 | But for a close female relation who is married he will not make himself unclean; he would profane himself. |
| TANK | 1985 | But he shall not defile himself as a kinsman by marriage, and so profane himself. |
| EB | 1987 | But a priest must not make himself unclean if the dead person was only related to him by marriage. |
| ETR | 1987 | But a priest must not make himself unclean if the dead person was only one of his slaves. |
| HIRS | 1989 | But a husband shall not render himself impure among his people regarding a marriage which was a desecration for him. |
| REB | 1989 | Nor is he to make himself unclean for any married woman among his father's kin, and so profane himself. |
| NRSV | 1990 | But he shall not defile himself as a husband among his people and so profane himself. |
| NCV | 1991 | But a priest must not make himself unclean if the dead person was only related to him by marriage. |
| WBC | 1992 | He may not make himself unclean for those related by marriage, for he would defile himself. |
| CEV | 1995 | Don't make yourself unclean by attending the funeral of someone related to you by marriage. |
| NIrV | 1996 | But he must not make himself "unclean" by going near the bodies of people who were only related to him by marriage. Going near them would make him "unclean." |
| STONE | 1996 | A husband among his people shall to contaminate himself to one who desecrates him. |

# 34 Translations Ignore the Subject!

The high priest was more severely restricted than the rest of the priesthood. He was not even to attend the funeral of his parents, or any relative, nor was he allowed to leave the sanctuary.

> **And he that is the high Priest among his brethren, upon whose head the anointing oil was poured, and that is consecrated to put on the garments, shall not uncover his head, nor rent his clothes: Neither shall he go in to any dead body, nor defile himself for his father, or his mother: Neither shall he go out of the Sanctuary, nor profane the Sanctuary of his God; for the crown of the anointing oil of his God is upon him: I am the Lord.[259]**

These severe restrictions placed on the High priest were to protect the same secret. The high priest should be the best priest, therefore, he should be the most gifted medium. Of course, this was not true. This secret forced the high priest to

---

[259] Leviticus 21:10 [KJV].

isolate himself from the people. This separation protected him from being asked questions he would be unable to answer.

To satisfy their desire for an easy lifestyle, priests played a deceitful trick on their followers and plunged them into ignorance. Priests successfully fooled the people with their "smoke and mirror" routine. People began to believe that the mirror image was real. People no longer went to mediums. They looked to priests to be the intermediaries between themselves and Spirit. Priests led people away from spiritual guidance, and plunged them into a world of darkness and ignorance. Millions of people were deprived of the opportunity to communicate with God to receive divine guidance.

Carl told me of a case in the New London area, where the members of the Catholic Church worked very hard to raise a large sum of money to purchase new carpeting for their church. When the parishioners had reached their goal, they arranged for a special ceremony to have the money blessed. When the bishop arrived, he walked down the aisle of the church to the altar, picked up the money, turned, and walked out of the church. The carpeting was never purchased. No member of the congregation dared to ask the bishop why he had taken their hard-earned money.

The whole world has followed the priest's pattern of greed. In our dog-eat-dog world, people have become self-absorbed, and are not concerned about their fellow-human beings. This is why our world is growing so unbalanced, and is ready to collapse upon us.

Fortunately, the day is rapidly approaching when this ancient conflict between priests and mediums will be over. When the New Age of Knowledge arrives, humankind will change. Priests will finally lose their control over people's minds. No longer will people believe the dark, ignorant views. People will turn their backs on the "smoke and mirror games." People will turn to face the light of knowledge. When this happens, mediumship will also die. People will no longer need an intermediary between themselves and the Spirit World. In this New Age of Knowledge, everyone will be his own medium. Everyone will be directly connected to the infinite wisdom of the universe that emanates from the World of Spirit.

# FIFTEEN

## I'm Outraged!

It was the spring of 1985. I was looking forward to summer vacation, especially since I had made plans to travel to Israel and Egypt. I wanted to visit the places I had read about in the Bible, and to explore the pyramids. I had already booked my trip with a travel agent when Carl called me with disturbing news. He was seeing American airplanes in the Middle East being hijacked, and the passengers held hostage. Two weeks later, terrorists hijacked a TWA airplane, the same airline on which I was scheduled to fly. Since it seemed possible that more hijackings could occur, I decided to change my plans. Reluctantly, I contacted the travel agent and canceled my trip. Luckily, TWA was giving full refunds to people who cancelled their travel plans to the Middle East. All of my travel plans evaporated with one brief phone call.

Three days later, I received another phone call from Carl. His voice could not conceal his excitement. "Yesterday I received a phone call from one of my clients who lives near Chicago. She told me she's discovered a psychic camp in Indiana, where trumpet séances are being held. I've decided to drive out there to attend some of these séances. Two of my students have decided to go. Would you be interested in going?"

"What exactly is a trumpet séance? Do you know anything about this camp?" I asked.

"It's in Chesterfield, Indiana, and was quite famous a while back," Carl replied, "but they did have some problems. People were faking mediumship. I understand that they've cleaned up their act. I cannot guarantee what we will find there, but why don't you come and we'll see what happens."

I agreed to go. Our drive to Indiana would take about two and a half days. As the four of us travelled though Pennsylvania, the lush green rolling hills made a beautiful backdrop for a lesson about trumpet mediumship.

The greatest trumpet séance in history took place during the lifetime of Moses. People steeped in the Judeo-Christian ethic are most familiar with the information known as *The Ten Commandments* that came through the trumpet from Spirit. God instructed Moses to build two trumpets.

**The Lord spoke to Moses and said: Make two trumpets of beaten silver and use them for summoning the community and for**

**breaking camp.**[260]

A medium's trumpet must be made of metal—not a ram's horn. God instructed Moses to make these trumpets so that Spirit could communicate with all Hebrews directly:

> **And the Lord said to Moses, Lo I am coming to you in a thick cloud, that the people may hear when I speak with you, and may also believe you forever.**[261]

When the Lord said, **"he was coming in a thick cloud,"** he was referring to ectoplasm. God understood the frailties of human beings, which prevent them from believing anything they can not see, hear, or touch. As the Hebrews proceeded on their long journey from Egypt to Israel, God gave instructions to Moses clairaudiently. Although Moses could hear God's voice, the rest of the Hebrews heard nothing. Moses enforced God's rules. It would have been easy for the Hebrews to resent these laws, to believe that Moses himself, was inventing them. God wanted to prove to the Hebrews that Moses was communicating with Him. God wanted the people to hear Him speaking the commandments with their own ears. Trumpet mediumship was utilized.

God gave Moses specific instructions explaining how the Hebrew people should prepare for this great trumpet séance.

> **Go down now and see that the people are ready for my visit. Sanctify them today and tomorrow, and have them wash their clothes. Then, the day after tomorrow, I will come down upon Mt. Sinai as all the people watch. Set boundary lines the people may not pass, and tell them beware do not go up into the mountain, or even touch its boundaries whoever does shall die. No hand shall touch him, but he shall be stoned or shot to death with arrows, whether man or animal.**[262]

No one could cross the boundary because the high amount of psychic energy needed to produce the ectoplasm, could kill a person, just as a high volt of electricity could. A disturbance of the ectoplasm would end the phenomena, and could be fatal to the medium.

> **So it came about on the third day, when it was morning, that there were thunder and lightning flashes and a thick cloud upon the mountain and a very loud trumpet sound, so that all the people who were in the camp trembled. And Moses brought the people**

---

[260] Numbers 10:1-2 [NEB].

[261] Exodus 19:9 [RSV].

[262] Exodus 19:9 [LIV].

**out of the camp to meet God, and they stood at the foot of the mountain. Now Mount Sinai was all in smoke because the Lord descended upon it in fire; and its smoke ascended like the smoke of a furnace, and the whole mountain quaked violently.**[263]

It is evident from these verses that the ancient Hebrews clearly understood that God was on Mount Sinai because there was smoke visible on the mountain. The smoke indicated the presence of God. Spirit had drawn ectoplasm from all the people, which is why they had had to prepare themselves for three days before this séance. The next verse is the all-important one. The NASB reads:

**When the *sound of the trumpet* grew louder and louder, Moses spoke and God answered him with *thunder*."**[264]

This small verse has tremendous importance. It is this verse that demonstrates how theologians have manipulated the original Hebrew to bury the psychic truth. This verse, when accurately translated, proves that God communicated to the Hebrews through trumpet mediumship. We will first examine the original Hebrew, using *The Interlinear Hebrew-English Old Testament*. This Bible has the English translation directly under each Hebrew word. Please note that the syntax (the word order) of Hebrew will be different than English. [You need to read this quotation from the right to the left.] Verse 19 reads:

| הוֹלֵךְ | הַשׁוֹפָר | קוֹל | וַיְהִי |
|---|---|---|---|
| growing | *the trumpet* | *sound of* | And he was |

| יְדַבֵּר | מֹשֶׁה | מְאֹד | וְחָזֵק |
|---|---|---|---|
| he spoke | Moses | very and | being loud |

| בְקוֹל | יַעֲנֶנּוּ | וְהָאֱלֹהִים |
|---|---|---|
| [265]*with thunder* | he answered him | and the God |

*The Interlinear Hebrew-English Old Testament* agrees with NASB in its translation of this verse. The significant Hebrew words in this verse are קוֹל (*Kol*)=*Sound*, בְקוֹל (*Vekol*)=*Thunder*, and הַשׁוֹפָר (*Hashofar*)=*Trumpet*.

But *The Englishman's Hebrew and Chaldee Concordance* provides the key to the psychically correct translation. It indicates that the word קוֹל (*Kol*) may be translated as:

**aloud, bleating, crackling, cry, cry out, fame, lightness, lowing,**

---

[263] Exodus 19:16-19 [NASB].

[264] Exodus 19:19 [NASB].

[265] Exodus 19:19 [Kohlenberger, John R., III. *The NIV Interlinear Hebrew-English Old Testament*. Vol. 1. Grand Rapids, MI: Zondervan, 1979.] p. 200.

noise, peace, proclaim, sing, sound, speak, thunder, thundering, *voice*, yell.[266]

This verse demonstrates how theologians, ignorant of the Gifts of the Spirit, stripped out the psychically correct meaning of the Hebrew text from the English translations of the Old Testament. Compare NASB with KJV, which contains the clear, psychically correct, translation. קוֹל הַשׁוֹפָר (*Kol Hashofar*) is translated as *Voice of the Trumpet*.

**And when the *voice of the trumpet* sounded long, and waxed louder and louder.**[267]

Let's examine the first half of this verse to see how the Hebrew phrase קוֹל הַשׁוֹפָר (*Kol Hashofar*) was translated.

# EXODUS CHAPTER 19 VERSE 19A

| KJV | 1611 | And when the ***voice of the trumpet*** sounded long, and waxed louder and louder |
| --- | --- | --- |
| LWYC | 1395 | And the ***sound of the clarion*** encreesside litil and litil, and was holdun forth lengere |
| TAV | 1539 | And the ***voice of the horn*** blew and waxed louder and louder |
| GEN | 1560 | And when the ***sound of the trumpet*** blew long, and waxed louder and louder |
| GEDD | 1792 | And the ***trumpet-like sound*** became progressive stronger and stronger |
| RAY | 1799 | And when the ***trumpet sounded*** long, waxing still louder, Moses said, I exceedingly fear and quake |
| THOM | 1808 | Still the ***sounds of the trumpet*** waxed louder and louder |
| BOTR | 1824 | And when the ***sound as of a trumpet*** grew stronger and stronger |
| LEES | 1856 | And the ***voice of the cornet*** went on, and waxed louder and louder |
| SPUR | 1885 | And when the ***blast of the trumpet*** went forth, and increased louder and louder |
| ROTH | 1897 | And as oft as the ***sound of the horn*** went on and became exceedingly loud |
| FENT | 1922 | And there was a continuous ***sound of a trumpet*** |
| MOFF | 1922 | As the ***trumpet blast*** grew louder and louder |
| MODL | 1945 | When the ***loud trumpet peal*** grew louder and louder |
| FRISH | 1977 | And then the ***voice of the shofar*** sounded louder and louder, |
| LIVT | 1981 | There was the ***sound of a ram's horn***, increasing in volume to a great degree. |
| NJER | 1985 | Louder and louder grew the ***trumpeting***. |
| TANK | 1985 | The ***blare of the horn*** grew louder and louder. |
| TFFR | 1986 | And as the ***voice of the clarion*** sounded long, and grew louder and louder, |
| ETR | 1987 | The ***noise from the trumpet*** became louder and louder. |

[266] *The Englishman's Hebrew and Chaldee Concordance of the Old Testament Vol 1.* London: Walton and Maberrly, 1866. p. 35.

[267] Exodus 19:19 [KJV].

| WBC | 1987 | The *sound of the ram's horn* meanwhile was moving, and growing very strong. |
|---|---|---|
| HIRS | 1989 | And while the *tones of the Shofar* waxed louder and louder |
| CEV | 1995 | The **trumpet blew** louder and louder. |
| FOX | 1995 | Not the **shofar sound** was growing exceedingly stronger |
| NLT | 1996 | As the *horn blast* grew louder and louder |
| STONE | 1996 | The *sound of the shofar* grew continually much stronger; |

# 26 Differing Translations

We discover that there are 26 variations in the translation of קוֹל הַשׁוֹפָר (*Kol Hashofar*). Some Bible translators wish to disguise the word הַשׁוֹפָר (*Hashofar*)/*Trumpet*, by using words such as **horn** or **cornet**.

WBC is interesting because it translates הַשׁוֹפָר (*Hashofar*) /*Trumpet* two different ways. In this verse הַשׁוֹפָר (*Hashofar*) is translated as **Ram's Horn**. Yet in Numbers 10:2 הַשׁוֹפָר (*Hashofar*) is translated as **Trumpet**.

> **And Yahweh spoke to Moses, saying, "Make for yourself two silver trumpets. You shall make them of beaten work.[268]**

What caused the confusion? What would cause the translators of WBC to translate the Hebrew word, הַשׁוֹפָר (*Hashofar*) differently in these two verses? Are they trying to conceal that the Ten Commandments came through trumpet mediumship, by bypassing the word "trumpet" and using "Ram's Horn" in Exodus 19:19?

The other variations, which use the words "sound" and "noise," are correctly translated in a technical sense, since these variations are found within *The Englishman's Hebrew and Chaldee Concordance*. It becomes apparent that the only correct translation for the words קוֹל הַשׁוֹפָר (*Kol Hashofar*) is the *Voice of the Trumpet*.

Let's examine the second half of the verse. Here the Hebrew word בְקוֹל (*Vekol*) is the key word. NASB reads:

> **While Moses was speaking and God answering him with thunder.[269]**

Compare this with the King James Version, which is psychically correct:

> **Moses spake, and God answered him by a voice.[270]**

Again, both, "Thunder" and "Voice" are technically correct translations of the Hebrew word בְקוֹל (*Vekol*). An understanding of psychic phenomena would

---

[268] Numbers 10:1-2 [WBC].

[269] Exodus 19:19 [NASB].

[270] Exodus 19:19 [KJV].

indicate that the only correct choice would be "Voice of the Lord." Study the chart and examine the 18 variations in the second half of the verse.

## EXODUS CHAPTER 19 VERSE 19B

| KJV | 1611 | Moses spake, and God answered him *by a voice*. |
|-----|------|------------------------------------------------|
| COV | 1535 | Moses spake, and God *answered him* loud. |
| HAAK | 1657 | Moses spake, and God answered him *with a voice* {in a softer way then by thunder, and the terrible noise of the trumpet } |
| GEDD | 1792 | While Moses spoke, and God *vocally answered him*. |
| LEES | 1856 | Moses spoke, and God answered him with *a loud voice*. |
| SMGO | 1939 | Moses spoke, and God answered him with *a thunder pea*l. |
| KNOX | 1944 | And then Moses spoke to the Lord, and the Lord's *voice was heard in answer*. |
| OGD | 1950 | Moses' words were answered by the *voice of God*. |
| RSV | 1952 | Moses spoke, and God answered him *in thunder*. |
| LIV | 1971 | Moses spoke and God *thundered his reply*. |
| BYIN | 1972 | Moses speaking and God *answering him with sound*. |
| NEB | 1976 | Whenever Moses spoke, God answered him in *a peal of thunder*. |
| ARATJ | 1987 | Moses spoke, and he received an answer from before the Lord *in a sweet and majestic voice, and sweet was the tone*. |
| ARATN | 1987 | Moses spoke in a pleasant voice, and from before the Lord answer was made to him *in thunder*. |
| ETR | 1987 | Every time Moses spoke to God, God answered him with *a voice like thunder*. |
| WBC | 1987 | Moses spoke, and God answered him in *a rumble of thunder*. |
| HIRS | 1989 | Moses spake and God answered him *loudly*. |
| FOX | 1995 | Moses kept speaking, and God kept answering him in the *sound (of a voice)*. |

## 18 Differing Translations

Six verses later, God delivers the Ten Commandments. This all-important communication is proceeded by the words:

**Then God spoke all these words saying...**[271]

This is another case where valuable information about psychic phenomena is embedded in the original Hebrew, but is absent in the English translation. *The Interlinear Hebrew English Old Testament* again unveils the hidden meanings in this small verse.

| לֵאמֹר | הָאֵלֶּה | הַדְּבָרִים | כָּל | אֵת | אֱלֹהִים | וַיְדַבֵּר |
|--------|----------|-------------|------|-----|----------|-----------|
| to say | the these | the words | all of | *** | God | and he spoke[272] |

---

[271] Exodus 20:1 [NASB].

Notice this Hebrew sentence (read from right to left) has two verbs that mean *spoke* and *say*! In chapter 10, I explained that in Hebrew there are families of words, based on a three consonant root. I discussed that there are two nouns meaning *oracle* דְּבִיר ((*debir* (noun)), דָּבָר ((*dâbâr* (noun)) and one verb דָּבַר ((*dâbar* (verb)). Notice that this Hebrew sentence begins with the Verb form of oracle—וַיְדַבֵּר (*vahydahbeir*). The Hebrew word הַדְּבָרִים (*had'veem*) translated as *the words* God spoke belongs to this same family of Hebrew words meaning *oracle*. An accurate translation of this verse would be, *"And the Gods (Spirit) using the psychic gift of trumpet mediumship, spoke the words of this oracle."*

God delivers the Ten Commandments through a medium's trumpet. These commandments are found in Exodus 20:2-17. The two verses [18-19] that follow the commandments reaffirm that God spoke to the people directly, with his voice coming through the trumpet. The Hebrews had heard the voice of God.

> **And all the people saw the thunderings, and the lightnings, and the voice of the trumpet, and the mountain smoking: and when the people saw it, they trembled, and stood afar off. And they said unto Moses, Speak thou with us, and we will hear: but let not God speak with us, lest we die.[273]**

It is sad to discover that theologians have twisted the language to hide the truth. The Hebrews were privileged to witness one of the highest forms of psychic phenomena—trumpet mediumship. For the first time they were able to hear the voice that guided Moses. This voice was responsible for their liberation from slavery in Egypt. The theologians who translated the King James Bible in 1611 had no problem translating this verse accurately. Many 20th century translators, with the benefit of newly discovered archaeological information, were so threatened by solid new evidence of psychic phenomena in the Bible that they deliberately chose other meanings for the Hebrew words to conceal the mediumship that God himself wanted the people to witness.

After two days of travel, we were finally on the road leading into Camp Chesterfield. We passed two rather rickety hotels, which reminded me of the hotel at Lilly Dale. Later we learned that the camp was ninety-nine years old—those hotels looked as if they had been standing there since the beginning. The rest of the camp was in much better shape. As we drove onto the grounds, we saw the administration building. We parked the car and walked over to it. We asked the silver haired lady behind the desk if there was anything planned for the evening. We were a bit shocked when she told us that a Vespers service would be starting in 15 minutes. She handed us a brochure that listed all the mediums who lived at the camp and their

---

272 Kohlenberger, John R., III. *The NIV Interlinear Hebrew-English Old Testament. Vol. 1.* Grand Rapids, MI: Zondervan, 1979. p. 200.

273 Exodus 20:18-19 [ERV].

gifts. Then she gave us directions to the small church in the middle of the grounds, where the service was to be held. We thanked her, and rushed to the service.

We entered the quaint white church, and sat in the last row. I was unfamiliar with the term *Vespers service*. I soon discovered that this service followed the same format as Carl's church services. The service began with a lecture given by a British medium. I vividly remember Gertrude Thomason, an auburn haired woman, dressed in an elegant evening gown, who spoke with a very pronounced English accent. We were very impressed with what she said.

After the lecture, a different medium did the message work. This is the part of the service where the medium becomes the bridge between the two realm. Spirits associated with individuals in the congregation take turns speaking to the medium, giving him personal information to relay. The message work medium that night was fascinating. Norman Williams was a psychic artist. He stood at the pulpit with his sketchpad. He would focus his attention on an individual and give a mini-reading, delivering messages from a departed loved one, or spiritual guide. As he talked with the person sitting in the church pew, he would sketch a picture of the Spirit that he was communicating with. When his mini-reading was over he would give the picture to the person in the congregation. It was quite fascinating.

At the conclusion of the service, our group remained behind. We wanted to talk to Gertrude Thomason. Carl did most of the talking. He discretely asked her which mediums she would recommend. We put this poor woman in a very awkward position, since all these mediums had a working relationship; she was very hesitant to say that one medium was better than another. We explained to her that we had come from New Jersey and Connecticut, and that this was our very first time visiting their camp.

She then said to us, "Are you aware that this is one of our convocation weekends? Many of the mediums of the camp will be teaching special weekend seminars dealing with all aspects of psychic phenomena. These classes will start tomorrow morning."

We were very surprised. There was a long pause, and then she said, "Well, you really should see Bill English." She explained to us that each medium has a book at the front of his or her house. Each séance is listed with the number of people allowed to attend. You simply sign the book to register for the séances that you wish to attend. The same was true for private readings. She then pointed us in the direction of Bill English's house. We thanked her for being so helpful.

We rushed over to Bill English's house. It was on the far end of the grounds. His book was in front of his house. As we thumbed through it we made a fantastic discovery. Bill English was a trumpet medium. He allowed only fifteen people to attend his séances. Miraculously, there were four openings remaining for his Monday morning trumpet séance. He was also doing another type of séance on Tuesday morning. We signed our names to attend both of these séances.

Now we had some time to explore. As we walked the grounds, the beauty of the camp impressed us. Camp Chesterfield was an amazing place; it had a very special, peaceful vibration. One felt a sense of pride—the lawns were immaculately trimmed, and there were flower arrangements wherever we turned.

There was a central green. Surrounding it were many small houses. This is where the mediums lived, and conducted their séances and readings. The cottages were very well maintained. Many had porches where people were sitting, waiting for their turn to see the medium. Many of the cottages had lavish gardens, all of which had small signs inviting people to come and enjoy the flowers and serenity. As we strolled the grounds, the hustle and bustle of daily life began to fade from our minds and bodies. Life at Camp Chesterfield was one of peace and tranquillity!

In addition to the mediums' cottages, there was a bookstore that sold hundreds of books dealing with psychic phenomena. The Cathedral was a large temple that could seat 1,000 people. It was there that special services were held on Saturday nights. There was a church where three services were held on a daily basis. There also was a small, peaceful, healing sanctuary, where people could go to meditate at any time, 24 hours a day.

It was the memorials that dotted the green that were so impressive. The title of one memorial was *The Trail of Religion*. It consisted of statues of nine great teachers who had came to bring truth and knowledge to us. Their teachings became the foundation of major religions. Eight of these teachers were in a semi-circle with a stone wall behind them. In the center of the semi-circle of his peers was the statue of Jesus. The following is a list of the great teachers depicted in this memorial:

**Vardhammana**  [848 B.C.] taught reincarnation and believed that trees, grass and even water had souls. **Jainism** grew from his teachings.

**GuatamaBuddah**  [500 B.C.] was one of the first teachers of reincarnation. Buddah means *enlightened one*. **Buddhism** is based on this great teacher's beliefs

**Confucius**  was a great scholar and teacher. **Confucianism** grew from his teachings.

**Lao-Tse**  [60 B.C.] founded the religion of **Taoism**. Lao-Tse believed that all of people's actions should be spontaneous, and that everything should be done on impulse.

**Zoroaster**  was a Persian prophet. He taught about an afterlife where people were judged according to how they lived their earthy life. **Zorasterism** was the religion that he founded.

**Osiris**  was the founder of sun worship in ancient Egypt.

**Abraham**  [1898 B.C.] was the Patriarch of the Jewish people. **Judaism** traces it heritage to him.

**Mohammed**  [589 A.D.] had a vision that explained that he was to be the prophet for Allah. The religion of **Islam** grew from his teachings.

**Zeus**  [980 B.C.] was the God of Greek myth.

**Jesus**  was the prophet of **Christianity**.

Although some of these statues looked a bit weather-beaten, they all emanated a vibration of reverence.

Close to *The Trail Of Religions* was a statue of a Native American invoking his Great White Spirit. There were many statues of Jesus on the grounds. The most unusual statue on the grounds was of an angel. I was puzzled by it for a while, because I didn't understand its significance. A few days later, I appreciated it. The angel held a trumpet in its left hand. This statue depicted a Spirit and the instrument of communication it used to talk to humanity.

Camp Chesterfield had an outstanding feature, the Hett Memorial Museum. It was captivating. The museum housed many valuable artifacts of mediums who had lived in the United States. Other interesting exhibits included pictures of materialized Spirits, and trumpets belonging to mediums who had worked at that camp.

The most impressive feature of this museum was the twenty-five portraits produced through the mediumship of the Bang sisters. Elizabeth S. and May E. Bang were very gifted mediums, and their gift was extremely unusual. They had the gifts of *direct* writing, drawing, and painting. In 1894 they developed a new technique, one, to my knowledge, that no other medium has demonstrated. They precipitated exquisitely beautiful color portraits of Spirit people.[274]

> **The portraits were produced as follows: two identical paper mounted canvases in wooden frames were held up face to face against the window with the lower half resting upon a table, and the sides held by each sister with one hand. A short curtain was hung on either side, and an opaque blind was drawn over the canvases. The light streamed from behind the canvases, which were translucent, and after a quarter of an hour the outline of shadows began to appear and disappear as the invisible artist made a preliminary sketch; then the picture began to grow at a feverish rate. When the pictures were separated, the portrait was found on the surface of the canvas next to the "sitter." Though the paint was greasy, and stuck to the finger on being touched, it left no stain on the paper, which covered closely the other canvas. Later, the works of art were openly precipitated as if by airbrush, and some took as a little as five minutes to complete and only one canvas was used.[275]**

As their gift developed, the sisters were able to do their Spirit portraits in full daylight, and discontinued the use of the cabinet. Art experts have examined these paintings and are quite baffled by them. The experts cannot determine what media

---

[274] Swann, Irene. *The Bang Sisters and the Precipitated Spirit Portraits.* Chesterfield, IN: Hett Memorial Art Gallery and Museum of Camp Chesterfield. n. d. p. 3.

[275] Swann, Irene. *The Bang Sisters and the Precipitated Spirit Portraits.* Chesterfield, IN: Hett Memorial Art Gallery and Museum of Camp Chesterfield. n. d. p. 3.

was used. In other words, they do not know if the paints on these portraits were oils, watercolor, pastels, charcoal, or some other type of material.[276] Upon close examination of the portraits, it is impossible to see any brush strokes. These Spirit portraits were on an artistic level comparable to famous artists such as Renior and Copley. They were as lifelike as photographs and the faces were breathtaking. The eyes of the people in the portraits seemed to stare straight into your soul.

People who went to the Bang sisters for a reading were asked to bring a photograph of departed relatives. They didn't show these pictures to the mediums. The precipitated portraits were not copies of the photographs. The facial features were close to the ones in the photograph but the colors in the Bang sisters' portraits were deeper in hue and richer. The subjects of the portraits are Spirits who were related to the sitters. The one exception was when the sitter was a widower, who had lost his twin daughters. A family portrait was precipitated, reuniting the whole family.[277]

**Many of the portraits changed when taken home. The hair on some would be altered to look as it had when the subject was on earth. A few blouses and dresses changed to seem more familiar, and in several cases the eyes would open and close. In one portrait of a spirit guide, pearls appeared around the neck a few days later when the "sitter" said that the girl always wore them. In another full-length picture, more flowers appeared on a rose bush.[278]**

Camp Chesterfield was the center for the Indiana Association of Spiritualists. I was surprised to find a very modern cafeteria was on the grounds of this 100-year-old Spiritualist camp. It reminded me of a cafeteria one might see in a public school. The one difference was that the tables had tablecloths on them. We learned that this cafeteria had been built recently. The Maxon family from Chicago had lost their only child, a son, in a tragic accident. This tragedy left them devastated. Through friends they learned about Camp Chesterfield. They decided they had nothing to lose and traveled to Indiana. It was during a trumpet séance that their son spoke to them. During their conversation he provided his parents with proof of his identity. He described events in his life that no one but his parents could know about. He told his parents that he was doing fine in his new home in the Spirit World. Then he encouraged them to stop their grieving, and to enjoy life the best they could. He was very happy they had come to Camp Chesterfield so he could speak with them.

---

[276] Swann, Irene. *The Bang Sisters and the Precipitated Spirit Portraits.* Chesterfield, IN: Hett Memorial Art Gallery and Museum of Camp Chesterfield. n. d. p. 4.

[277] Swann, Irene. *The Bang Sisters and the Precipitated Spirit Portraits.* Chesterfield, IN: Hett Memorial Art Gallery and Museum of Camp Chesterfield. n. d. p. 4.

[278] Swann, Irene. *The Bang Sisters and the Precipitated Spirit Portraits.* Chesterfield, IN: Hett Memorial Art Gallery and Museum of Camp Chesterfield. n. d. p. 4.

That profound experience changed these people's convictions about life and death. As they strolled the grounds, they noticed that there was no place for visitors to eat. This man wrote a check for $100,000, donating the money to the camp to build a cafeteria. Today this cafeteria is a living memorial to his son, and the comfort this family received though trumpet mediumship.

That night when we returned to the hotel, I couldn't sleep. I was too excited, as I thought of finally attending a trumpet séance. Tomorrow, at the Cathedral service, I would hear the voice of Spirit with my own ears! On that beautiful summer night in 1985, all I knew about trumpet mediumship was what Carl had recently taught me. I had a clear understanding of the mechanics of trumpet mediumship, and knew I would be hearing Spirit voices. However, I wasn't prepared for the shock I would receive, and the discovery I was about to make. For Carl had accidentally omitted one very powerful piece of information about this amazing form of mediumship.

Saturday morning our entire group attended the class we had signed up for. The teacher was quite informative and I thoroughly enjoyed the class. After class we spent some time exploring the camp, and studying what types of gifts different mediums had, and checking to see if they had openings in their schedules in the next few days. Since Carl was the only one of us who had experienced trumpet mediumship, he signed the four of us up for séances with three different trumpet mediums.

On Saturday night our group attended a special service in The Cathedral. When I saw the program for the service I became very excited. The service was going to be divided into three parts. The first was a lecture by a medium. The second was clairvoyant messages delivered by a second medium, and the third was a demonstration of trumpet mediumship.

As the service progressed, I was getting more and more excited. The lecture and clairvoyant messages were quite good. But they were "old hat" for me. I had seen these done hundreds of times before. It finally came time for the trumpet work. Assistants wheeled a cabinet out into the middle of the stage. A medium entered into the cabinet. There were guards posted at each of the building's entrances, and one on each stairway leading up to the stage. This was done to protect the medium, and to deter any trickery. The lights were shut off, leaving the auditorium in utter darkness. This was necessary so that the ectoplasm could be withdrawn from the medium's body to form the voice box. Any light entering the auditorium would destroy the ectoplasm and could kill the medium. Spirit placed the ectoplasmic voice box inside the trumpet in order to amplify the sound.

Before I knew it, I heard a voice. I don't have a vivid memory of this séance, because of what I experienced afterwards. I do know that some people in the audience were lucky enough to get a message from the trumpet voice. Someone would speak through the trumpet and say, "I want to speak to Sally." Then a conversation would take place between the Spirit and Sally. I must admit that I wasn't very impressed with the first message that came through the trumpet. It was like eavesdropping on a phone conversation. I heard two people talking about personal information and memories.

However, as the second Spirit began to speak, I nearly jumped out of my seat! I couldn't believe my ears! It was amazing! Could this be true? The second voice from the trumpet sounded different than the first. Each of the Spirits that came through the trumpet that night had a different voice!

The service ended, and we left the cathedral. We had to cross the entire camp to get to our rental car. Carl suggested that the four of us go for a cup of coffee. I was not in the mood to socialize. Carl looked at me with a puzzled expression. Then he said to the rest of the group, "Why don't you go to the cafeteria, and we will catch up with you later. I have something to discuss with Sidney." Then Carl and I walked in silence.

I was beyond words, in an emotional turmoil and in the throes of a great synthesis. Everything I had learned about mediumship was surfacing in my mind.

What I witnessed could have been experienced by billions of people during the last two millenniums, if religions' leaders had not been the enemy of the Gifts of the Spirit.

Thoughts kept angrily swarming my mind, as if they were bees, and I had just destroyed the hive. Each one delivered its sting of irony as it pierced my consciousness.

**The medium of Endor was called a witch.**[279]

**Find me a familiar Spirit vs. find me a Spirit of prophecy**[280]

**You must not suffer a witch to live.**[281]

**Anyone with a familiar Spirit must be stoned to death, their blood is upon them.**[282]

**Hilkiah just happen to find a scroll in the basement of the Temple, saying that all mediums should be executed.**[283]

**You must not bring God a defective animal to sacrifice.**[284]

**The way to have a stronger communication with your deceased relatives is to give a donation to the synagogue.**

**God does not talk to us any more because we are not worthy.**

---

[279] 1 Samuel 28:7 [MOFF].

[280] 1 Samuel 28:7 [KJV] and [COV].

[281] Exodus 22:18.

[282] Leviticus 20:27.

[283] 2 Kings 23:24.

[284] Deuteronomy 17:1.

**A Jewish priest can't go to the cemetery.**[285]

**The priests burned Joan of Arc as a witch, heretic and sorceress.**

**It is God's will to bring a hurricane or tornado to destroy your house, but it's the work of the devil to have a medium tell your future.**

**Don't ask questions about God's will.**

**The Bible is the word of God, it has not been changed or altered.**

The lies! The lies! How priests have lied! How religions have lied to billions upon billions of people! How could they be that deceptive? Priests labored so strenuously to bury the truth, leaving us in total ignorance, placing us in their control. Priests instilled the fear that terrorized us, chaining us to the false superstitions of limbo, purgatory, and a hell brimming with devils and demons.

I wish everyone could experience a trumpet séance and talk directly with loved ones that have passed over. They would hear for themselves a description of the Spirit World as a wonderful, peaceful place, and their fears of death would dissolve.

We had come to a beautiful fountain. I was leaning against a tree, kicking the dirt, and swearing. Carl had a puzzled look on his face. "What in the world is wrong? Why do you look like you are ready to eat nails and spit out battleships? You have just witnessed the real thing—a genuine trumpet séance. Why in the world would are you so angry?"

"Those bastards!" I said, "How could priests do this? How could they hide this from humanity? I'm outraged! I have never witnessed such strong and convincing mediumship, such undeniable evidence of life after death." Carl was amazed by my reaction, but understood it. He was flying high from witnessing such fantastic mediumship. Instead of sharing his high, I was outraged, and depressed.

For the first time, I felt the powerful realization of truth deep in my bones. Hearing the voice of the trumpet had suddenly transformed my faith and spirituality. Paul must have experienced a similar transformation, when he heard Jesus' voice on the road to Damascus. The event inspired him to teach the Gifts of the Spirit. This is why the priesthoods of organized religions prohibited mediumship, covered it up in the Bible, and still preach against it today.

---

[285] Leviticus 21:1-4.

# SIXTEEN

## My Father Speaks through the Trumpet

Monday morning, Carl and our group had an appointment with Bill English for a trumpet séance at 9:00 a.m. Needless to say, I was filled with anticipation. As we walked into the séance room, I was unaware that I still had much to learn about trumpet mediumship. This séance would become very significant in my education. Bill had built this séance room as an addition to his house. It had a separate entrance, so it didn't disturb his living quarters. It was a rather large, rectangular room, without any inside dividers or columns to hold up the roof. There were no windows in the room—when the lights were turned off it would be pitch black. The extreme darkness allowed Bill to work without the use of a cabinet. In effect, his whole séance room was his cabinet. There were many high, straight-backed wooden chairs, lining the perimeter of the walls. There was multi-colored wall to wall carpeting on the floor, and a rather ornately carved wooden chair to one side. The only furnishing in the room, was a very small round table. There were two items on the table—a bottle of ink and a stack of white polyester cloth, each piece cut to the same size.

I was unaware that Carl was trying to conceal his identity as a medium from Bill. Carl and Bill exchanged quips. I had no idea that Carl's purpose was to mentally control the light around his body. The aura around a medium is unique, making it easy for one clairvoyant to recognize another. Carl later explained to me that he had only been able to hide his identity from Bill for a few minutes. I remember Bill saying, "Oh no, I have to deal with another medium."

Carl and Bill English shared other qualities besides mediumship. Bill had a very easy-going personality. He was a rather tall, slim, middle-aged man. His wavy black hair did not reveal his age, nor did his eyeglasses conceal the twinkle in his eyes. Bill welcomed us, and asked us to take a seat anywhere we wished.

As soon as all fifteen people had arrived, Bill started to explain what would happen during the séance. He would lock the room and turn out the lights. We would be sitting in a pitch-black room, a requirement for trumpet mediumship. Bill picked up one of his three trumpets. They were about thirty-six inches tall. They looked like giant funnels, or perhaps a more accurate description would be giant, aluminum ice-cream cones. Bill had applied three strips of phosphorus tape, which glows in the dark, around each of the trumpets. As he was explaining all this to us, he held up each trumpet, one at a time, to the illuminated light bulb. He explained that he was charging the phosphorus. After the house lights were turned off, the Spirits would lift the trumpets off the ground and move them around. We would be able to keep track of where the trumpets were in the room because of the glow from the phosphorus tape.

Bill would sit in his chair and go into a deep trance state, allowing his Spirit to leave his body. Then Spirit would extract ectoplasm from his body and form a voice box to put inside one of the trumpets. A specific spirit, Dr. Louis, would come through the trumpet first. He would serve as the master of ceremonies for the séance, greet us, and announce who would receive the next message. We would then see the trumpet traveling over to the person receiving the message. When that Spirit finished his message, he would step back, or disconnect from the trumpet. Dr. Louis would announce the next Spirit to speak through the trumpet.

When Bill had finished charging the phosphorus bands on the three trumpets, he turned off the lights. It was time for the séance to begin! After a few moments, the three trumpets began to float off the ground. It was a remarkable sight. Then the trumpets began moving around the room. They moved in such a way that if Bill had been trying to fake this séance, he would have needed three hands to control the trumpets. The trumpets moved independently of each other in three distinct patterns. There was no way anyone could have faked this!

Slowly, two of the trumpets drifted to the ground. A voice came through the remaining trumpet, suspended in midair. It was Dr. Louis, who welcomed us. Then he asked us to cooperate with him and sing the song, "You are my Sunshine." We all sang the song in the dark room.

*[This puzzled me, so when I had the chance, I asked Awan why Dr. Louis had asked us to sing at this séance. Awan told me that singing causes the people in the room to harmonize their vibrational rate. It also provides energy that Spirit needs. Spirit accumulates the sound waves that the singers produce, and manipulates this energy to energize the voice in the trumpet. Even in ancient times, when people went to a medium, they would sing songs or chant. The sole purpose was to build up energy in the room, thus making it easier for the medium and the Spirit to communicate. This is why Christians included singing hymns during their church services. This is simply a carry over from ancient times, when the Gifts of the Spirit were practiced.]*

After our poor, out of tune rendition of the song, Dr. Louis thanked us for our cooperation. Then he asked if there was a Ellen in the room. Ellen responded by saying that she was present. The trumpet glided over to Ellen, and remained in midair. Dr. Louis announced that a relative of hers wanted to speak with her. Within moments the voice came through the trumpet, and the two of them began reminiscing about their time together.

I was a bit puzzled, as Ellen's relative's voice was similar to Dr. Louis's voice. Yet, for the moment, my wonder eclipsed my puzzlement. I just sat and listened.

During the séance, Carl's father spoke to him. Later my grandfather, who had died when I was ten years old, came to talk to me. It was difficult for me to remember his voice. All the voices sounded very much alike.

When the séance concluded, we walked towards the car. Although Carl was a medium himself, nothing pleased him more than finding another genuine medium. Carl's face seemed to light up as he watched another medium demonstrate the Gifts of the Spirit. Often when Carl discovered an outstanding medium, he would invite that medium to work at his church. Since I first met Carl, he had constantly pointed out the real mediums from the people trying to fake it. When we were in Lilly Dale, Carl sat next to me and discussed the quality of the messages each medium gave. Because of his tutelage, I was learning to determine if a person was faking it. Carl said to me, "Well how do you feel this time?"

"That wasn't the real thing, was it?" I asked.

"What do you mean," Carl said, with much agitation in his voice, "Of course that was the real thing."

"But the voices didn't sound different from one another." I exclaimed.

"I can't explain this at the moment, but I assure you that Bill English is a fantastic trumpet medium. In fact he is the best one I have ever seen!" said Carl.

I felt robbed. Again I should have been riding high from this séance, yet I wasn't. I was still disturbed. I hoped that tomorrow, when we had a second séance with Bill, I would feel differently—which is exactly what happened. Tuesday morning's séance was a very special moment in my life.

The Tuesday morning séance was a different type. It was called a precipitation séance. We were each given a 9 inch square piece of white polyester cloth. Bill told us we were to hold this cloth tautly by the sides. He then uncapped a bottle of India Ink and placed it on a table at the side of the room. During this séance, Spirit would take bits of ink and draw pictures on our cloth. Again Bill charged up the phosphorus on the trumpets, and the séance began.

As on the previous day, we sang to build up the energy. Although I had seen it the day before, my heart skipped a beat as the trumpets levitated up off the floor and sailed into the air. As they swirled around our heads I was filled with anticipation. Dr. Louis began speaking through one of the trumpets. He announced who would receive the first message. The trumpet went to the person. The voice started speaking. A bolt of electricity ran through my body. Today the voices all sounded different from each other!

Trumpet mediumship is a type of physical mediumship. Physical mediumship means that the Spirits move objects, or manipulate objects. Spirits physically make themselves known to the sitters of the séance. Physical mediumship is much more taxing and strenuous on the medium's body. There are many more variables than in mental mediumship. This was the reason the voices hadn't changed the day before. Conditions were not perfect. Perhaps there were too many skeptical people sitting in the séance. Their negative thoughts would be a drain on the psychic energy. That drain of energy might be enough to cause the voices to sound the same. In any event, there was no doubt at this séance. All the voices that came through the trumpet sounded different.

About mid-way through the séance, Dr. Louis sounded a bit concerned. "Oh, oh," he said, "we have a Native American here." The trumpet went silent, then suddenly there was a tremendous thundering **BOOM** that blasted through the trumpet. The sound just reverberated though the room. It was like an atomic explosion. I was so startled that I jumped out of my seat. The trumpet slowly began spinning around, almost like a majorette's baton in slow motion, or as if a person were dancing around a campfire. A Native American chant was coming from the trumpet. "Ah ye ya ha you he yaa." This lasted about a minute, then the Native spoke.

"My name is Lone Eagle, and I wish to speak to my beloved medium." It was Carl's Spirit control, coming to communicate with Carl.

"I am here, Lone Eagle." Carl replied.

An exchange followed. Carl had heard that voice all his life. It had become very familiar to him. But until this point, he had only heard the Chief's voice clairaudiently. This was the first time that Carl had heard the sound of Lone Eagle's voice. I don't remember the entire conversation. I do remember Carl sliding forward in his chair. He said, "I feel that I want to get down on my knees before you."

The Chief replied, "No, that will not be necessary, I do not wish you to do that."

The conversation lasted for a few more minutes. Then Lone Eagle said to Carl, "You have much work ahead of you. You are to be a spiritual farmer, planting spiritual seeds of truth. Do not let anyone's criticism or negativity prevent you from teaching the Gifts of the Spirit."

Lone Eagle's words sent shivers down my spine. At dinner the night before, Carl had told me of an experience he had had when he was nine years old. He was working on his father's farm, hoeing corn. An entity appeared to him and said, "You will not be this type of farmer in the future. You will become a spiritual farmer planting spiritual seeds in the minds of people."[286] Now Lone Eagle was giving Carl the same message.

Lone Eagle withdrew, allowing another Spirit to use the trumpet. A few more people, including the other two members of our group communicated with guides or loved ones. Suddenly Carl whispered to me, "I see your father. He is with his two brothers."

My father and his two brothers were in the Spirit World.

Carl continued, "I see them running from house to house, looking in at the mediums at work. Your father is shaking his head. He cannot accept that this is happening. Now I see him coming into this séance room. He is being hooked up to the trumpet."

Dr. Louis said, "I have someone here who wishes to talk to a man in the room, I believe his name is Sidney."

"Hello," I said.

Carl continued, "They are telling him to speak as if he were talking on the telephone."

"Hello," said the voice through the trumpet.

The voice startled me. That hello was exactly the way my father said hello.

"Hello," I said.

I don't remember all the details of that conversation. I wished it could have been taped, but that was against the rules of the camp. I remember my father discussed my mother, and the fact that I loved to travel. He thought that was a good opportunity to learn about other people and places.

---

[286] This refers to parables in Matthew 13.

I cannot say that the voice through the trumpet sounded exactly like my father's voice. It did not. Today there is such a thing as a voiceprint. It is like the fingerprint of a voice. If it were possible to make a comparison of the voiceprints of my father's voice and the voice of the trumpet, I know it would not have been an exact match. Although the voice was coming out of an ectoplasmic voice box, instead of the medium's voice box, some of the medium's qualities blend with the voices from Spirit. However, I *know* it was my father speaking through the trumpet. I know this because of his choice of words, the expressions that he used, the grammar that he used, and the enunciation of his words. And finally, no one said hello to me the way my father did.

There is one is fragment of our conversation that I clearly remember. No matter how hard I had tried, I could not convince my father when he was alive, that he would live on after he died. This is why the mediumship at Camp Chesterfield flabbergasted my father and his brothers. My father considered mediumship to be a bunch of hogwash.

"Well, Dad, you used to say that when you are dead, you are dead. Have you changed your mind yet?" I asked.

Without a moment's hesitation, my father said, "Some people say you have to live to learn, in my case I had to die to learn."

I suddenly remembered sitting in the synagogue, nearly two years before, listening to the rabbi say that the only way for a Jewish person to have a conversation with a deceased relative was through the *Yiskor* service. He had wanted me to give a donation to the synagogue to speak with my father. If I had, I certainly would not have heard my father's voice, as I just had. In the synagogue, I might have imagined his voice in my mind. In the séance room I heard his voice with my ears. And the rabbi was expecting far more than the $15 donation I gave to Bill English.

My conversation was the last one of the séance. After Dr. Louis finished saying good-bye to us, the séance ended. Bill English came out of his deep trance. He gave us specific instructions on what to do with the cloth before he turned on the lights.

My conversation was the last one of the séance. After Dr. Louis finished saying good-bye to us, the séance ended. Bill English came out of his deep trance. He gave us specific instructions on what to do with the cloth before he turned on the lights.

The images on the cloth would need about twelve hours to dry before they would become permanent. Before then, it was important that direct light be kept from them. Therefore, as if we were in a photographic darkroom, Bill turned on a "safe" red light. He came to each one of us, with the red light so we could see what was on our cloths. I was amazed. There were four pictures on my cloth, which looked like photographs! I didn't recognize any of the faces. However, other people attending the séance did recognize their loved ones.

We each received a piece of construction paper, and placed our cloth on top of it. Then we rolled our cloth up and put a rubber band around the roll. Only after our cloths were protected from daylight were the lights turned on.

This séance was the most remarkable experience of my life. I had spoken with my father, who had died two years before. No one could tell me that there is no afterlife, I had more than enough proof to know that we live after we die.

Carl and I went to the cafeteria to have some lunch. As we were sitting at a table, I received more interesting information.

"Your grandmother is here," Carl said.

"She is, where?" I replied.

"She's by the door, she just entered the building. Apparently she doesn't know that she can walk right through the door, because she waited for that man to open the door to walk in. She has been watching what we've been doing in the past few days, and has learned a lot. [Pause] This is strange. Did your grandmother have a window in her kitchen?" Carl asked.

"Yes, she did." I replied.

"And did it face a brick wall?" Carl asked.

"The apartment house she lived in was in the shape of a U. There was a brick wall about ten yards from her kitchen window."

"This is very strange indeed," Carl continued. "I see her throwing her dishes and pots and pans out her kitchen window. They are smashing against the brick wall. Apparently she's furious. She's just discovered that all the man-made rules of keeping kosher aren't worth a pile of beans. She has learned that she has been lied to."

I certainly empathized with my grandmother, for I also felt that I had been lied to. That's why I was so outraged a few nights ago. My experiences at Camp Chesterfield did more than shake me up. They shook up "the Jewish side of heaven."

Carl and I left the camp for a few days to do some research in Chicago. We returned late Saturday afternoon, in time to attend the Saturday night Cathedral service.

The first medium on the Cathedral program would be Bill English. He would conduct a card writing séance. Card writing is a modern version of slate writing. Years ago, when I attended Carl's psychic development classes, Carl had taught me about slate writing, which took place in the late 1800's and early 1900's.

The people who gathered for a séance would sit in a circle. The medium was part of that circle. One of the people would act as the assistant, and take a small slate and put it inside a box with a few pieces of chalk. The box would be sealed, so that no light could get into it. Then the séance began. After a few moments, the medium would go into a trance. If Spirit were going to write messages to the people in the circle, there would the scratching sounds of the chalk writing on the black board. These sounds would continue for a few minutes, then the pings of chalk being dropped would be heard. Then there was silence.

A few moments later, the medium would come out of the trance. The assistant would usually ask another person to open the box, take out the slate and read it. In most cases, there were messages for everyone in the circle written on the slate.

The card writing we were about to witness in Chesterfield was a modern version of slate writing. Instead of a slate, Bill placed a *sealed* cellophane package of 3x5 index cards into a basket. Then, he put a handful of different colored felt-tipped markers with their caps still on into the basket. The basket was covered with a thick cloth so that the inside of the box was in absolute darkness. In effect, Bill created a cabinet where the phenomena would take place. He then went into a trance and, seconds afterwards, noise emanated from the basket. It sounded as if a couple of kittens were rambunctiously playing. Suddenly, Bill began speaking. He was announcing the names of the Spirit people who were present. I was astounded to hear the names of my uncles, father, and grandparents mentioned. I turned to Carl and said, "I wonder if those names belong to me?"

About 10 minutes later, the noise from the basket stopped, and Bill came out of his trance. It was then that two of the ladies from the audience were asked to come up and remove the black cloth from the basket.

One of the ladies picked up the sealed package of cards and opened the cellophane. The first few cards were still blank. Then a card had writing on it, including the name of a person in the audience. The woman announced the person's name, who immediately came to the stage to receive her card. About three of four cards later, my name was called. I eagerly left my seat to pick up my card.

I was amazed. The card had a vase of flowers drawn on it. Along the sides were the names Ben and Abe, who were my uncles; Harry, who was my father; and Joseph and Sylvia, who were my grandparents. (See picture on page 140.)

For people who are skeptical, and think that perhaps Bill English remembered my father's and grandfather's name from the trumpet séance, I had never mentioned any of my family's names to him. He had no way of knowing that Ben and Abe were my father's brothers.

We had one last appointment for a trumpet séance with Gilbert Burke, another one of Camp Chesterfield's respected mediums. There were seven people signed up to attend this séance. Although it was early on a Sunday morning, it was a dark, gloomy day. There was a gray cast to the air, as if a storm were approaching.

The other three people did not arrive for the séance. So the medium, Carl, and our group were the only people there. Unfortunately this séance is not very clear in my mind. I do remember that the voices changed for each Spirit that came through. But there was one indelible impression that I did have of this séance. I remember vividly the loud claps of thunder that occurred as the voices were speaking through the trumpet. The irony made me chuckle, as a little voice in my head dramatically started reciting the Bible.

> **And it came to pass on the third day in the morning, that there were thunders and lightnings, and a thick cloud upon the mount and the voice of the trumpet exceedingly loud; so that all the people that were in the camp trembled.**[287]

> **And when the voice of the trumpet sounded long, and waxed louder and louder, Moses spake, and God answered him by a voice.**[288]

---

[287] Exodus 19:16 [KJV].

[288] Exodus 19:19 [KJV].

This demonstrated exactly what Carl had said so many times. What happened in Biblical times, can still happen today. The Bible recorded a famous séance that occurred three thousand four hundred years ago, high on a mountaintop.[289] The ancient Hebrews trembled with fear as they heard God's own voice recite the Ten Commandments through a trumpet.[290] For, despite their familiarity with the Gifts of the Spirit, they were ignorant of the laws of psychic science.

Now, that ancient scene was being recreated, as I heard the claps of thunder reverberate while the קוֹל הַשׁוֹפָר (*Kol Hashofar*), the *Voice of the Trumpet* spoke. As I listened to the trumpet's voice I too began trembling. However, my reaction differed greatly from that of my ancestors. Excitement, not fear, caused me to tremble.

Since so few people have this rare opportunity to hear Spirits' voices, I felt very privileged. I also felt very fortunate that I would not live my life confined by religious dogmas and rituals. I had begun expanding my spiritual horizons. My disillusionment with religion during my college years had opened the door. I no longer had to rely on information coming from a Bible, rabbi, priest, or minister. The knowledge I had acquired by personally witnessing the workings of Spirit had erased all my fear of death and dying. I became overjoyed as these realizations flooded my mind. "My cup runneth over."

As my research expanded to additional Bible passages, my dialogues with the Angel Without A Name grew more detailed and comprehensive. Each new discovery whet my insatiable thirst for knowledge of these ancient teachings and wisdom. As I continue to uncover psychic knowledge, I invite you to accompany me on this path to a greater understanding of the long *hidden* truth.

---

[289] Exodus 19:9-Exodus 20:21.

[290] Exodus 20:18 [RSV]

# EPILOGUE

## Conflict Between the Priest and the Medium — A Personal Battle

As I look back, I realize that the first reading I had with Rev. Carl Hewitt was a turning point in my life. It was my first encounter with a legitimate medium, one that did not fake the gift of mediumship. My first encounter with Awan sent tremors though my life as powerful as an earthquake, shaking all my beliefs, forcing me to examine the validity of what I considered the truth. As my knowledge of psychic science grew, I was impelled into a venture I never expected—writing a book about my experiences. The most uncomfortable aspect of this new knowledge was that it placed me in the middle of an age-old conflict.

The more I learned about psychic phenomena, the more I felt betrayed by orthodox religions. I could no longer walk into a synagogue and attend a service. I saw the errors, the misinterpretations. If I went to the High Holiday service, I would hear the Kol Hashofar/קוֹל הַשׁוֹפָר which, in synagogues of the 20th century was the sound of the *ram's horn*. Yet, I knew that I was supposed to be hearing the Voice of Spirit coming out of a *Trumpet*. I had a hard time dealing with the frustration that I felt about the destruction of vital spiritual truths. I watched others blindly participating in the rituals, totally unaware they were mimicking communication with the Divine. It felt as though everyone was admiring a beautiful 100-carat diamond. I was the only one who knew it was only a cubic zirconium. It looked genuine, but it wasn't.

I recently had the privilege of attending the bat mitzvah of a close friend's daughter. Since I no longer attend services, being in a synagogue was unusual for me. I found the experience like riding a bicycle—no matter how long you don't ride, you still remember how. It was an intense, emotional experience. I became swept up in the wonderful melodies and the chanting of the same prayers that I had said when I was a child. The feeling of awe was suddenly rekindled. It felt like home, very warm and comforting. Yet, as I was floating up, in this emotional high, I was also being pulled down by the gravity of an intellectual low. On an intellectual level, I saw again how far my religion had veered from its psychic origins—the clairaudience of Abraham, its founder.

As these polarities, the medium and the rabbi, pulled on me, I realized that for me there is no resolution. I will forever be stuck in this conflict. However, my newly gained knowledge allows me to look forward with excitement and joy. It allows me to have a deeper understanding of the events recorded in the Bible. It allows me to step away from old, lifeless rituals and to embrace something that is much more important—an eternal Spirituality.

If you analyze what is left after you strip away the man-made dogmas and superstitious rituals from orthodox religions, you discover the residuals of an ancient psychic science. You are left with the understanding that all people, whether they are Catholics, Jews, Protestants, Muslims, Buddhists, Confucians, Taoists, Hindus, or atheists, are all the same—spiritual, divine beings manifested in a physical body. Everyone has the ability to communicate with the Divine, with God, and with the heavenly realms where the angels and our ancestors dwell. The truth is that mediums only enhance the spiritual energies that are already present within and around us.

With this enhanced knowledge of psychic science, I now feel more responsible for my actions than I ever did. I can no longer collect a list of sins and have them forgiven on Yom Kippur, the Day of Atonement by a God sitting outside of myself. Now if I sin against someone, I need to ask for his or her forgiveness. No longer do I walk down a path that was prescribed by my ancestors—one that once dictated my conscious behavior. I no longer look to God or the Bible to tell me what to wear, eat, when to work or rest, or who to associate with. I take full responsibility for every aspect of my life and work in harmony with God and the Divine through the various communication channels that have now become so much a part of my life.

* * * * *

It was a month after my visit to Camp Chesterfield, Indiana, and my emotionally charged encounter with trumpet mediumship. I had decided to do some further research in the Library of Congress, in Washington D. C. During my return trip home my mind automatically drifted back to those powerful experiences. I reviewed all of the information that I had learned about mediumship. I suddenly realized that materialization was the only type of mediumship I had not witnessed. As I contemplated that thought, I began seeing in my mind's eye the famous pictures of Silver Belle's ectoplasmic form standing in front of the cabinet. I had a flash of realization: wait a minute—I was in Maryland! I could easily change my route and drive to Ephrata, Pennsylvania to visit Camp Silver Belle. I wondered what type of mediums are there now? (Unfortunately, within the past few years, Camp Silver Belle has permanently closed.) I stopped in the first rest area along the highway, studied my road atlas, and plotted my new route to Ephrata.

For the sake of brevity, I will not discuss my entire experience at Camp Silver Belle. I did, however, upon my arrival at the camp, make a rather startling discovery. Dan Taggert, a medium from Norfolk, Virginia, was working at the camp. He was giving private, individual trumpet readings! I was totally amazed, since I thought trumpet mediumship was only done for a group of people. I immediately booked a reading with him.

Dan was a pleasant young man, about my age. As we entered the seance room, Dan turned and asked me, "Have you ever experienced trumpet mediumship?"

"Yes," I enthusiastically replied, "In fact, last month I attended several trumpet seances, with Bill English, a medium at Camp Chesterfield, Indiana."

"You did!" he exclaimed, "Isn't that interesting. I used to be one of Bill's students!"

Obviously, I was totally amazed at what seemed to be a coincidence. We sat down to begin my reading. Dan charged up the phosphorus on his trumpet, and turned off the lights, which caused the room to be in utter darkness. Several Spirit people spoke to me during this reading. The voice of each Spirit had a distinct sound. Yet, I was totally startled when I suddenly heard a familiar voice speak through the trumpet.

"Hello again, Sidney, this is Dr. Louis."

"Hi, Dr. Louis! What are you doing out here? I thought you would be busy in Indiana, assisting Bill English."

"Well I have left my medium [Bill English] in good hands (another Spirit would be 'watching over Bill' in Dr. Louis' absence.) You know that I have other interests and duties in this dimension. I am not always with my medium."

"I find that very interesting," I said, "especially since you are speaking through another medium."

Dr. Louis replied, "Well, as you have discovered, this medium is no stranger to me. Many Spirits have more that one medium that they work through. This medium was one of my medium's students. I have come here today to speak briefly with you. Those of us in this realm became aware that you would be having this reading and it provided us the opportunity to check in with you. We wanted to let you know that even though you feel that you have learned so much about the spiritual realm, you really have just begun your journey towards enlightenment. We are very pleased with your progress, and your career in teaching has just begun."

This trumpet reading was a very profound experience for me. In the past year or so, I have come to the conclusion that Dr. Louis was not referring to my public school teaching when he said my career in teaching had just begun. A more profound message was embedded in the experience with Dr. Louis that day. I had what I can only assume to be a very rare experience—a conversation with the same Spirit person through two trumpet mediums in two locations. I can only compare it with our telephone system. We find nothing "strange" if John calls Mary from San Francisco, and a month later he calls her from Paris, France. When Mary hears John's voice, she can recognize it without any difficulty. His voice has the identical sound, despite the fact that John used two different telephones from two locations, and his voice traveled through different wires. Yet, it surprised me that this held true for mediumship. I heard Dr. Louis' voice through two different instruments (different mediums and trumpets), and yet his voice was easily recognizable, because it had the identical sound on both occasions. This lends evidence to the fact that the Spirits have distinct, recognizable voices, just as physical people do. It also proves that mediums are just instruments, acting as telephones between the two dimensions of life. This experience deeply enhanced my understanding of mediumship.

# APPENDIX

## So You Want a Psychic Reading

**About gifts of the Spirit, there are some things of which I do not wish you to remain ignorant.**[291]

This book about my experiences with psychic phenomena and research about Biblical psychic phenomena may have peaked your interest in having a psychic reading. Unfortunately, there are many charlatans who claim to be psychic or mediumistic, just as there were false prophets in Biblical days. These fraudulent mediums are interspersed with the genuinely gifted people. Therefore, I thought it important to provide readers with advice to help determine if a particular reader is genuine or not. The following are guidelines you may choose to use when selecting a psychic reader.

1. Just as two thousand years ago, Jesus' reputation had spread far and wide, a genuine medium will be known through word of mouth. He or she will not have to put advertisements in newspapers, or flyers of any kind.

Awan's medium, Carl Hewitt, has never advertised his abilities. He simply has a small sign, "Mr. Hewitt's office," on the gate outside his office. Yet, clients have traveled to his doorstep from all over the United States, and as far away as the Philippines, Hong Kong, Guana, Lebanon, and Saudi Arabia.

In more recent times, some genuine mediums do have web sites on the internet. Also, some communities have New Age newspapers in which legitimate mediums sometimes choose to advertise. You may also find a legitimate psychic at a Spiritualist camp. There are a few of these camps around the United States, some of which can be found on the internet.

2. If the medium will not allow you to tape your reading, it should be a warning to you that the medium may have something to hide. After researching mediumship for many years, I have learned that legitimate mediums welcome taping. It is the frauds, who wish to hide their inaccurate predictions. Impostors are only looking for your money, and will not allow any physical evidence, such as tape recordings, which could be used against them in a court of law.

---

[291] 1 Corinthians. 12:1 [NEB].

In the 24 years I have known Carl Hewitt, he has always insisted on taping the readings he gives. His recording system sits prominently on his desk. He even has a battery back up system in case of a loss of electricity. However, there is an exception. If you visit a psychic camp where the camp rules prohibit taping, usually, the mediums there are genuine.

3. Some people choose gypsies, palm readers, and fortunetellers for psychic readings. This can have dire consequences. Many of these types of readers mislead their clients. They claim that they can remove curses, or spells for a fee. This is impossible. Everyone on this planet operates on his or her own unique frequency, just as everyone has his or her own fingerprints and personality. If Mary set out to cast a spell on Alice, Mary would create the spell on her own vibration. Mary's negative thought would go out into the universe, where it would draw more negative energy to it. This negative thought could not change its frequency to any other than its own creator—Mary. Eventually it would boomerang back to Mary and she would suffer the consequences of the negative thought that she had initiated.

If a reader talks of spells and curses you would be wise to get up and walk out immediately. This is just a ruse to frighten clients and to extort money from them. Be extremely careful if you choose to visit this type of reader.

4. Frame your questions in such a way that you do not give the reader all the information. A legitimate reader will fill in the missing pieces. It is a way to test the reader's abilities.

5. Be aware if the reader goes fishing for information, by asking vague questions, until he or she hits on a correct response.

6. A genuine medium is interested in helping you. Be aware that some mediums are interested in being the instrument that enables you to communicate with a deceased loved one. That is their primary focus. Other mediums have a different focus, where they are interested in providing their clients with guidance on how to handle the future. Both of these types of mediums are genuine, but you may be more interested in one over the other. You may wish to ask the reader at the time you make the appointment what you can expect from the reading.

7. Be aware of where the medium chooses to work. A genuine medium needs to work in quiet surroundings to be able to focus on only one vibration. Usually genuine mediums will not choose to work in bars or restaurants that are open to the public. Some mediums may choose to work at private parties and give short mini-readings to the guests. There are also psychic fairs, where some mediums may choose to work. Usually these are short readings. I would be wary of a medium that does longer readings in a noisy environment.

8. A genuine medium can only do a limited amount of this work, because of the energy that it requires. In the Bible, Joshua was the medium in the meeting tent where Spirit spoke with Moses. Afterwards, Joshua was so exhausted he did not leave the tent.[292]  I have known many mediums who have overworked themselves and had a premature death. Therefore, it is highly unlikely that the best mediums would be associated with phone/hot line services.

Saint Paul wanted all people educated in the Gifts of the Spirit. He was emphatic about this because of his personal psychic experience on the road to Damascus, which changed the course of his life.[293]

After reading this book, it should be evident to the reader that orthodox religions all over the world do not want the public to understand the Gifts of the Spirit. If a clergy person does not have these spiritual gifts, as found in the Bible, that person will try to convince you that the Gifts of Spirit are the work of the devil. If that were true, then the Pharisees were correct when they said Jesus invoked with the devil to do healings.

> **As they went out, behold, they brought to him a dumb man possessed with a devil. And when the devil was cast out, the dumb spake, and the multitudes marveled, saying, It was never so seen in Israel. But the Pharisees said, He casteth out devils through the prince of devils.[294]**

Jesus performed all of the Gifts of the Spirit, which were of God. In John 4:16-29 Jesus gave a Samaritan woman a psychic reading. He told her she had five husbands, without the woman telling him. The woman recognized that Jesus was a prophet, and exclaimed that he had told her everything she had ever done. After experiencing a psychic reading by a genuine medium, you will be as excited and inspired as this Samaritan woman. This is very possible. Jesus stated:

> **Verily, verily, I say unto you, He that believeth on me, the works that I do shall he do also; and greater works than these shall he do; because I go unto my Father.[295]**

---

[292] Exodus 33:11.

[293] Acts 9:1-9.

[294] Matthew. 09:32-34 [KJV].

[295] John 14:12 [KJV].

# SUGGESTED READING

## SPIRITUALISM

Andreae, Christine. *Seances & Spiritualists*. Philadelphia, PA: Lippincott, 1974.

Babbitt, Edwin D. *Religion as Revealed by the Material and Spiritual Universe*. NY: Babbitt & Co.,1881.

Bander, Peter. *Voices from the Tapes: Recordings from the Other World*. NY: Drake Publishers, 1973.

Barbanell, Maurice. *This is Spiritualism*. NY: Award Books, 1959.

Doyle, Arthur Conan, Sir. *The History of Spiritualism*. NY: George H. Doran Company, 1926.

Findlay, James Arthur. *The Psychic Stream: The Source and Growth of the Christian Faith*. London: Psychic Press, 1947.

Findlay, James Arthur. *The Rock of Truth: Spiritualism the Coming World Religion*. London: Psychic Press, 1968.

Findlay, James Arthur. *The Way of Life: a Guide to the Etheric World, Giving 419 Extracts from the Verbatim Records of Sittings with John Campbell Sloan, the Famous Glasgow Direct Voice Medium*. London: Psychic Press, 1956.

Findlay, James Arthur. *The Curse of Ignorance: A History of Mankind from Primitive Times to the End of the Second World War*. London: Psychic Press, 1948.

Findlay, James Arthur. *Where Two Worlds Meet: The Verbatim Record of a Series of Nineteen Seances with John Campbell Sloan, the Famous Glasgow Direct Voice Medium*. London: Psychic Press, 1951.

Hall, Trevor H. *The Spiritualists: The Story of Florence Cook and William Crookes*. London, G. Duckworth, 1962.

McHargue, Georgess. *Facts, Frauds, and Phantasms: A Survey of the Spiritualist Movement.* Garden City, NY: Doubleday, 1972.

Underhill, Ann Leah. *The Missing Link in Modern Spiritualism.* NY: Arno Press, 1976.

# MEDIUMS

Adare, Viscount. *Experiences in Spiritualism with Mr. D. D. Home.* NY: Arno Press, 1976.

Altea, Rosemary. *Proud Spirit: Lessons, Insights & Healing from "the Voice of the Spirit World."* NY: Eagle Brook: William Morrow and Co., Inc., 1997.

Altea, Rosemary. *The Eagle and the Rose: A Remarkable True Story.* NY: Warner Books, 1995.

Bird, J. Malcolm, ed. *The Margery Mediumship: A Complete Record from January 1st, 1925.* NY: American Society for Psychical Research, 1928.

Brown, Rosemary. *Generic Immortals at My Elbow, Immortals By My Side.* Chicago: H. Regnery Co., 1975.

Brown, Rosemary. *Unfinished Symphonies: Voices from the Beyond.* NY: W. Morrow, 1971.

Browning, Norma Lee. *Peter Hurkos: I Have Many Lives.* Garden City, NY: Doubleday, 1976.

Browning, Norma Lee. *The Psychic World of Peter Hurkos.* Garden City, NY: Doubleday, 1970.

Christopher, Milbourne. *Mediums, Mystics, & the Occult.* NY: Crowell, 1975.

Cook, Ellen A. Pennau. *The Voice Triumphant: The Revelations of a Medium, by Mrs. Cecil M. Cook.* NY: A. A. Knopf, 1931.

Editors of Time-Life Books. *The Psychics.* Alexandria, VA: Time-Life Books, 1992.

Edwards, Harry. *The Mediumship of Arnold Clare: Leader of the Trinity of Spiritual Fellowship.* London: Rider, 1942.

Eisenbud, Jule. *The World of Ted Serios: "Thoughtographic" Studies of an Extraordinary Mind.* 2nd ed. Jefferson, NC: McFarland, 1989.

Fleckles, Elliott V. *Willie Speaks Out! the Psychic World of Abraham Lincoln.* St. Paul, MN: Llewellyn Publications, 1974.

Flint, Leslie. *Voices in the Dark: My Life as a Medium*. London: Macmillan, 1971.

Ford, Arthur A. *The Life Beyond Death*. NY: Putnam, 1971.

Ford, Arthur A. *Unknown but Known: My Adventures into the Meditative Dimension*. NY: New American Library, 1969.

Fornell, Earl Wesley. *The Unhappy Medium: Spiritualism and the Life of Margaret Fox*. Austin, TX: Austin University of Texas Press, 1964.

Garrett, Eileen Jeanette Lyttle. *Many Voices: The Autobiography of a Medium*. NY: Putnam, 1968.

Garrett, Eileen Jeanette Lyttle. *My Life as a Search for the Meaning of Mediumship*. NY: Oquaga Press, 1939.

Hall, Trevor H. *Generic Spiritualists, the Medium and the Scientist: The Story of Florence Cook and William Crookes*. Buffalo, NY: Prometheus Books, 1984.

Hall, Trevor H. *The Enigma of Daniel Home: Medium or Fraud?* Buffalo, NY: Prometheus Books, 1984.

Hapgood, Charles H. *Voices of Spirit: Through the Psychic Experience of Elwood Babbitt*. NY: Delacorte Press, 1975.

Holzer, Hans. *The Clairvoyant*. NY: Mason/Charter, 1976.

Home, Daniel Dunglas. *Incidents in My Life*. Secaucus, NJ: University Books, Inc., n.d.

Jackson, Herbert G. *The Spirit Rappers*. Garden City, NY: Doubleday, 1972.

Jenkins, Elizabeth. *The Shadow and the Light: a Defense of Daniel Douglas Home, the Medium*. London: H. Hamilton, 1982.

Knight, J. Z. *A State of Mind, My Story: Ramtha: the Adventure Begins*. NY: Warner Books, 1987.

Manning, Matthew. *In the Minds of Millions*. London: W. H. Allen, 1977.

Manning, Matthew. *The Link: Matthew Manning's Own Story of His Extraordinary Psychic Gifts*. NY: Holt, Rinehart and Winston, 1975.

Maynard, Henrietta Sturdevant Colburn. *Was Abraham Lincoln a Spiritualist?* Philadelphia, PA: R. C. Hartranft, 1891.

Montgomery, Ruth Shick. *A Gift of Prophecy: The Phenomenal Jeane Dixon.* NY: Morrow, 1965.

Montgomery, Ruth Shick. *A World Beyond: A Startling Message from the Eminent Psychic Arthur Ford from Beyond the Grave.* NY: Coward, McCann & Geoghegan, 1971.

Nichols, Thomas Low. *A Biography of the Brothers Davenport. With Some Account of the Physical and Psychical Phenomena which have Occurred in Their Presence, in America and Europe.* NY: Arno Press, 1976.

Parrott, Ian. *The Music of Rosemary Brown.* London: Regency Press, 1978.

Podmore, Frank. *Mediums of the 19th Century.* New Hyde Park, NY: University Books, 1963.

Pollack, Jack Harrison. *Croiset, the Clairvoyant.* Garden City, NY: Doubleday, 1964.

Price, Harry. *Stella C. : An Account of Some Original Experiments in Psychical Research.* London: Souvenir Press, 1973.

Robbins, Anne Manning. *Past and Present with Mrs. Piper.* NY: H. Holt and Company, 1922.

Smith, Susy. *The Mediumship of Mrs. Leonard.* New Hyde Park, NY: University Books, 1964.

Spraggett, Allen. *Arthur Ford: The Man Who Talked with the Dead.* NY: New American Library, 1973.

Stearn, Jess. *A Prophet in His Own Country: The Story of the Young Edgar Cayce.* NY: Morrow, 1974.

Stearn, Jess. *Edgar Cayce, the Sleeping Prophet.* Garden City, NY: Doubleday, 1967.

Sullivan, Eileen. *Arthur Ford Speaks from Beyond.* Chicago: J. P. O'Hara, 1975.

Tietze, Thomas R. *Margery.* NY: Harper & Row, 1973.

Twigg, Ena. *Ena Twigg: Medium.* NY: Hawthorn Books, 1972.

Van der Hurk, Pieter. *Psychic: The Story Of Peter Hurkos.* Indianapolis, Bobbs-Merrill, 1961.

# PSYCHIC PHENOMENA

Agee, Doris. *Edgar Cayce on Esp.* NY: Hawthorn Books, 1969.

Bradley, Dorothy Bomar. *Psychic Phenomena: Revelations and Experiences.* West Nyack, NY: Parker Pub. Co., 1967.

Cayce, Hugh Lynn, ed. *The Edgar Cayce Reader.* NY: Paperback Library, 1969.

Cerminara, Gina. *Many Mansions.* NY: Morrow, 1968.

Editors of Time-Life Books. *Ancient Wisdom and Secret Sects.* Alexandria, VA: Time-Life Books, 1989.

Editors of Time-Life Books. *Cosmic Connections.* Alexandria, VA: Time-Life Books, 1988.

Editors of Time-Life Books. *Dreams and Dreaming.* Alexandria, VA: Time-Life Books, 1990.

Editors of Time-Life Books. *Mind Over Matter.* Alexandria, VA: Time-Life Books, 1988.

Editors of Time-Life Books. *Mysterious Lands and Peoples.* Alexandria, VA: Time-Life Books, 1991.

Editors of Time-Life Books. *Mystic Places.* Alexandria, VA: Time-Life Books, 1987.

Editors of Time-Life Books. *Phantom Encounters.* Alexandria, VA: Time-Life Books, 1988.

Editors of Time-Life Books. *Psychic Powers.* Alexandria, VA: Time-Life Books, 1987.

Editors of Time-Life Books. *Psychic Voyages.* Alexandria, VA: Time-Life Books, 1987.

Editors of Time-Life Books. *Search for Immortality.* Alexandria, VA: Time-Life Books, 1992.

Editors of Time-Life Books. *Search for the Soul.* Alexandria, VA: Time-Life Books, 1989.

Editors of Time-Life Books. *Spirit Summonings.* Alexandria, VA: Time-Life Books, 1989.

Editors of Time-Life Books. *The Mind and Beyond.* Alexandria, VA: Time-Life Books, 1991.

Editors of Time-Life Books. *The Mysterious World.* Alexandria, VA: Time-Life Books, 1992.

Editors of Time-Life Books. *Visions and Prophecies.* Alexandria, VA: Time-Life Books, 1988.

Fodor, Nandor. *Between Two Worlds.* West Nyack, NY: Parker Pub. Co., 1964.

Forman, Henry James. *The Story of Prophecy in the Life of Mankind from Early Times to the Present Day*. NY: Toronto, Farrar & Rinehart, Inc., 1936.

Glass, Justine. *They Foresaw the Future: the Story of Fulfilled Prophecy*. 1st American ed. NY: Putnam, 1969.

Greenhouse, Herbert B. *The Book Of Psychic Knowledge: All Your Questions Answered*. NY: Taplinger Pub. Co., 1973.

Holzer, Hans. *Born Again*. Garden City, NY: Doubleday, 1970.

Holzer, Hans. *ESP and You*. NY: Hawthorn Books, 1968.

Holzer, Hans. *Life Beyond Life: the Evidence for Reincarnation*. West Nyack, NY: Parker Pub. Co., 1985.

Holzer, Hans. *The Psychic World of Bishop Pike*. NY: Crown Publishers, 1970.

Holzer, Hans. *The Psychic Side of Dreams*. Garden City, NY: Doubleday, 1976.

Holzer, Hans. *The Truth About ESP: What it Is, How it Works, and How You Develop It*. Garden City, NY: Doubleday, 1974.

Kettelkamp, Larry. *Sixth Sense*. NY: W. Morrow, 1970.

Knight, David C., ed. *The ESP Reader*. NY: Grossett & Dunlap, 1969.

Lodge, Oliver, Sir. *Raymond*. NY: George H. Doran Company, 1916.

MacLaine, Shirley. *Dancing in the Light*. NY: Bantam Books, 1985.

MacLaine, Shirley. *Out on a Limb*. NY: Bantam Books, 1983.

Montgomery, Ruth Shick. *A Search for the Truth*. NY: Morrow, 1967.

Montgomery, Ruth Shick. *Here and Hereafter*. NY: Coward-McCann, 1968.

Montgomery, Ruth Shick. *The World Before*. NY: Coward, McCann & Geoghegan, 1976.

Pike, James A. *The Other Side: An Account of My Experiences with Psychic Phenomena*. Garden City, NY: Doubleday, 1968.

Robinson, William E. *Spirit Slate Writing and Kindred Phenomena*. NY: Munn & Company, 1898.

Rosher, Grace. *Beyond the Horizon: Being New Evidence from the Other Side of Life Communicated by Gordon Burdick in Automatic Writing.* London: James Clarke & Co. Ltd., 1961.

Smith, Susy. *The Book Of James.* NY: Putnam, 1974.

Stearn, Jess. *Adventures Into The Psychic.* NY: Coward-McCann, 1969.

Worrall, Ambrose A. *Explore Your Psychic World.* NY: Harper & Row, 1970.

Wright, Theon. *The Open Door: A Case History of Automatic Writing.* NY: John Day Co., 1970.

# PSYCHIC PHENOMENA IN THE BIBLE

Carrington, Hereward. *Loaves and Fishes: A Study of the Miracles, of the Resurrection, and of the Future Life, in the Light of Modern Psychic Knowledge.* NY: C. Scribner's Sons, 1935.

Ebon, Martin. *Beyond Space and Time: An ESP Casebook.* NY: New American Library, 1967.

Ebon, Martin. *Prophecy in Our Time.* NY: New American Library, 1968.

Ebon, Martin. *The Psychic Reader.* NY: World Pub. Co., 1969.

Editors of Psychic Magazine. *Psychics.* NY: Harper & Row, 1972.

Elliott, Graeme Maurice. *Spiritualism in the Old Testament.* London: Psychic Press, 1938.

Elliott, Graeme Maurice. *The Bible as Psychic History.* London: Rider, 1959.

Elliott, Graeme Maurice. *The Psychic Life of Jesus.* London: Spiritualist Press, 1938.

Heron, Laurence Tunstall. *ESP in the Bible.* Garden City, NY: Doubleday, 1974.

Hull, Moses. *Encyclopedia of Biblical Spiritualism.* Cassadaga, FL: National Spiritualist Association of Churches, 1962.

Sprague, E. W. Rev. *All the Spiritualism of the Christian Bible and the Scripture Directly Opposing it.* Detroit, MI: (self-published), 1922.

Tooley, Sarah A. *Psychic Phenomena in the Old Testament.* London: Psychic Book Club, 1957.

# HEALING

Cerutti, Edwina. *Olga Worrall: Mystic with the Healing Hands*. NY: Harper & Row, 1975.

Chapman, George. *Surgeon from Another World*. San Bernardino, CA: Borgo Press, 1988.

Editors of Time-Life Books. *Powers of Healing*. Alexandria, VA: Time-Life Books, 1989.

Edwards, Harry. *A Guide to Spirit Healing*. London: Spiritual Press, 1955.

Edwards, Harry. *The Science of Spirit Healing*. London: Rider and Company: 1953.

Fuller, John Grant. *Arigo: Surgeon of the Rusty Knife*. NY: Crowell, 1974.

Kraft, Dean. *Portrait of a Psychic Healer*. NY: Putnam, 1981.

Montgomery, Ruth Shick. *Born To Heal: The Astonishing Story of Mr. A. and the Ancient Art of Healing with Life Energies*. NY: Coward, McCann & Geoghegan, 1973.

# About the Author

Mr. Sidney Schwartz earned a Bachelor's degree in history from the University of Bridgeport, and a Master's degree in educational media from Boston University. He currently resides in northern New Jersey where he teaches history and is a middle school librarian.

# About the Medium

Rev. Carl Hewitt's career as a medium began when he was 23 years old. A friend asked Carl to accompany his wife to a lecture. Carl agreed without knowing the subject of the lecture. He had no idea this event would change the course of his life.

The lecturer was a medium, a person who could hear and see entities who lived in another dimension. When the lecture ended, the medium delivered Spirit Messages, which is advice for members of the audience from their deceased loved ones. Carl was the fourth person to receive a message that night. The medium announced to a room packed with people that Carl also had the ability to be the medium or messenger between the two dimensions of life. One day, he would stand before large audiences delivering Spirit Messages.

It took years for this prediction to manifest. Gaining the confidence in himself was a slow process for Rev. Hewitt, because he had to overcome his negative past.

Rev. Hewitt grew up in Shallotte, North Carolina, a small and poor rural community. He was born endowed with several Gifts of the Spirit. At the age of three, Carl's clairvoyance (clear seeing, or second sight), and clairaudience (hearing the voices of Spirit similar to Joan of Arc) got him into trouble. One day little Carl suddenly began crying and announced to his mother that his sister had died. Goldie, Carl's mother, became enraged with him, and spanked him for telling such a dreadful lie. Twenty minutes later, word arrived that Carl's sister had indeed died. As one would expect, this astonished Carl's parents.

Unfortunately for Carl, their astonishment transformed into disapproval. Living in the midst of the Bible belt, would become a tremendous burden for a psychically gifted child. Carl remembers sitting along side his father in a Southern Baptist church, whose minister was furiously delivering his message of "Hell fire and brimstone." Carl heard the voice of Spirit tell him that the minister's message was incorrect. Carl turned and tugged on his father's suit-sleeve and said, "Daddy, what the minister says is not right!" His father, Alvie, became very upset with Carl. Alvie believed, as most of the Southern Baptists, that everything that did not have a logical explanation must be the work of the devil. Since the townspeople considered Carl's predictions as demonic, they ostracized Carl. They thought if they merely talked to Carl, they would be inviting the devil into their lives. Alvie and Goldie often told Carl that he should stop his predicting, or he would be locked up in an insane asylum. Carl, his parents, and the rest of the community did not understand that psychic phenomena were the source of these events.

It was not surprising that Carl began to withdraw, spending much time alone. He enjoyed climbing into a tall, live-oak tree that was near the inland waterway. It was in that tree that an Native American boy would visit with Carl. They would talk and play together. This Native American boy was about the only friend that Carl had. It took two decades until Carl finally learned the Indian boy's true identity: he was the Spirit that guards and guides Carl's life.

In 1974, Carl was ordained as a minister. Then, after decades of Spirit's pleading, Rev. Hewitt founded The Gifts of the Spirit Church in 1977, where he is the pastor. Between 1979-1981 Rev. Hewitt was interviewed repeatedly, and his life's story became the basis of the NBC movie entitled *The Gifted One*. Rev. Hewitt has taught audiences throughout the United States, about mediumship and the Gifts of the Spirit.

For the last 35 years, Rev. Hewitt has been demonstrating mediumship. People from all walks of life: doctors, lawyers, professors, people working in the media, delegates to the United Nations, and even a former head of OPEC, have sought his spiritual guidance. People journeyed to Rev. Hewitt's office in Connecticut, from all parts of the United States, and as far away as Saudi Arabia, Hong Kong, and Africa. Yet, Rev. Hewitt never advertised his services as a medium, or erected a neon sign over his doorway. There is just a simple sign on the front gate that says, "Mr. Hewitt's Office."

Rev. Hewitt is currently collaborating with Mr. Schwartz on his autobiography, which will be entitled: *And Now They Know*.